UNDERSTANDING THE END TIMES

UNDERSTANDING THE END TIMES

Available from Amazon.com and other online stores

TABLE OF CONTENTS

INTRODUCTION

Why at this juncture in human history is it important for every Christian to have a heart for—and a proper understanding of—the Bible's prophesied end-times events? Why should the Church once again be stirred by the prophetic Word of God? One reason stands out: Christ's sobering challenge to today's Christian in the Parable of the Ten Virgins.

In Matthew's New Testament Gospel, Jesus presents twelve parables which deal with a previously undisclosed kingdom—an *inter-advent* "kingdom of heaven"—which He will bring forth on earth between His two advents. Today this kingdom is known as Christianity or Christendom. Significantly, one of these parables—the Parable of the Ten Virgins—describes the precise condition of early twenty-first century Christendom: *"The kingdom of heaven will be comparable to ten virgins, who took their lamps and went out to meet the bridegroom. And five of them were foolish, and five were prudent. For when the foolish took their lamps, they took no oil with them, but the prudent took oil in flasks along with their lamps. Now while the bridegroom was delaying, they all became drowsy and began to sleep" (Matt. 25:1-5)*. Christ compares His followers to ten virgins. Just as a Jewish virgin in Christ's day was to be prepared for, and joyously awaiting, the final consummation of her marriage upon the return of her loved one for her at the end of the betrothal period (always an undisclosed length of time), the ten virgins (those who call themselves Christians) are likewise to be alert and ready for Christ when He returns *unexpectedly* (a common romantic practice among first-century Jewish bridegrooms) to take His Bride to heaven. But look what happens to the virgins in Christ's parable: *"Now while the bridegroom was delaying, they all became drowsy and began to sleep."*

The five virgins having the "oil" represent those within Christendom who are born-again—those Christians who have invited Christ into their hearts and who are indwelled with the Holy Spirit ("oil" is uniformly a picture of the Holy Spirit in the Scriptures). The five virgins not having the oil represent those within Christendom who call themselves Christians but who are *not* born-again and who are not indwelled with the Holy Spirit. Yet, incredibly, Christ states that *all* of the virgins—including His true sheep, the born-again Christians—will become drowsy and begin to sleep rather than being alert for his return, an event which could happen at any moment.

Does this parable describe the condition of Christians today? The answer, lamentably, is yes. Christendom at this juncture of its history is largely unprepared for, and noticeably disinterested in, the end-times events: the return of the Jesus Christ for His own at the Rapture of the Church; the horrible time of judgment (a seven-year period called the "Tribulation") which will come upon those left on earth after the Rapture; the subsequent bodily return of Jesus Christ after the Tribulation to save Israel from annihilation; Christ's defeat of the armies fighting against Israel (the so-called Battle of Armageddon); Christ's gathering of all remaining earthlings to Jerusalem in order to evaluate their heart condition with regard to the gospel of Jesus Christ; and Christ's establishment of His Millennial Kingdom on earth.

That part of Christendom which does not possess the "oil"—the apostate, liberal Christian movement—by definition is unprepared for the Lord's return. Because these Christians have never invited Christ into their hearts, they do not have the indwelling Holy Spirit to illumine their hearts to the truths of God's Word (I Cor. 2:14). Before apostate, liberal Christendom can awaken from its sleep with regard to the End Times, it must first correct its entire doctrine of salvation, which typically is a works-performance system rather than a grace-faith system.

Sadly, however, even that part of Christendom which does possess the "oil"—evangelical, born-again Christianity—likewise has, in the main, become drowsy or asleep with regard to the end-times events. For example, many highly regarded, born-again theologians hold to an amillennial position with regard to Christ's reign over the earth: these otherwise wonderful teachers of God's Word deny that Christ will reign over the earth for a thousand years, despite several dozen prophecies to the contrary. They choose to spiritualize or allegorize these prophecies rather than taking them at face value—contending, for example, that Christ's Millennial reign is presently taking place in heaven and that the term "millennial" is not to be taken as a literal 1,000 year period of time. In addition, many amillennial theologians assert that the Church, because of Israel's corporate rejection of Christ, has now inherited the covenant promises which God made to Abraham—utterly contradicting the explicit, unambiguous teaching of Romans 11:1-32. In short, amillennial theologians have fallen into a deep slumber with regard to the true nature of the end-times events. Accordingly, the young men who study under these theologians and who go on to become pastors and otherwise wonderful men of the gospel are themselves robbed of the truth about the end times and in turn unwittingly rob their respective flocks of preparedness.

Christians who sit under this type of teaching invariably are not looking for the imminent return of Christ and typically do not even consider it to be important. Yet Christ Himself taught just the opposite. On a number of different occasions, Christ exhorted His followers to be alert for His return: *"Then there will be two men in the field; one will be taken and one will be left. Two women will be grinding at the mill; one will be taken and one will be left. Therefore, **be on the alert**, for you do not know which day your Lord is coming. But be sure of this, that if the head of the house had known at what time of the night the thief was coming, **he would have been on the alert** and would not have allowed his house to be broken into. For this reason, **you also must be ready**; for the Son of Man is coming at an hour when you do not think He will"* (Matt. 24:40-44).

Still other born-again theologians hold to a postmillennial position with regard to Christ's reign over the earth. These Christians likewise do not believe in a literal millennial reign of Christ over the earth after a second coming, but instead see the kingdom of God (Christianity) being victoriously extended in the present world through the preaching of the gospel. These Christians believe that much of the world will be Christianized prior to Christ's return. Postmillennialists also assert that the Church will eventually enter into a spiritual "millennium" of Christians and Christianity reigning throughout the earth (not necessarily for a thousand-year duration) and that Christ will return after this Christian reign to take His sheep home to heaven forever. Such a position, however, is not supported in prophetic Scripture. For example, the chronology of end-times events given to Christendom by the Lord Himself in the book of Revelation clearly teaches that He will return to the earth *before* He sets up His Millennial Kingdom. Moreover, though many postmillennialists believe that they will be the ones who will win the world to Christ before His return, Jesus teaches that much of mankind will reject the gospel between His two advents (Matt. 13:18-23). Jesus corroborates this position when He asks His disciples rhetorically, *"but when the Son of Man comes, will He find the faith on earth?" (Luke 18:18)*. In short, postmillennialists, while perhaps having a commendable zeal for evangelism, have nevertheless fallen into a deep sleep with regard to the true nature of the end-times events and the return of Christ.

Even among those Christians who believe (correctly, in the writer's view) that Christ will return to the earth before He establishes His 1,000-year reign over the earth from Jerusalem (the premillennial position), the vast majority of these Christians have unwittingly become drowsy or have fallen asleep to both the imminency and the importance of the return of Christ. Today the politically correct view of many premillennial evangelicals seems to be that a careful understanding of the end-times events is neither important to the Christian life nor relevant to daily living. So the question must be asked: Is an accurate knowledge of the end times relevant to the Christian life? The Apostle Peter taught that it was when he exhorted believers as follows: *"But according to His promise we are looking for new heavens and a new earth, in which righteousness dwells. Therefore, beloved, since you look for these things, be diligent to be found by Him in peace, spotless and blameless" (II Peter 3:13-14)*. What could be more relevant to the Christian life than an unshakable inner peace and a life that seeks to be spotless and blameless? Could it be that a proper understanding of the end times (*"since you look for these things"*) is a catalyst to inner peace and to a life that is increasingly freed from the pull of sin? Peter seemed to think so, and so should you and I.

In conclusion, just as Christ and the Apostle Peter challenged those who had access to the Scriptures two thousand years ago to know and to understand the prophetic Word of God, so too do Christ and Peter challenge you and me today to know and understand the prophetic Word of God. Let *none* of us be drowsy or asleep with regard to Christ's imminent return for His own and the end-times events which follow.

THE FOUR REQUISITES TO UNDERSTANDING THE END TIMES

For many Christians nothing is more daunting in Scripture than the study of Eschatology—the study of the "end times." Who is the "beast" in the book of Revelation? Who are the "two witnesses"? How does one make sense out of the "seals," the "trumpets," and the "bowls"? What happens when?

Yet, are the end-times prophecies actually that difficult to understand? Could it be that God, over the past sixty or seventy years, has begun to unseal these prophecies? Could it be that world events and the current configuration of nations are so in line with Bible prophecy that the end-times events—or at least the broad panorama of these events—can now be fairly easy to grasp? Listen to what God told the prophet Daniel 2,600 years ago: *" 'But as for you, Daniel, conceal these words and seal up the book until the end of time; many will go back and forth, and knowledge will increase. . . .' As for me, I heard but could not understand; so I said, 'My lord, what will be the outcome of these events?' And he said, 'Go your way, Daniel, for these words are concealed and sealed up until the end time'"* (Dan. 12:4, 8-9). In the verses leading up to this passage, God had given Daniel a glimpse of the end-times Tribulation judgments. But when Daniel replies that he cannot understand what he has just seen in the vision, God tells His puzzled prophet not to fret over this lack of understanding because these prophecies will not make sense until the "end time."

Four hundred years ago, during the time of the Reformation, the ultimate military weapon was perhaps the crossbow—not exactly a weapon of mass destruction. Accordingly, it would have been difficult for a Reformer to take a literal view of the Tribulation judgments portrayed in Revelation. Given the weaponry of that day, it was virtually impossible for one-half of the earth's population to be killed (the death toll depicted in the book of Revelation's Seal and Trumpet judgments) by the earth's sixteenth-century armies. Thus, the Reformers placed little emphasis on Eschatology in their theological systems; furthermore, because they could not see how the horrors depicted in Revelation could be fulfilled literally (in fact, according to Daniel 12, *no one* during the Reformation days could readily understand the end times prophecies), these men chose to spiritualize or allegorize most of these prophesies rather than to take them at face value.

Today, however, the ultimate fighting weapon is, let us say, a United States Trident submarine. This submarine, virtually undetectable under the earth's oceans and carrying twenty-four Trident ballistic missiles, each armed with ten independently-targeted hydrogen warheads, can, in thirty minutes, destroy nearly two hundred fifty of the world's cities. If targeted at cities with populations averaging a million people, then *one* Trident submarine could kill a quarter of a billion people. Not only is the Trident submarine an immeasurable leap forward from the crossbow of the Reformation, but for the first time in human history—and in this generation—all of the end-times prophecies can be fulfilled *literally*. There is no need to spiritualize or allegorize these prophecies as the Reformers chose to do. Four hundred years ago everyone would have had good reason to question a literal interpretation of the book of Revelation. But now, *no one* should reject the literal interpretation: the ramifications of the world's military capabilities are right before our eyes, if we choose to acknowledge their prophetic significance.

With these thoughts in mind, let us set out in the following pages to enable each reader to gain a workable grasp of the end-times events. To this end, four building blocks are essential to a proper understanding of the End Times—building blocks that will be substantiated throughout the book: (1) a literal interpretation of prophetic Scripture (i.e., taking all words and figures of speech in their plain, normal, and literal sense); (2) a clear distinction between Israel and the Church; (3) a pre-tribulation Rapture of the Church; and (4) a still-future, literal Millennial Kingdom on earth. *Unless the reader can embrace each of these four essentials, he will never gain a proper understanding of the End Times.*

First, the reader must take prophetic Scripture at face value. When the book of Revelation states that one-fourth of the earth's population will be killed during the Seal judgments of the end times, today's reader can be certain, given the current military hardware of the world, that the carnage depicted will take place exactly as prophesied. Thus, just as all of the prophecies relating to Christ's first advent were fulfilled *literally*, so too will all of the prophecies relating to His second advent. There is no longer a need for today's Christian to spiritualize or allegorize any of the end-times prophecies or to cling to, for example, the four-hundred-year old Eschatology of the Reformation. God has been gradually unsealing the end-times prophecies during the past century, and the twenty-first century reader can now, without hesitation, interpret the language of prophetic Scripture in a plain, normal, straightforward way.

Second, the reader must understand the distinction between the Church and Israel. The Church is a *spiritual* entity made up of Jewish and Gentile born-again believers (indwelled with the Holy Spirit). Israel, on the other hand, is a *national* entity. It is also the recipient of several yet-to-be fulfilled (but irrevocable) promises of God, and it still awaits a seven-year period of judgment *"to finish the transgression, to make an end of sin, to make atonement for iniquity, to bring in everlasting righteousness, . . ." (Dan. 9:24)*. Romans 9-11 makes the distinction between the Church and Israel unequivocally clear (a topic which will be examined at length in Chapter 7).

Third, the reader, upon weighing the Scriptural evidence for "imminency" (the any moment return of Jesus Christ for His Bride, the Church), should come to embrace a "pre-tribulation" Rapture (a topic which will be examined in Chapters 6 and 10).

Fourth, the reader, in view of the preponderance of Bible prophecy on the topic, should accept and embrace the doctrine of a future literal Millennial Kingdom on earth—ruled over from Jerusalem by the resurrected Jesus Christ (after His Second Coming), as King of kings and Lord of lords. Appendix D lists some of the prophecies which attest to this literal Millennial Kingdom.

Finally, let us understand that God, through His prophets, has already *announced* the end-times judgments. These judgments have been *impending* for the past nineteen hundred years and, because of the conditions beginning to burst forth on the world scene, are now *imminent* (a topic to be discussed in Chapter 33). Are *you* prepared for the return of Jesus Christ at any moment? Are you living your life by His Word? Are you abiding in the grace of Jesus Christ? Are you genuinely others-centered (versus self-centered) in your approach to life? Are you willing to serve rather than be served? Are you willing to become of no reputation in order to advance the gospel? Is your life "salt and light" to the hurting world around you—a world which desperately needs the Savior? Is your heart completely sold-out to Jesus Christ? Has your heart ever addressed the following question: "How can I best live the rest of my life in view of Christ's imminent return?"

THE FOUR REQUISITES TO UNDERSTANDING THE END TIMES

1. **A LITERAL INTERPRETATION OF BIBLE PROPHECY**
   (i.e., taking all words and figures of speech in their plain, normal sense)

2. **A CLEAR DISTINCTION BETWEEN ISRAEL AND THE CHURCH**

3. **A PRE-TRIBULATION RAPTURE**

4. **A FUTURE MILLENNIAL KINGDOM ON EARTH**

<u>Overarching Interpretive Principle</u> for the Bible's End-Times Prophecies:

If all of the prophecies relating to Christ's first coming were fulfilled *literally*—and they were—then we can be certain that all of the prophecies relating to His second coming will likewise be fulfilled *literally*. There is no need or reason to spiritualize them or to treat them allegorically (e.g., to treat them as nothing more than a grand metaphor of good winning out over evil).

DANIEL'S "SEVENTY WEEKS" PROPHECY

During Judah's (southern Israel's) captivity in Babylon, a Jewish prophet named Daniel—under the inspiration of the Holy Spirit approximately 570 years before the Crucifixion and Resurrection of Jesus Christ—gives mankind one of history's greatest prophecies. This proclamation is found in Daniel 9:24-27, and it is often called Daniel's "Seventy Weeks" prophecy. Out of this prophecy come a number of foundational truths about Messiah and the end-times events.

In the latter years of Judah's captivity, Daniel, upon reading an earlier prophecy given by the prophet Jeremiah (Dan. 9:1-2) and upon discerning that the time of the Jews' captivity in Babylon is nearly over (Jer. 25:11-12), cries out to God on behalf of his people—confessing the sins of the Jews and asking God for forgiveness:

O Lord, in accordance with all Your righteous acts, let now Your wrath turn away from Your city Jerusalem, Your holy mountain—for, because of our sins and the iniquities of our fathers, Jerusalem and Your people have become a reproach to all those around us. . . . O my God, incline Your ear and hear! Open Your eyes and see our desolations and the city which is called by Your name, for we are not presenting our supplications before You on account of any merit of our own, but on account of Your great compassion. O Lord, hear! O Lord, forgive! O Lord, listen and take action! For Your own sake, O my God, do not delay, because of Your city and Your people are called by Your name (Dan. 9:15-19).

God then answers Daniel's plea by revealing to him the broad brush of the future history of the Jewish people and Jerusalem:

Seventy weeks have been decreed for your people and your holy city, to finish the transgression, to make an end of sin, to make atonement for iniquity, to bring in everlasting righteousness, to seal up vision and prophecy, and to anoint the Most Holy. So you are to know and discern that, from the issuing of a decree to restore and rebuild Jerusalem until Messiah the Prince, there will be seven weeks and sixty-two weeks; it will be built again, with plaza and moat, even in times of distress. Then after the sixty-two weeks the Messiah will be cut off and have nothing, and the people of the prince who is to come will destroy the city and the sanctuary. And its end will come with a flood; even to the end there will be war; desolations are determined. And he will make a firm covenant with the many for one week, but in the middle of the week he will put a stop to sacrifice and grain offering; and on the wing of abominations will come one who makes desolate, even until a complete destruction, one that is decreed, is poured out on the one who makes desolate (Dan. 9:24-27).

Included in this broad brush of Israel's future history are statements about the rebuilding of Jerusalem, the coming of Messiah, the death of Messiah, the destruction of Jerusalem, and a future opponent of the Jews who would both make and break a covenant with them.

A. A Brief Analysis of Daniel's Prophecy

Keeping in mind its Messianic, historical, and end-times ramifications, let us make some observations about this seminal prophecy, beginning with verse 24: *"Seventy weeks have been decreed for your people and your holy city, to finish the transgression, to make an end of sin, to make atonement for iniquity, to bring in everlasting righteousness, to seal up vision and prophecy, and to anoint the Most Holy" (Dan. 9:24).* "Seventy weeks" literally means "seventy sevens." God had instructed the Jews in the Mosaic Law to work the land (the land of Canaan) for six years and then to allow the land to rest during the seventh—or Sabbath—year (Lev. 25:1-7). The Jews, however, ignored all seventy of these Sabbath years during the 490 years prior to their Babylonian captivity. Accordingly, God tells Daniel that, although the seventy years of captivity are nearly over, another seventy years *times seven* (in accordance with the punishment prescribed in Leviticus 26:18) will enfold the Jews and Jerusalem (*"have been decreed"*) for the following six reasons: (1) to finish the transgression of the Jews (their failure to keep the Sabbath years during the 490 years); (2) to bring an end to the penalty of sin (at the Cross); (3) to make atonement for iniquity (so that man can be reconciled to God); (4) to bring in everlasting righteousness (at the Coming of Messiah to set up His Davidic [Millennial] Kingdom on earth [II Sam. 7:8-29]); (5) to seal up vision and prophecy (visions and prophecies will no longer be needed when Messiah reigns from Jerusalem in fulfillment of prophecy); and (6) to anoint the Most Holy (either the dedication of the Millennial Temple or the establishment of Christ's reign from Jerusalem). Of major significance, we see *both* advents of Christ foreshadowed in verse 24—His first coming as the Lamb of God who takes away the sins of the world ("to make atonement for sin") and His Second Coming as righteous Sovereign over the earth ("to bring in everlasting righteousness").

In verse 25, God informs Daniel that 483 years (sixty-nine seven-year periods, or sixty-nine "weeks" of years) will take place between the issuing of a decree to restore and rebuild Jerusalem and the coming of Messiah: *"So you are to know and discern that, from the issuing of a decree to restore and rebuild Jerusalem until Messiah the Prince, there will be seven weeks and sixty-two weeks; it [Jerusalem] will be built again, with plaza and moat, even in times of distress" (Dan. 9:25).* The first half of the verse was fulfilled literally, *to the day*, when Jesus Christ entered Jerusalem on a donkey nearly two thousand years ago—to the clamor of crowds proclaiming *"Hosannah to the Son of David; BLESSED IS HE WHO COMES IN THE NAME OF THE LORD"* (a prophecy reserved exclusively for the coming of Israel's Messiah). How do we know that what we call "Palm Sunday" today was the *exact* fulfillment of this part of Daniel's prophecy? Listen to Christ's rebuke of the Pharisees, who understood the Messianic implications of what the crowds were shouting (and who were therefore asking Jesus to quiet the crowds): *"I tell you, if these [people] become silent, then the stones will cry out" (Luke 19:40).* Christ in effect says that not only is this day exactly 483 years from the time of the issuing of the decree by Artixerxes Longimanus of Persia to restore and rebuild Jerusalem, but that God would have had the rocks announce Christ's entrance into Jerusalem as Israel's Messiah (in fulfillment of this prophecy) had the crowds not done so!

In verse 26, Daniel prophesies that, after His coming, Messiah will be "cut off"—an Old Testament expression meaning "to be killed by the people." Daniel also prophesies that, after Messiah is killed, an invading people—out of whom would ultimately come a treacherous end-times leader—will destroy Jerusalem: *"Then after the sixty-two weeks the Messiah will be cut off and have nothing, and the people of the prince who is to come will destroy the city and the sanctuary." (Dan. 9:26).* In view of the fact that Titus and his Roman armies destroyed Jerusalem in 70 A.D., we know with certainty the identity of *"the people of the prince who is to come"*—the people of the ancient Roman Empire. Accordingly, we know that the end-times "prince who is to come" (the Antichrist) will be a descendent of the ancient Roman Empire and will be one of the following: narrowly, an Italian; or more broadly, a "Japhethite" (to be discussed in Chapter 14).

In verse 27, Daniel describes the final "week" of seven years which God has decreed for Israel (and which we know to be still future). This part of Daniel's prophecy focuses on the activities of a charismatic end-times world political leader, known elsewhere in Scripture as the Antichrist: *"And he will make a firm covenant with the many for one week, but in the middle of the week he will put a stop to sacrifice and grain offering; and on the wing of abominations will come one who makes desolate, even until a complete destruction, one that is decreed, is poured out on the one who makes desolate" (Dan. 9:27).* Daniel states that the Antichrist *("the prince who is to come")* will make a seven-year peace treaty with Israel and her surrounding neighbors *("the many").* At the mid-point of the seven-year timeframe, the Antichrist will break the treaty and will bring a close to the Levitical sacrifices which have once again commenced in a Jerusalem temple *("but in the middle of the week he will put a stop to sacrifice and grain offering").* Daniel also prophesies that the Antichrist will ultimately meet his end: *"even until a complete destruction . . . is poured out on the one who makes desolate."*

[Note: In verse 26, Daniel has prophesied that the Jerusalem temple will be destroyed by the people who will one day spawn the Antichrist, only to prophesy one verse later that the worship sacrifices will be halted by this end-times Antichrist—thus telling us today that the temple which was destroyed in 70 A.D. must be rebuilt during the end times. Jesus Himself teaches the same thing in His Olivet Discourse: *"Therefore, when you see the ABOMINATION OF DESOLATION,*

which was spoken of through Daniel the prophet, standing in the holy place . . .
then let those who are in Judea flee to the mountains" (Matt. 24:15-16). In other
words, Jesus states that the Antichrist will enter and desecrate the innermost part
of a *Jerusalem* temple. Because a Jerusalem temple does not presently exist, one
must be rebuilt if Daniel's prophecy and Christ's exhortation are to be fulfilled in
the future.]

B. A Summary of the "Seventy Weeks" Chronology

Before concluding this section let us review the sequence of events given
in Daniel's "Seventy Weeks" prophecy. The events, in chronological order, are as
follows: (1) the issuing of a decree to restore and rebuild Jerusalem; (2) the coming
of Messiah to Jerusalem; (3) the death of Messiah; (4) the destruction of Jerusalem
and its temple by the people who will beget the end-times Antichrist; (5) the signing
of a seven-year peace treaty between the Antichrist, Israel, and her neighbors; (6)
the Antichrist's halting of the regular temple sacrifices—and his setting up of the
"abomination of desolation" in the temple—mid-way through the seven-year treaty
(Dan. 12:11; Matt. 24:15); and (7) the eventual destruction of the Antichrist. These
events are diagrammed chronologically in Chart 2-A.

Because the date of the decree of Artixerxes Longimanus to rebuild Jerusalem is known to secular historians (445 B.C.) and the date of the destruction of Jerusalem by the Romans is also known (70 A.D.), it can be concluded, according to the
chronology of Daniel's "Seventy Weeks" prophecy, that Messiah has already come
to Israel in fulfillment of this prophecy. Indeed, how tragic it is for any Jew living
today to still be looking for some yet-to-be-revealed Messiah, in view of the fact that
Israel's true Messiah has already presented Himself to the nation. In turn, only one
historical figure fulfills the prophecy: Jesus Christ—the carpenter from Nazareth
who, born of a virgin, healed the sick, raised the dead, cast out demons, confounded
the Pharisees, and Himself was crucified for your sins and mine, only to be raised
from the dead three days later to offer eternal life to all who would turn to Him.

Finally, let it be stated categorically that Daniel's "Seventy Weeks" prophecy has not yet been fulfilled entirely. One "week" of seven years yet remains in
God's 2,600-year-old decree toward Israel and Jerusalem *"to finish transgression,
. . . to bring in everlasting righteousness, to seal up vision and prophecy, and to
anoint the Most Holy."* This "week" of seven years includes events 5 and 6 shown
on Chart 2-A: the signing of the seven-year peace treaty and the Antichrist's halting
of the regular temple sacrifices in Jerusalem midway through this seven-year treaty.
How severe is the final three and a half years of the Tribulation? Hear again how
Jesus Himself describes the last half of Daniel's Seventieth Week: *"Therefore,
when you see the abomination of desolation, which was spoken of through Daniel
the prophet, standing in the holy place (let the reader understand), then let those
who are in Judea flee to the mountains. But pray that your flight may not be in the*

winter or on a Sabbath, for at this time there will be great tribulation—such as has not occurred since the beginning of the world until now, nor shall ever be again. And except those days be cut short, no life would be saved" (Matt. 24:15-16, 20-22). Jesus plainly states that, unless God cuts short the days of this future calamity, *everyone* would die.

Note: To suggest that the three-and-a-half years following Titus' invasion of Jerusalem in 70 A.D. fulfilled this prophecy, as some Christians assert, demeans Christ's explicit warning. Why? It should be obvious to any twenty-first century student of the Bible that, however devastating the destruction spread by Titus, no Roman armies in 70 A.D. could reach (let alone kill) civilizations living thousands of miles away from the Roman Empire (such as the Chinese or the various Western Hemisphere tribal cultures). Today, however, the armed forces of the United States and Russia *do* have the capacity to reach the entire globe with weapons of mass destruction and *do* have the capacity to accomplish precisely what Christ prophesied.

Chart 2-A

DANIEL'S "SEVENTY WEEKS" CHRONOLOGY

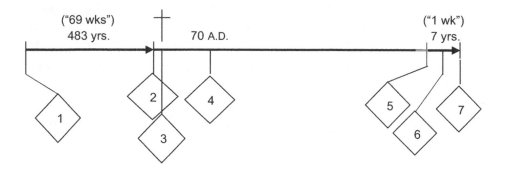

1.   The issuing of the decree to restore and rebuild Jerusalem

2.   The coming of Messiah to Jerusalem

3.   The death of Messiah

4.   The destruction of Jerusalem—and its temple—by the people who will beget the end-times Antichrist

5.   The signing of a seven-year peace treaty between the Antichrist and Israel

6.   The Antichrist's halting of the regular temple sacrifices in Jerusalem— and his setting up of the "abomination of desolation" in the temple— midway through the seven-year treaty

7.   The destruction and end of the Antichrist

Chart 2-B

OBSERVATIONS FROM DANIEL 9:24-27

- Seventy years times seven (or 490 years) have been decreed for the Israelites (and for Jerusalem) to finish their transgression and to bring in everlasting righteousness. [483 years (or 69 "weeks") have already taken place; seven years (or one "week") yet remain—the precise length of the Tribulation period; a nearly 2,000-year time gap has now taken place between Daniel's 69th and 70th weeks]

- Messiah will be presented to Israel 483 years after the decree to restore and rebuild Jerusalem. [The decree to rebuild Jerusalem was issued by Artixerxes Longimanus of Persia in 445 B.C.]

- Jerusalem and the temple will be rebuilt before Messiah is presented to Israel at the end of the 483 years

- Messiah will be presented to Israel—and subsequently killed—*before* Jerusalem and the temple are once again destroyed

- An invading people, from whom will come the 70th week Antichrist, will destroy Jerusalem and the temple. [Jerusalem and its temple were destroyed in 70 A.D. by the Romans]

- A time gap of an unspecified length of time will occur between the 69th and 70th weeks during which time Messiah will be killed and the temple will be destroyed

- The Antichrist will be a descendent of the ancient Roman Empire

- The Antichrist will sign a seven-year peace treaty with Israel and her neighbors

- The Antichrist will break the peace treaty at its mid-point

- Upon breaking the peace treaty, the Antichrist will put an end to Israel's Levitical worship system

- Jerusalem will have a temple during the Tribulation period

- The Antichrist will desecrate the temple

- The Antichrist will make Israel and Jerusalem desolate after the mid-point of the Tribulation

- The Antichrist will eventually be destroyed

THE DUALISM OF MESSIANIC PROPHECY

The chronology of events in Daniel's "Seventy Weeks" prophecy implies a time gap of an undisclosed length of time between the 69th and 70th "weeks" decreed for the Israelites. With the benefit of 20-20 hindsight, today's student of Bible prophecy knows that the time gap has now covered nearly 2,000 years. In the next several chapters we will discover God's purposes for the gap as well as the gap's end-times implications. Fundamental to our understanding of this interval, however, is the dual nature of Christ's advents and the dualism of Messianic prophecy itself—namely, that Christ would first come as a suffering servant but would later come again as a reigning king.

Perhaps the key Messianic prophecy reflecting this dualism is Zechariah 9:9-10: *"Rejoice greatly, O daughter of Zion! Shout in triumph, O daughter of Jerusalem! Behold, your king is coming to you; He is just and endowed with salvation—humble, and mounted on a donkey, even on a colt, the foal of a donkey. And I will cut off the chariot from Ephraim and the horse from Jerusalem; and the bow of war will be cut off, and He will speak peace to the nations; and His dominion will be from sea to sea, and from the [Euphrates] River to the ends of the earth."*

Zechariah 9:9 announces that Israel's Messiah (*"your king"*) would come in peace on a lowly donkey rather than coming as a conquering warrior on a horse. Unlike most other kings of the day, Israel's Messiah would be humble. Moreover, He would be endowed with *salvation*—in fulfillment of (1) God's promise of a Redeemer in Genesis 3:15 and (2) God's promise in Genesis 12:3 that all the nations would be blessed through a person coming from Abraham's seed.

Zechariah 9:10, on the other hand, provides a significantly different picture of the coming of Israel's Messiah: He will reign over the entire earth (*"from sea to sea . . . to the ends of the earth"*). He will bring an end to war on earth (*"will cut off the chariot and the horse"*). And His rule will bring peace to all the nations of the earth (*"He will speak peace to the nations"*). Thus, we can see that Zechariah 9:9-10 pictures two different advents of Messiah the King—the first bringing an offer of salvation from sin and the second bringing a reign of peace over the entire earth.

The Jews of Christ's day were fixated on the second half of this prophecy but blind to the first half. Simply put, they wanted a Messiah who would rid them of the yoke of Rome and simultaneously reign over the known world. Thus, most of the Jews who welcomed Christ into Jerusalem on Palm Sunday and proclaimed Him to be Israel's Messiah were looking for the beginning of a Davidic political kingdom. When Christ was crucified four days later as the "Lamb of God who takes away the sins of the world," most of the Jews grew disillusioned and fell away. Most of them wanted no part of a kingdom which called for *repentance unto salvation*—a turning of their hearts to receive Jesus Christ as their Savior from sin.

Many other Bible passages point to this dual nature of Messiah's advents. Some of these prophecies are listed in Charts 3-D and 3-E. It is also apparent from several of these prophecies that a far more visible (worldwide and startling) coming of Messiah will one day take place (e.g., Isa. 13:9-13; Ezek. 32:7; Amos 5:20; and Joel 3:14-15). Because Scripture describes two different advents of Jesus Christ— one in which He comes to offer salvation from sin and the other in which He comes as the sovereign King of the earth, mankind can be certain of a future second coming of Jesus Christ to reign over the earth.

Chart 3-A

ZECHARIAH 9:9-10

AT CHRIST'S 1ST COMING: (v.9)   *[SAVIOR !]*

      HE IS JUST

      HE IS ENDOWED WITH <u>SALVATION</u>

      HE IS HUMBLE

AT CHRIST'S 2ND COMING: (v.10)   *[KING ! PRINCE OF PEACE !]*

      HE WILL BRING AN END TO WAR

      HE WILL BRING <u>PEACE</u> TO ALL NATIONS

      HE WILL <u>RULE</u> OVER THE ENTIRE EARTH

Chart 3-B

PROPHECIES RELATING TO CHRIST'S 1ST ADVENT

- He would be born of a woman

- He would be from the line of Abraham

- He would be from the tribe of Judah

- He would be from the house of David

- He would be born of a virgin

- He would be called Emmanuel

- He would be born in Bethlehem

- He would be worshiped by wise men and presented gifts as an infant

- He would be in Egypt for a period of time

- His birthplace would suffer a massacre of infants

- He would have a forerunner

- He would be called a Nazarene

- He would be filled with God's Spirit

- He would heal many

- He would speak in parables

- He would make a triumphal entry into Jerusalem

- He would be mounted on a donkey during this entry

- His miracles would not be believed

- He would be betrayed for 30 pieces of silver

- He would be rejected by his own

- He would be the rejected cornerstone

- He would be a man of sorrows

- He would be scourged and spat upon

Chart 3-B

- His betrayal money would be used to buy a potter's field

- He would be crucified between two thieves

- He would be given vinegar to drink

- He would suffer the piercing of his hands and feet

- His garments would be taken from him and gambled for

- He would be surrounded by his enemies

- He would thirst

- He would commend his spirit to the Father

- His bones would not be broken

- He would be buried with the rich

- He would be raised from the dead

- He would ascend

- He would be seated at God's right hand

Taken from Wilmington's Book of Bible Lists, H.L. Wilmington, Tyndale House Publishers, Inc., Wheaton, 1987, pp.260-263

Chart 3-C

PROPHECIES RELATING TO CHRIST'S 2ND ADVENT

- Christ will return to the earth to save Israel from annihilation at the hands of the Gentile armies of the world (Zech. 9:14-16; 12:2-3).

- Immediately after the assembling of nations in Megiddo and the destruction of half of Jerusalem, (1) the sun will be darkened; (2) the moon will not give off its light; (3) the stars will fall from the sky; and (4) the powers of the heavens will be shaken (Isa. 13:9-13; Ezek. 32:7; Amos 5:20; 8:9; Joel 3:15; Acts 2:20; Matt. 24:29; Mark 13:24,25; Hebrews 12:26; Haggai 2:6,21).

- Immediately after the four items above, (1) a supernatural phenomenon pointing to the return of Jesus Christ will appear in the sky; and (2) Christ Himself will return out of the clouds to the earth (Matt. 24:30,31; 26:64; Mark 13:26; 14:62)

- Christ will return bodily to the earth thirty days after the end of the Tribulation period (Dan. 12:11,12; Matt. 24:29-30).

- Christ will return to the Mount of Olives (Zech. 14:4) and will descend to the earth in the same manner in which He ascended (Acts 1:4-11).

- The Mount of Olives will be split open upon the Lord's return, with half of it moving toward the north and half of it toward the south, thus forming a large valley (Zech. 14:4).

- Many Jews who have been fighting the Gentile invaders in Jerusalem when Christ returns will flee to safety through the newly-formed valley (Zech. 14:5).

- On the day of the Lord's return, the sun, moon, and stars will not give off their light, but the entire earth will be illumined instead by the Lord Himself (Zech. 14:6,7) and His angels (II Thes. 1:7).

- Every person remaining on earth will see Christ's bodily return (Rev. 1:7).

- Christ and His angels will return to the earth in flaming fire (II Thes. 1:7).

- Resurrected believers will return with Christ and will have the glory of Christ (Col. 3:4; I Thes. 3:13).

- When the Lord appears at His Second Coming, all resurrected believers with Him will be like Christ, having been transformed into His image (I John 3:2; Romans 8:29).

Chart 3-C

- God will pour out His grace upon Israel; and Israel, at Christ's Second Coming, will mourn Him whom they once crucified (Zech. 12:10).

- When Israel sees Christ at His Second Coming, Israel will say, "Blessed is He who comes in the name of the Lord!" (Luke 13:35).

- Whoever on this earth today is ashamed of Jesus Christ and His Word will discover that the Lord will be ashamed of him when He returns (Mark 8:38; Luke 9:26).

- Those who do not abide in Christ will shrink away from Him in shame at His coming (I John 2:28).

- Christ will destroy all persons who have come to Megiddo to fight against Israel (Zech. 12:9).

- Christ will strike many of the invaders with madness (Zech. 12:4).

- Christ will cause the invading soldiers of the land of Magog and her allies to kill each other while positioned in the mountains of Israel (Ezek. 38:21).

- Christ will bring a supernatural fire down upon the invading soldiers of Magog and her allies (Ezek. 38:22).

- The corpses of the invading troops of Magog will be eaten by predator birds and beasts of the field (Ezek. 39:4).

- Christ will also bring fire down upon the land of Magog as well as many other countries (Ezek. 39:6).

- Jesus Christ will defeat the Antichrist (II Thess. 2:8-10).

- The Antichrist and his kingdom will be destroyed forever (Dan. 7:26;11:45).

- All the nations will know that Christ is Lord (Ezek. 39:9).

- Israel will know from this time forward that Christ is her Messiah and Lord (Ezek. 39:22).

- Christ will be given the throne of David (II Sam. 7:12-16).

- Christ will rule over the entire earth (Zech. 9:10; Ps. 2:9).

- Christ will bring peace to the nations (Zech. 9:10).

- Christ's throne will be an eternal throne (II Sam. 7:12,16).

Chart 3-C

- Christ will be called Wonderful Counselor, Mighty God, Eternal Father, Prince of Peace (Isa. 9:6)

CHRIST'S "KINGDOM OF HEAVEN" PARABLES

God's prophets in the Old Testament not only revealed the immediate future of the nation of Israel, but also her far-off future. This distant future would include the coming of Messiah to reign over the earth from Jerusalem and to rid Israel of her foreign oppressors (Micah 4:1-3; Zechariah 14:9; Daniel 2:36-44). As just mentioned, it was this Messianic Kingdom that many of the Jews who saw and heard Jesus were expecting. Indeed, most who followed Christ were neither looking for, nor wanted, a Messiah who would save them from their sins. Instead, they wanted Jesus to set up a Messianic Kingdom to rid them of the yoke of Rome. To their dismay this hoped-for political Messiah was crucified.

As a result, the Jewish audience to whom Matthew writes wants to have one crucial question answered: "If Jesus Christ is Israel's Messiah, then why isn't He reigning from Jerusalem this very moment?" Matthew answers this question by unveiling in the second half of his Gospel the unforeseen Inter-Advent Kingdom of Messiah, a kingdom designed to take root in the heart of any person—Jew or Gentile—who would put his faith in Jesus Christ as Savior from sin. This kingdom had not been revealed to Israel's prophets.

Jesus discloses a number of the principal characteristics of this inter-advent kingdom through the use of twelve parables—similes which begin with the words "the kingdom of heaven is like" or "the kingdom of heaven is comparable to." These twelve parables are found in chapters 13, 18, 20, 22, and 25 of Matthew's Gospel. Eleven of these parables describe a spiritual kingdom of Christ's that will exist on earth *between* His two advents. A twelfth parable describes an event which takes place immediately after Christ's second coming. Today this kingdom is known as Christianity or Christendom—and consists of all persons who call themselves Christians. Christianity and Christendom stand in contrast to Islam, Buddhism or Hinduism, for example, whose adherents call themselves Muslims, Buddhists or Hindus. Let us look briefly at some of these parables.

The parable of the Sower reveals that the gospel message will be met with a continuum of response between the two advents of Christ—from outright rejection, to shallow profession, to carnal reception, to wholehearted belief. The parable of the Mustard Seed teaches that Christ's kingdom ("Christendom") will begin as the tiniest of movements but will grow to be the largest religion on earth before His Second Coming. The parable of the Wheat and the Tares explains that Christ's kingdom will contain true adherents and counterfeit adherents. The parable of the Leaven makes it clear that Christ's kingdom will grow inexorably over time but will also become infiltrated with false teaching and destructive heresies. The parable of the Hidden Treasure and the parable of the Pearl of Great Value explain that a personal relationship with Christ will have incalculable value to the adherent and is worth laying aside all other pursuits in order to have it to the fullest. The parable of the Landowner who Offers Work teaches that Christ's kingdom is available even to those who put their faith in Christ late in life. The parable of the Talents shows that Christ will reward faithful service in His kingdom. Significantly, the parable of the Ten Virgins not only pictures Christ's coming for born-again believers (His Bride) at the Rapture, but it also suggests that most of Christ's followers will not be alert for his return.

Nevertheless, Christ makes it clear in the gospels that this inter-advent kingdom of heaven is not a political kingdom: *"My kingdom is not of this world. If my kingdom were of this world, then My servants would be fighting, that I might not be delivered up to the Jews. But as it is, My kingdom is not of this realm" (John 18:36).* Instead, Christ's inter-advent kingdom is a spiritual kingdom designed to take root in the hearts of men and women—Jew or Gentile—anywhere on earth who put their faith in Jesus Christ and His finished work on the Cross for their sin problem. Chart 4-A lists the twelve kingdom of heaven parables. [Note: by comparing both the parable of the Sower and the parable of the Mustard Seed in Mark and Luke, we can conclude that the terms "kingdom of heaven" (used in Matthew) and "kingdom of God" (used in Mark and Luke) have the same meaning and are interchangeable terms.]

It is also important at this juncture for the reader to recognize that the New Testament portrays *three* different "kingdoms of heaven" (or "kingdoms of God"). The first kingdom is the **Inter-Advent Kingdom**—known today as Christianity or Christendom. This kingdom deals with the sowing of, and response to, the gospel message between Christ's two advents. This kingdom includes true adherents (the "wheat") and counterfeit adherents (the "tares"). The tares will be left behind on earth at the Rapture of the Church (Matt. 25:1-13). The second kingdom is the **Millennial Kingdom**, a kingdom established and ruled over by Jesus Christ *after* His Second Coming (Rev. 20:1-6) in fulfillment of numerous Old Testament prophecies, including the Davidic Covenant (II Sam. 7:8-29). The third kingdom is the **Eternal Kingdom**, a kingdom established by God (for believers from every generation of human history) *after* the destruction of the present heavens and earth—and after the creation of the new heavens and earth (where sin will no longer exist) (Rev. 21:1 - 22:5). It is critical that a student of the End Times understands these distinctions. Chart 4-B lists the three kingdoms.

Finally, four of Christ's twelve "kingdom of heaven" parables in Matthew have significant end-times implications, and two of these will be examined at length in upcoming chapters. It should be mentioned at this point, however, that the parable of the Mustard Seed—in which Christendom is seen as beginning as a tiny religion only to become the largest of the earth's religions before Christ's second coming—implies the passage of a significant amount of time for the message of the good news of Jesus Christ to reach throughout the earth. It took nearly fifteen hundred years, for example, for the gospel to reach the Western Hemisphere. Today, Christianity is the largest of the world's religions, both numerically and geographically, just as Christ prophesied, and a long period of time—nearly 2,000 years—has passed since His first advent. The growth of Christianity has been a major world phenomenon during the past two millennia.

Chart 4-A

MATTHEW'S INTER-ADVENT "KINGDOM OF HEAVEN" PARABLES

- **THE SOWER**
  (Matt. 13:3-9,18-23; Mark 4:3-8,14-20; Luke 8:5-8)

- **THE MUSTARD SEED**
  (Matt. 13:31-32; Mark 4:30-32; Luke 13:18-19)

- **THE WHEAT & THE TARES**
  (Matt. 13:24-30,36-43)

- **THE LEAVEN**
  (Matt. 13:33; Luke 13:20-21)

- **THE HIDDEN TREASURE**
  (Matt. 13:44)

- **THE PEARL OF GREAT VALUE**
  (Matt. 13:45-46)

- **THE KING WHO SETTLES ACCOUNTS**
  (Matt. 18:23-35)

- **THE LANDOWNER WHO OFFERS WORK**
  (Matt. 20:1-16)

- **THE TEN VIRGINS**
  (Matt. 25:1-13)

- **THE TALENTS**
  (Matt. 25:14-30)

- **THE WEDDING FEAST**
  (Matt. 22:2-14)

- **THE FISHING NET**
  (Matt. 13:47-50)

Chart 4-B

THE TWO "KINGDOMS OF GOD" IN THE OLD TESTAMENT

- **THE MESSIANIC KINGDOM**
  (MESSIAH'S REIGN OVER THE EARTH FROM JERUSALEM)

- **THE ETERNAL KINGDOM**
  (THE ETERNAL HOME OF EVERY BELIEVER FROM ALL GENERATIONS)

THE THREE "KINGDOMS OF GOD" IN THE NEW TESTAMENT

- **THE INTER-ADVENT KINGDOM: CHRISTIANITY OR "CHRISTENDOM"**
  (CHRIST'S KINGDOM ON EARTH BETWEEN HIS TWO ADVENTS. THIS
  KINGDOM WAS NOT REVEALED IN THE OLD TESTAMENT [EPH.3:1-11;
  COL. 1:25-28])

- **THE MESSIANIC (MILLENNIAL) KINGDOM**
  (CHRIST'S 1,000-YEAR REIGN OVER THE EARTH FROM JERUSALEM)

- **THE ETERNAL KINGDOM**
  (THE ETERNAL HOME OF EVERY BELIEVER FROM ALL GENERATIONS)

THE DAY OF PENTECOST

Jesus also told the disciples of His two advents: *"Little children, I am with you a little while longer. You shall seek Me; and as I said to the Jews, I now say to you also, 'Where I am going, you cannot come'. . . . Let not your heart be troubled; believe in God, believe in Me also. In My Father's house there are many dwelling places; if it were not so, I would have told you; for I go to prepare a place for you. And if I go and prepare a place for you, then I will come again and receive you to Myself, that where I am, you may be also"* (John 13:33; 14:1-3).

Because of their likely concern over the pronouncement that He would be leaving them for an unspecified period of time, Jesus then made a startling promise to his disciples. Specifically, He revealed that He would send the Holy Spirit to comfort them, to lead them, and to *indwell* them during His absence: *"And I will ask the Father, and He will give you another Helper, that He may be with you forever— that is, the Spirit of truth, whom the world cannot receive, because it does not behold Him or know Him, but you know Him because He abides with you and will be in you. . . . And the Helper, the Holy Spirit, whom the Father will send in My name, will teach you all things and bring to your remembrance all that I said to you"* (John 14:16-17,26). Jesus would later add: *"But when He, the Spirit of truth comes, He will guide you into all the truth"* (John 16:13). Thus, the Holy Spirit—whom Jesus would send—would forever indwell believers, comfort them, guide them, teach them, and lead them into all truth.

In addition, Jesus explained another ministry of the Holy Spirit:

> *And He, when He comes, will convict the world concerning sin, and righteousness, and judgment: concerning sin, because they do not believe in Me; concerning righteousness, because I go to the Father, and you no longer behold Me; and concerning judgment, because the ruler of this world has been judged (John 16:8-11).*

The Holy Spirit, during the inter-advent period, would convict the world of sin, righteousness, and judgment. To be sure, when unbelievers are confronted with the truth about their sin, their unrighteousness compared to the perfect righteousness of Christ, and the judgment which awaits those who refuse to avail themselves of God's grace at Calvary's Cross, this moving of the Holy Spirit (often through the witness of believers) has a *restraining* influence on sin. The Apostle Paul alludes to the Holy Spirit as the One who restrains lawlessness (II Thess. 2:6-7).

When did the promised Helper—the indwelling Holy Spirit—come to the believers in Jerusalem? The Holy Spirit descended to the earth fifty days after the Resurrection of Jesus Christ on the Jewish feast day known as Pentecost. Approximately a hundred and twenty of Christ's disciples (including the Apostles) were present together in Jerusalem (Acts 1:15) awaiting the coming of the Holy Spirit:

> *And when the day of Pentecost had come, they were all together in one place. And suddenly there came from heaven a noise like a violent, rushing wind, and it filled the whole house where they were sitting. And there appeared to them tongues as of fire distributing themselves, and they rested on each one of them. And they were all filled with the Holy Spirit and began to speak in other languages, as the Spirit was giving them utterance (Acts 2:1-4).*
>
> *Now there were Jews living in Jerusalem, devout men, from every nation under heaven. And when this sound occurred, the multitude came together, and were bewildered, because they were each one hearing them speak in his own language. And they were amazed and marveled, saying, "Why, are not all these who are speaking Galileans? And how is it that we each hear them in our own language to which we were born? Parthians and Medes and Elamites, and residents of Mesopotamia, Judea and Cappadocia, Pontus and Asia, Phrygia and Pamphylia, Egypt and the districts of Libya around Cyrene, and visitors from Rome, both Jews and proselytes, Cretans and Arabs—we hear them in our own tongues speaking of the mighty deeds of God (Acts 2:5-11)."*

Coinciding with this supernatural event and in response to the crowd's bewilderment-amazement, Peter, indwelled and filled with Holy Spirit, proclaims the gospel message to the large number of Jews gathered in Jerusalem, and 3,000 of them put their trust in Jesus Christ for salvation: *"Now when they heard this, they were pierced to the heart and said to Peter, 'Brethren, what shall we do?' And Peter said to them, 'Repent, and let each of you be baptized in the name of Jesus Christ for the forgiveness of your sins, and you shall receive the gift of the Holy Spirit'" (Acts 2:37-38).* Thus, on this first Pentecost after Christ's Resurrection and Ascension, the Church (all persons indwelled with the Holy Spirit) is born and the "mustard seed" (Christendom) begins to grow.

This inter-advent period, now nearly 2,000 years in length, stands unique in human history because of the coming of the Holy Spirit to *indwell* born-again believers in Jesus Christ. The moment a person—by faith—invites Christ into his heart, God the Father imparts to him the indwelling Holy Spirit (John 14:17) and makes him a new creature in Christ (II Cor. 5:17). It is a supernatural transaction from above (John 3:4-8). The person is now a spiritual babe, whom Christ desires to grow up to spiritual maturity through a process of feeding on His Word (the Bible), fellowshipping with other believers, worshipping together, praying earnestly to the Father, loving and serving others, being a living sacrifice, experiencing trials and testing, and being ready to share with others the hope that is within him.

Finally, by using Daniel's "Seventy Weeks" chronology as our frame of reference, we can readily see where the coming of the indwelling Holy Spirit at

Pentecost fits into the timeline of God's inter-advent purposes (and ultimately God's end-times purposes) (see Chart 5-A).

DANIEL'S "SEVENTY WEEKS" CHRONOLOGY (INCL. PENTECOST)

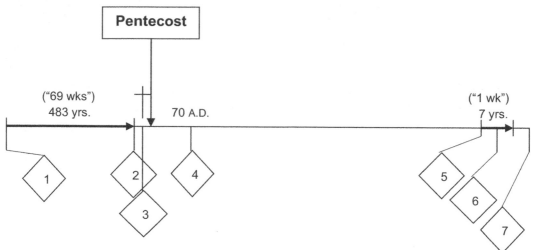

1.   The issuing of the decree to restore and rebuild Jerusalem

2.   The coming of Messiah to Jerusalem

3.   The death of Messiah

   PENTECOST (the coming of the indwelling Holy Spirit)

4.   The destruction of Jerusalem—and its temple—by the people who will
     beget the end-times Antichrist

5.   The signing of a seven-year peace treaty between the Antichrist and
     Israel

6.   The Antichrist's halting of the regular temple sacrifices in Jerusalem—
     and his setting up of the "abomination of desolation" in the temple—
     midway through the seven-year treaty

7.   The destruction and end of the Antichrist

THE RAPTURE—AND ITS TIMING

A. The Two Phases of the Lord's Return

The tenor of New Testament Scripture indicates that the return of Jesus Christ takes place in two different phases. One phase involves the Lord's coming in the air *for* His Church (those persons, dead or living, who, from Pentecost until this unannounced return, have put their faith in Jesus Christ for salvation). The other phase involves the Lord's bodily return to the earth *with* His Church (as well as pre-Pentecost believers and Tribulation martyrs/saints) to save Israel from annihilation, to judge the earth's remaining inhabitants, and to establish His Millennial Kingdom on earth. The first phase is typically called the "Rapture" and the second phase is typically called the "Second Coming." (See Chart 6-A.) [Note: Matthew's Gospel presents these two phases of the Lord's return as two entirely different, *mutually exclusive* comings of the Son of Man—a topic which will be examined in Chapter 10, "The Olivet Discourse"]

B. Contrasts between the Rapture and the Second Coming

The two different phases of the Lord's return are best understood when the contrasts between the two are noted. Christ's return at the Rapture will be *unannounced*, just as a thief's stealthy entrance into a home at night is unannounced (Matt. 24:43-44; I Thess. 5:2-3). Christ's return at the Second Coming, however, will be *announced*—by signs in the sky (Matt. 24:29; Zech 14:6-7; and others). Christ's return at the Rapture will be in the air (I Thess. 4:15-18); Christ's return at the Second Coming will be to the earth (Zech. 14:4; Acts 1:4-11). Christ's return at the Rapture will be instantaneous and *invisible*, in the "twinkling of an eye" (I Cor. 15:51-52). Christ's return at the Second Coming will take several minutes (if not several hours) and will be *visible*—every person still alive on earth will see His return (Acts 1:9-11; Rev. 1:7). (See Chart 6-B.)

When examining these contrasts, it is readily apparent that the two events cannot be simultaneous. Rather, some passage of time necessarily must take place between the events (e.g., for the condition on earth to deteriorate from "marrying and giving in marriage" to "unless those days had been cut short, no life would have been saved").

C. The Certainty of the Rapture

The Apostle Paul describes the Rapture in two separate New Testament passages. In I Thessalonians, Paul describes it as follows:

> *For the Lord Himself will descend from heaven with a shout, with the voice of the archangel and with the trumpet of God; and the dead in*

Christ shall rise first. Then we who are alive and remain shall be caught up together with them in the clouds to meet the Lord in the air, and thus we shall always be with the Lord. Therefore, comfort one another with these words. (I Thess. 4:15-18)

In I Corinthians, Paul offers additional information about the Rapture:

Now I say this, brethren, that flesh and blood cannot inherit the kingdom of God; nor does the perishable inherit the imperishable. Behold, I tell you a mystery; we shall not all sleep, but we shall all be changed, in a moment, in the twinkling of an eye, at the last trumpet; for the trumpet will sound, and the dead will be raised imperishable, and we shall be changed. (I Cor. 15:50-52).

The Rapture, then, is an invisible, unannounced (Matt. 24:43), instantaneous "catching up" into heaven of all dead and living born-again believers, who in this moment receive their eternal, imperishable resurrection bodies. The *certainty* of the Rapture cannot be debated by Christians; it is the plain, straight-forward teaching of the Scriptures. The only item for debate is the Rapture's *timing* relative to the Tribulation.

D. The Different Views on the Timing of the Rapture

Five viewpoints with regard to the timing of the Rapture exist in Christian circles today. These five viewpoints are as follows: (1) the "pre-tribulation" Rapture; (2) the "mid-tribulation" Rapture; (3) the "post-tribulation" Rapture; (4) the "pre-wrath" Rapture; and (5) the "partial" Rapture. The first view contends that the Rapture—this invisible, unannounced, instantaneous catching up into heaven of all dead and living born-again believers from the day of Pentecost until the instant of the Rapture—takes place before the Tribulation begins (hence the name, pre-tribulation Rapture). The second view contends that the Rapture takes place at the mid-point of the Tribulation. The third view contends that the Rapture takes place at the end of the Tribulation. The fourth view contends that the Rapture takes place before God pours out His wrath upon mankind near the end of a Christ-shortened Tribulation (hence the name, pre-wrath Rapture). The fifth view contends that only those who are faithful in the Church will be raptured before the Tribulation begins (and that the remaining believers will be raptured either during, or at the end of, the Tribulation). All five of these positions acknowledge the reality and certainty of the Rapture—the instantaneous "catching up" into heaven of all dead and living born-again believers.

E. Eight Reasons why a Pre-Tribulation Rapture is the Best View

One of the essential components to a correct understanding of the End-Times events is the adoption of a pre-tribulation Rapture. Though other reasons can be rendered, the following eight arguments explain why the pre-tribulation Rapture is the best position.

First, the Lord's exhortations in Matthew 24 & 25 that His coming for His Bride (born-again believers) will be sudden, unannounced, and as unexpected as a thief entering a home at night are meaningless except in the context of a pre-tribulation Rapture. Once the Middle-East peace treaty between the Antichrist and Israel is signed, the Christian knows from Scripture that Christ will return bodily to the earth exactly 2,550 days after the signing of the treaty—1,260 days to the breaking of the treaty and 1,290 days from the breaking of the treaty to the bodily return (Dan. 12:11-12). Thus, a person who holds to a mid-tribulation Rapture need not be looking for an any-moment Rapture, but instead need only be looking for the signing of the Antichrist's peace treaty with Israel. Moreover, such Christians could "live it up" until just before the mid-point of the Tribulation, should they choose to do so, and then "clean up their act" for the Rapture. Likewise, a person who holds to the post-tribulation position need not be looking for an imminent, unexpected, any-moment Rapture of the Church, but need only be looking for the Antichrist's peace treaty. Such Christians could also live it up until the end of the Tribulation, should they choose to do so, and then get ready for the Rapture. The pre-wrath position is similarly flawed because the whole concept of "imminence"—the Lord's coming for His "Bride" (the Church) unannounced and at any moment, as taught by Christ in the Gospels and as pictured in the parable of the ten virgins (Matt. 25:1-13)—is negated by this position. *Only the pre-tribulation Rapture challenges the Christian to be alert and ready for an unannounced, unexpected, any-moment return of Christ for the Church.* [Note: the "partial" Rapture must be also rejected because Christ states that He will come for *all* of His sheep not just some of them (John 14:1-3).]

Second, the Lord Himself promises that Church Age believers will not go through the Tribulation. Jesus tells His sheep: *"Because you have kept the word of My perseverance, I also will keep you from the hour of testing, which is about to come upon the whole world, to test those who dwell upon the earth" (Rev. 3:10).* Jesus states unequivocally that He will keep His children—born-again Christians—from the "hour of testing." Because this hour of testing is to come upon the whole world (and because the context of the Lord's promise is the book of Revelation, which deals almost exclusively with the end times and the Tribulation judgments), it is clear that Christ is talking about the Tribulation. Only the pre-tribulation Rapture coincides with Christ's promise. *All other Rapture positions invalidate this promise.* Critics of this verse often state that Christ does not promise to take his children out of the Tribulation but only to protect them during the Tribulation. Yet such an argument wholly contradicts certain passages in Revelation which state that tens of millions of Christians will be murdered and martyred during the Tribulation. How has Christ thus "protected" Christians during Tribulation if millions of Christians are slaughtered? In contrast, under a pre-tribulation position Christ takes all born-again Christians with Him at the Rapture, thus leaving, at the instant of the Rapture, no true Christians on earth. Those who subsequently come to faith in Christ during the Tribulation through, for example, the ministry of the 144,000 Jewish Tribulation evangelists, only to be killed because of their new-found faith in Christ, are the martyrs pictured in Revelation. We need not try to finesse Christ's plain teaching. Christ has stated that He will keep His sheep from the horrors of the Tribulation—and we can trust that He will do just that. *Only the pre-tribulation position takes Christ's promise at face value.*

Third, the Apostle Paul teaches that Church Age believers will not go through the Tribulation. Paul states in I Thessalonians 5:9: *"For God has not destined us for wrath, but for obtaining salvation through our Lord Jesus Christ."* Paul presents exactly the same promise as Christ: believers (the "us" in Paul's passage) are not destined to go through "wrath" (the Tribulation). Instead, each Church Age believer's salvation will be *completed* (1) at the Rapture when he or she receives an eternal, imperishable resurrection body and (2) at the judgment seat of Christ when the dross of his or her Christian life is removed for all eternity (II Cor. 5:10; I Cor. 3:10-15).

Fourth, the substance and tenor of Daniel's Seventy Weeks prophecy calls for a pre-tribulation Rapture. On the Day of Pentecost in 30 A.D., God interrupted His prophetic plan for Israel so that He could begin to fulfill His salvation purposes in Gentile nations as well (Romans 11:25-26). When God finishes this Gentile grace, He will Rapture the Church and will then once again undertake for His people Israel in order to bring Daniel's "Seventy Weeks" prophecy to completion. Furthermore, because the Church (all born-again Christians from Pentecost until the Rapture) had no role whatsoever in the first 483 years of Daniel's prophecy, then logic would suggest that the Church would likewise have no role whatsoever in the final seven years of the prophecy. The only Rapture position which harmonizes with Daniel's Seventy Weeks prophecy (God's previous and still-future dealings with Israel [with a now nearly 2000-year Church Age "parenthesis" in the middle]) is the pre-tribulation Rapture. (See Charts 6-C & 7-B.)

Fifth, the metaphor of the Betrothal, Marriage, and Marriage Supper of Christ (the Bridegroom) and His Church (the Bride) readily suggests, if not demands, a pre-tribulation Rapture (Matt. 25:1-13; Rev. 19:6-9). According to born-again commentator Zola Levitt, the first century Jewish betrothal was unlike the typical Gentile engagement of today. In a Jewish betrothal, the bridegroom, after proposing to his loved one, would "go away" to his "father's house" to "make a place" for them to live on the father's land. Often he would be away for a year while he completed their home. Then, when the home was ready and all the arrangements had been made for a wedding feast, the bridegroom, in a touch of Jewish romance, would come for his bride *unexpectedly*, usually in the middle of the night. The bride, of course, was to be alert and ready for his return, eager to have their marriage consummated. To be fully prepared (in case her groom would come for her at night), she would have to have her lamp trimmed with oil so that she would have sufficient light to go out to greet him. And so it is to be with the Church, the Bride of Christ (Eph. 5:22-32; Rev. 19:7). All persons indwelled with the Holy Spirit (the "oil") are to be alert and ready for an any-moment coming of the Bridegroom (Christ) to take them to the Father's home for the consummation of their wedding (the completion and perfection of their salvation) and for the subsequent wedding feast prepared for them by the Father. The pre-tribulation Rapture best fits this picture.

[Note: Because Christ knows that He will not return for many centuries (Matt. 24:45-51; 25:14-19) when He presents the Parable of the Ten Virgins (Matt. 25:1-13)—and because He knows that the vast majority of His Bride (the true Church of born-again believers) will have died before He returns—He apparently chooses to describe the *living* members of the true Church when He comes at the Rapture as five "prudent" virgins. The prudent virgins have the "oil"—a picture of the indwelling Holy Spirit—and are that part of living Christendom which will be translated into heaven at the Rapture. In contrast, Jesus describes that part of living Christendom which will be left behind on earth at the Rapture as five "foolish" virgins. The foolish virgins have no "oil"—no indwelling Holy Spirit—because they have not come to Christ on the basis of faith in His finished work (but instead have come to Christ on their own terms, typically by sacraments, good works, church membership, or universalism).]

Sixth, the Holy Spirit—the restrainer of evil (Gen. 6:3)—must be taken out of the way *before* the "lawless one" (the Antichrist) can be revealed (II Thess. 2:7-10). In addition, the lawless one—the Antichrist—in turn must be revealed *before* the Tribulation begins so that he can have time to rise to power and eventually sign the peace treaty with Israel, the event which inaugurates the Tribulation. States Paul: *"For the mystery of lawlessness is already at work; only he who now restrains will do so until he is taken out of the way. And then that lawless one, the one whose coming is in accord with the activity of Satan, will be revealed, whom the Lord will slay with the breath of His mouth and bring to an end by the appearance of His coming."* Paul's argument is straightforward: the One who restrains lawlessness (the Holy Spirit) must be taken out of the way before the Antichrist can be revealed. Because the Holy Spirit indwells believers (who in turn are part of the restraining influence of sin), the restraining influence of the Holy Spirit cannot be removed to make way for the coming of the Antichrist unless the Church (whom the Holy Spirit indwells) is also removed. (See Chart 6-D.) Only the pre-tribulation Rapture lines up with Paul's argument.

Seventh, the calling out of the 144,000 Jewish virgin males in the book of Revelation (Rev. 7:1-8; 14:1-5) readily suggests, if not demands, a pre-tribulation Rapture. It is clear that the 144,000 are saved *before* the Tribulation begins: *"do not harm the earth or the sea or the trees until we have sealed the bond-servants of our God on their foreheads"* (Rev. 7:3). Moreover, it should be noted that the 144,000 Jewish males are not only saved before the Tribulation period begins (i.e., before the earth is harmed), but in fact are the *first persons saved* after the Rapture occurs: *"These have been purchased from among men as first fruits to God and to the Lamb."* Because the 144,000 are described as "first fruits" of a harvest, this narrative necessitates that a *previous* harvest of some sort has taken place. This previous harvest is the Rapture of the Church, a harvest which leaves *no* believers on earth. [Note: In contrast, the first persons saved during the Church Age (i.e., the "first fruits" of the Church Age harvest) were the 120 disciples (including Peter and several women) in the Upper Room, then the 3,000 Jews who responded to Peter's sermon on the Day of Pentecost, then the ones who were being added day by day (Acts 2:47), and then the 5,000 Jews (including widows—Acts 6:1) who responded the Peter's second sermon a few weeks later. Thus, it is clear that the calling out of the 144,000 Jewish males as "first fruits to God and to the Lamb" cannot refer to the Church Age.] It should be noted, moreover, that the calling out of the 144,000 *before* the earth or sea or trees are harmed (Rev. 7:3) renders—because of the Law of Non-Contradiction—the pre-wrath and post-tribulation Rapture positions Biblically impossible: by the time a pre-wrath or post-tribulation Rapture takes place, one-half of the earth's population will have been killed (Rev. 6:3-8; 9:13-18); Israel will have been denuded by the Antichrist; a worldwide earthquake will have taken place (Rev. 6:12-14); a third of the earth, a third of the trees, and all the green grass will have been burned up (Rev. 8:7); a third of the sea will have become blood (Rev. 8:8); a third of all marine life will have died (Rev. 8:9); and a third of the rivers and lakes will have become bitter (Rev. 8:10-11). Thus, for an expositor of Scripture to suggest that the earth has not yet been harmed by the time a pre-wrath or post-tribulation Rapture takes place—a stance which pre-wrath and post-tribulation proponents would have to take if they are to interpret God's word at face value—is wholly untenable.

Eighth, the Lord Himself teaches a pre-tribulation Rapture in the Olivet Discourse (Matthew 24 & 25). In two of the Discourse's parenthetical passages (Matt. 24:36-44; 25:1-13), Christ (1) describes the *human condition* prior to the Rapture—people will be eating and drinking, and marrying and giving in marriage (i.e., it will be "business as usual" on earth at the time of this unexpected coming); (2) describes *what happens* at the Rapture—some will be taken and some will be left behind; (3) teaches *who* will be taken into heaven at the Rapture—born again believers in Jesus Christ (those having the indwelling Holy Spirit)—and *who* will be left behind on earth—counterfeit "Christians" (those not having the indwelling Holy Spirit) and all other unbelievers; and (4) explains that the Rapture will occur *before* the Tribulation judgments. Christ's Olivet Discourse presentation will be analyzed further in Chapter 10.

F. Conclusion

The pre-wrath and post-tribulation Rapture positions, while well-meaning, have serious flaws and must be laid aside by born-again Christians. Both positions (1) fail to recognize Christ's revelation of a pre-tribulation Rapture in the Olivet Discourse; (2) reject Christ's straightforward teaching about the unannounced, unexpected, any-moment nature of the Rapture; (3) reject Christ's unequivocal statement that He will keep believers "from the hour of testing, which is to come upon the whole world" (the Tribulation period); (4) fail to harmonize with Daniel's Seventy Weeks prophecy; (5) fail to harmonize with Paul's teaching that the restrainer must be removed *before* the Antichrist can be revealed; and (6) contradict Christ's revelation to John that the 144,000 Jewish "first fruits" of God's Tribulation harvest will be called to salvation *before* the earth is harmed.

The partial Rapture position, even though it recognizes the efficacy of the pre-tribulation Rapture, must also be rejected because Christ clearly teaches in the Olivet Discourse and in John 14:1-3 that He will come for *all* born-again believers, not just some of them.

The mid-tribulation position has some merit, but (1) fails to recognize Christ's disclosure of a pre-tribulation Rapture in the Olivet Discourse; (2) lacks the doctrine of imminency; (3) places the removal of the Restrainer at the mid-point of the Antichrist's public presence rather than *before* his emergence on the world scene—thus contradicting II Thess. 2:7-10; and (4) does not harmonize with Daniel's "Seventy Weeks" prophecy.

The pre-tribulation position, on the other hand, harmonizes seamlessly with the various similes, metaphors, promises, statements, and exhortations which deal with the Lord's unexpected, unannounced, invisible, any-moment return for His own—and can be trusted unreservedly by born-again Christians as the best eschatological position.

Chart 6-A

THE TWO PHASES OF CHRIST'S RETURN

PHASE 1: THE "RAPTURE"

- **HE WILL MEET RESURRECTED CHRISTIANS IN THE AIR
(I THESS. 4:13-18; I COR. 15:50-58)**

PHASE 2: THE SECOND COMING

- **HE WILL RETURN BODILY TO THE MOUNT OF OLIVES
(ACTS 1:11; II THESS. 1:6-10; ZECH. 14:4)**

Chart 6-B

CONTRASTS BETWEEN THE RAPTURE AND THE SECOND COMING

THE RAPTURE:	THE SECOND COMING:
BEFORE THE TRIBULATION "just like the days of Noah . ."	AFTER THE TRIBULATION "immediately after the tribulation . . "
RETURNS FOR HIS SAINTS	RETURNS WITH HIS SAINTS
UNANNOUNCED (LIKE THIEF . .)	ANNOUNCED (SIGNS IN THE SKY)
UNEXPECTED	EXPECTED
UNKNOWN DAY OR HOUR	KNOWN DAY

CONDITION ON EARTH PRIOR:
  business as usual
  eating & drinking
  marrying & giving in marriage
	CONDITION ON EARTH PRIOR:
	  not business as usual
	  massive death tolls
	  torture, fear, fright, panic

INVISIBLE RETURN	VISIBLE RETURN (EVERY EYE . .)
IN THE AIR	TO THE EARTH
A CATCHING UP	A COMING DOWN
FOR DELIVERANCE	FOR JUDGMENT

Chart 6-C

DANIEL'S "SEVENTY WEEKS" CHRONOLOGY (INCL. THE RAPTURE)

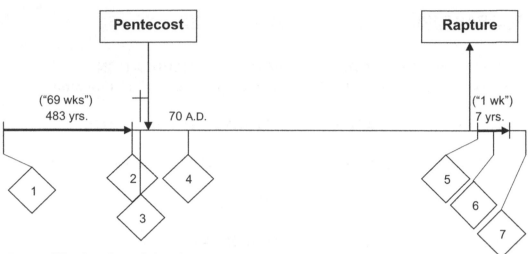

1.   The issuing of the decree to restore and rebuild Jerusalem

2.   The coming of Messiah to Jerusalem

3.   The death of Messiah

PENTECOST (the coming of the indwelling Holy Spirit)

4.   The destruction of Jerusalem—and its temple—by the people who will
        beget the end-times Antichrist

**THE RAPTURE (the removal of those persons indwelled with the
Holy Spirit)**

5.   The signing of a seven-year peace treaty between the Antichrist and
        Israel

6.   The Antichrist's halting of the regular temple sacrifices in Jerusalem—
        and his setting up of the "abomination of desolation" in the temple—
        midway through the seven-year treaty

7.   The destruction and end of the Antichrist

Chart 6-D

THE INDWELLING HOLY SPIRIT DURING THE CHURCH AGE

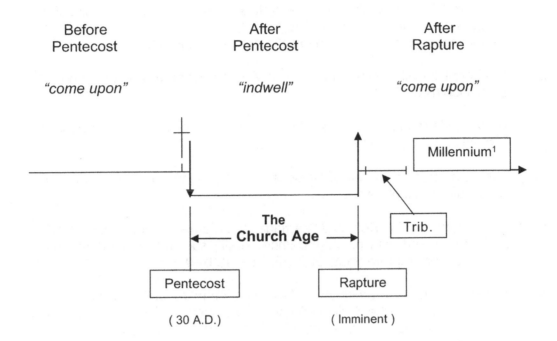

Before Pentecost

"come upon"

After Pentecost

"indwell"

After Rapture

"come upon"

Millennium[1]

The
Church Age

Trib.

Pentecost

(30 A.D.)

Rapture

(Imminent)

[1] All Jews who enter the Millennial Kingdom (as well as all of their offspring) will be indwelled and filled with the Holy Spirit during the Millennial Kingdom (Jer. 31:31-34; 32:39; Ezek. 11:19-20; Ezek. 36:26-27; 37:14); Gentiles apparently will not (Rev. 20:7-9). All resurrected believers who have returned to the earth with Christ and are living in the Millennial Kingdom (e.g., Matt. 19:27-28) will not only be filled with the Holy Spirit but will be like Christ Himself (I John 3:2; II Cor. 3:18; Rom. 8:29)

Chart 6-E

EIGHT PRINCIPAL REASONS FOR A "PRE-TRIBULATION" RAPTURE

1. The Lord's four Olivet Discourse exhortations that His coming for His Bride will be sudden and as unexpected as a thief entering a home at night are meaningless except in the context of a pre-tribulation Rapture.

2. The Lord Himself promises that Church Age believers will not go through the Tribulation (Rev. 3:10).

3. The Apostle Paul teaches that Church Age believers will not go through the Tribulation (I Thess. 5:9).

4. The substance and tenor of Daniel's Seventy Weeks prophecy calls for a pre-tribulation Rapture.

5. The metaphor of the Betrothal, Marriage, and Marriage Supper of Christ (the Bridegroom) and His Church (the Bride) readily suggests, if not demands, a pre-tribulation Rapture (Matt. 25:1-13; Rev. 19:6-9).

6. The Holy Spirit as the restrainer of evil must be taken out of the way *before* the "lawless one" (the Antichrist) can be revealed (II Thess. 2:7-10)—and the Antichrist in turn must be revealed *before* the Tribulation begins (so that he has time to rise to power and sign his peace treaty with Israel, the event which commences the Tribulation). Moreover, the Holy Spirit as the restrainer of evil cannot be taken out of the world unless the Church, whom the Holy Spirit indwells, is translated at the same time.

7. The calling out of 144,000 Jewish males during the Tribulation (Rev. 7:1-8; 14:1-5) as "first fruits" before the "earth or sea or trees" are harmed demands a pre-tribulation Rapture.

8. The Lord Himself teaches the disciples a pre-tribulation Rapture in two parenthetical sections of the Olivet Discourse (Matt. 24:36-44; 25:1-13)

ROMANS 9 - 11: THE TEMPORARY SETTING ASIDE OF ISRAEL

A particularly crucial ingredient in arriving at an accurate understanding of the end-times events involves the question of how one deals with the issue of Jewish unbelief at the time of Christ's first advent. Has God cast off Israel because of her corporate rejection of Messiah? What about Israel versus the Church?

The Old Testament clearly teaches that God selected Israel to be His special people on earth: God purposed for Israel to lead other nations to Himself; God selected Israel to be the repository of His Word; God promised spiritual blessings to Israel; and God promised many literal earthly blessings to Israel which have not yet been fulfilled. Why then, if God ordained Israel to be His people, did He not cause them to believe that Jesus Christ, at His first advent, is Israel's promised Messiah? What advantage are all of the Old Testament Covenants between God and Israel if God has now permanently cast off Israel? How can God reject the nation whom He elected? Each of these questions is answered in Chapters nine through eleven of Paul's letter to the Romans.

Chart 7-A presents this writer's outline of Romans 9 - 11, an outline which is built around the two critical questions posed in Romans 9 - 11: (1) "Has the Word of God failed with regard to Israel?" and (2) "Has God rejected His people Israel?" The answer to both questions is an emphatic no. To be sure, the Word of God has not failed with regard to Israel and its corporate unbelief in Jesus Christ; instead, the Word of God foresaw the unbelief (and even foretold God's grace toward the Gentiles). Equally important, God has not rejected His people Israel; instead, He has only temporarily set them aside "until the fullness of Gentiles comes in" (Rom. 11:25).

Paul answers the first question—"Has the Word of God failed with regard to Israel?"—by enlisting five specific proofs: First, the Scriptures have always made it clear that national posterity is not identical with spiritual posterity. Each person, regardless of nation, must come to grips with God's assessment of his own personal sin condition and must avail himself of God's provision for sin. Second, the Scriptures foretold God's grace to the Gentiles. Third, the Scriptures foretold that God would keep for Himself a remnant of believers in Israel, regardless of Israel's corporate disposition. Fourth, the Scriptures foretold Israel's unbelief. Fifth, the Scriptures have always made it clear that the gospel is for anyone—Jew or Gentile—and that it is made effective through faith not works.

Paul answers the second question—"Has God rejected His people Israel?"—even more directly: *"May it never be!" (Rom. 11:1)*. Paul then explains why God has not rejected Israel:

> *"For I do not want you, brethren, to be uninformed of this mystery, lest you be wise in your own estimation, that a partial hardening has happened to Israel until the fullness of the Gentiles has come in; and thus all Israel will be saved, just as it is written, 'THE DELIVERER WILL COME FROM*

ZION; HE WILL REMOVE UNGODLINESS FROM JACOB. AND THIS IS MY COVENANT WITH THEM, WHEN I TAKE AWAY THEIR SINS.' From the standpoint of the gospel they are enemies for your sake, but from the standpoint of God's choice they are beloved for the sake of the fathers, for the gifts and the calling of God are irrevocable (Rom. 11:25-29)."

Nothing could be clearer in Scripture: The gifts and the calling of God toward Israel are *irrevocable* (v. 29). God has not permanently rejected Israel; He has only set her aside temporarily (*"a partial hardening has happened to Israel"*) in order to make the offer of salvation available to the Gentiles (*"until the fullness of Gentiles comes in"*). When God has finished this Gentile grace, He will once again take up for Israel (during Daniel's 70th week, thus enabling Israel to complete her Sabbath transgressions), and He will then fulfill all of His Old Testament Kingdom promises to Israel after the return Jesus Christ to the earth. During Christ's Millennial reign over the earth, Israel will be the head of the nations, and righteousness will fill the earth from sea to sea (Isa. 2:3-4; 9:7; 72:1-19; Joel 9:10).

Sadly, many Christians have surrendered to a theological belief called "Replacement Theology," which contends that the Church has inherited all of God's Old Testament promises to Israel because of Israel's corporate rejection of Christ. Yet Romans 9 - 11 teaches just the opposite. God has not permanently rejected Israel, but has only set her aside for a season until He finishes His offer of salvation to the Gentiles. So the question must be asked: Where do *you* stand on this vitally important question?

Finally, Chart 7-B shows how a pre-tribulation Rapture and Daniel's "Seventy Weeks" prophecy harmonize perfectly with Paul's teaching in Romans 9 - 11.

Chart 7-A

ROMANS 9 - 11

SUBJECT: THE SETTING FORTH OF ISRAEL'S PROPER PLACE IN THE HISTORY OF NATIONS

KEY VERSE: 11:25

I.   HAS THE WORD OF GOD FAILED WITH REGARD TO ISRAEL?
     (CHAPTERS 9 - 10)   *[ANSWER: NOT AT ALL! (9:14)] [NIV]*

   A.   THE SCRIPTURES HAVE ALWAYS MADE IT CLEAR THAT NATIONAL POSTERITY IS NOT IDENTICAL WITH SPIRITUAL POSTERITY (ROM. 9:6-18)

   B.   THE SCRIPTURES FORETOLD GOD'S GRACE TOWARD THE GENTILES (ROM. 9:19-26)

   C.   THE SCRIPTURES FORETOLD GOD'S "REMNANT" IN ISRAEL (ROM. 9:27-29)

   D.   THE SCRIPTURES FORETOLD ISRAEL'S UNBELIEF (ROM. 9:30-33)

   E.   THE SCRIPTURES HAVE ALWAYS MADE IT CLEAR THAT THE GOSPEL IS FOR ANYONE—JEW OR GENTILE—AND THAT IT IS MADE EFFECTIVE THROUGH FAITH NOT WORKS (ROM. 10:1-21)

II. HAS GOD REJECTED HIS PEOPLE ISRAEL?
     (CHAPTER 11)   *[ANSWER: BY NO MEANS! (11:1)]   [NIV]*

   A.   ISRAEL HAS BEEN TEMPORARILY SET ASIDE, NOT PERMANENTLY REJECTED (ROM. 11:25-32)

Chart 7-B

DANIEL 9:24-27 & ROMANS 9 - 11

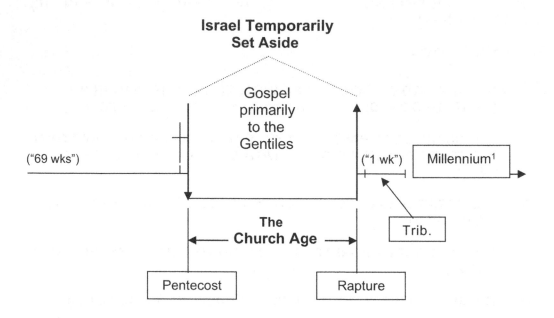

[1] All covenants between God and Israel are fulfilled during the Millennial Kingdom; Israel will be the head of the nations (Isa. 49:22-23; 60:14-17; 61:6-9); and Jerusalem will be the worship center of the world (Isa. 2:2-3; Mic. 4:1-2)

THE PRINCIPAL END-TIMES BOOK OF THE BIBLE: <u>REVELATION</u>

The New Testament book of Revelation stands alone as the major end-times book of the Bible. In this prophetic unveiling, God presents the entire panorama of end-times events to His creature man, including all of the judgments which He has ordained for unrepentant mankind. Tragically, most of the earth's population is altogether ignorant of the horrors that await them at some point in the future. These judgments have been impending for nearly two thousand years and are now *imminent* (as we will see in Chapter 33). Though judgment and justice are the primary themes of Revelation, the book nevertheless closes with a glorious picture of God's Eternal Kingdom, the kingdom which awaits all persons who turn their hearts to Christ. Let us review some of the high points of this great prophetic revelation.

The book of Revelation—the final book of the New Testament—is a book of *endings*. The book consummates the following major themes:

- Jesus Christ, the King of kings and Lord of lords
- The Church—the Bride of Christ
- The Resurrection/Rapture of the Bride
- Apostate Christendom (the "Harlot")
- The Antichrist
- The Antichrist's Empire ("Babylon the Great")
- The Tribulation Period (Daniel's Seventh Week)
- The Second Coming of Christ
- The Victory of Christ Over All of His Enemies
- The Millennial Kingdom on Earth
- Israel's Covenants
- Satan—and Satan's Final Demise
- The Second Resurrection—and Final Judgment
- The Eternal Kingdom in Heaven

The text of Revelation is primarily chronological in format, but it also contains several non-chronological (or "parenthetical") descriptions and vignettes. These parenthetical sections *do not advance the chronological sequence of events* but merely describe, in greater or lesser detail, certain key personages, institutions, places, or events which relate in some way to the chronology of the end-times events. It is thus crucially important that the reader of Revelation be able to recognize which parts of the book are **chronological** in nature and which parts are **non-chronological** (i.e., parenthetical).

The human author of Revelation is the Apostle John. John receives three major visions from Jesus Christ and then records them on parchment for circulation among seven first century churches in "Asia" (western Turkey) (Rev. 1:9-11). The three visions are as follows: (1) a vision of the resurrected, glorified Christ walking amidst Christendom at the end of the first century (beginning at Revelation 1:10); (2) a vision of the end-times events (beginning at Revelation 4:2); and (3) a vision of the New Jerusalem (beginning at Revelation 21:10). The "end-times events" are those events which begin with the Rapture of the Church and which include the ensuing Tribulation judgments, the Second Coming of Christ to the earth (after the Tribulation), the Battle of Armageddon, the judgment of the earth's remaining population, the binding of Satan, the Millennial Kingdom, the final rebellion and defeat of Satan, the Second Resurrection, the destruction of the present heavens and earth, the Great White Throne Judgment, the creation of the New Heavens and New Earth, and the Eternal Kingdom in Heaven.

Revelation has a God-given outline (Rev. 1:19): *"Write, therefore, the things which you have seen, the things which are, and the things which shall take place after these things."* Consequently, we can outline the major sections of Revelation as follows:

> Chapter 1: "The Things Which You Have Seen"
>
> Chapters 2-3: "The Things Which Are"
>
> Chapters 4-22: "The Things Which Shall Take Place After
> These Things"

We could also outline the book like this:

> Chapter 1: Things Past
>
> Chapters 2-3: Things Present
>
> Chapters 4-22: Things Future

Most of the end-times scenes in Revelation *alternate between heaven and earth*. This pattern is readily apparent when the parenthetical portions of Revelation are removed from the text:

- The scene in *heaven* before the First Series of Judgments

- The First Series of Judgments on *Earth*

- The scene in *heaven* before the Second Series of Judgments

- The Second Series of Judgments on *Earth*

- The scene in *heaven* before the Third Series of Judgments

- The Third Series of Judgments on *Earth*

- The Scene in *heaven* before the Second Coming of Christ

- The Second Coming of Christ to the *Earth*

- The Battle of Armageddon—and Christ's Victory over All His Enemies (including the binding of Satan)

- The Millennial Kingdom on Earth

- The Release, Final Rebellion, and Defeat of Satan

- The Second Resurrection

- The Destruction of the Present Heavens and Earth

- The Great White Throne Judgment

- The Creation of the New Heavens and New Earth

- The Eternal Kingdom in Heaven

Three important facts about the end times can be gleaned from the chronology of Revelation. First, the Battle of Armageddon takes place *after* the Tribulation period rather than during the Tribulation. [Note: Many Christians mistakenly believe that "Armageddon" is a colossal conflagration which takes place during the Tribulation. In truth, the Battle of Armageddon begins in Israel immediately after the end of the Tribulation. It is this conflict which prompts the return of Christ to the earth—the Second Coming of Christ—in order to save Israel from annihilation.] Second, the Millennial Kingdom takes place *after* the Second Coming of Christ. Therefore, postmillennialism contradicts John's straightforward presentation of the end-times sequence of events. Third, Revelation describes a *literal* Millennial Kingdom on earth reigned over by Jesus Christ (Rev. 20:1-7). Consequently, amillennialism likewise stands in opposition to John's presentation of the events.

Much of Revelation—Chapters 6 through 18—takes place during a seven-year period known as the "Tribulation." The chronology of the Tribulation is characterized by three series of judgments upon mankind:

> Chapter 6: the seven Seal judgments
>
> Chapters 8-9: the seven Trumpet judgments
>
> Chapter 16: the seven Bowl judgments

The Seal judgments show unregenerate man's inhumanity against his fellow man (Rev. 6:1-8). The Trumpet judgments depict Satan's torment, deception, and destruction of man (Rev. 8:2-13; 9:1-11; 9:13-16). The Bowl judgments portray a long-suffering God's personal judgment of unrepentant man (Rev. 15:1, 5-8; 16:1-21).

The second half of the Tribulation is known as the "Great Tribulation." This expression comes from Jesus' admonition in Matthew 23:21-22: *"for then there will be a great tribulation, such as has not occurred since the beginning of the world until now, nor ever shall be. And except those days be cut short, no life would be saved."* Because the magnitude of human loss described in the last fifteen verses of Chapter 6 of Revelation is so unprecedented in human history, it can also be said that *most of Chapter 6 and all other chronological passages through Chapter 18* take place during this second three-and-a-half-year period. How severe is the Great Tribulation? Revelation tells us that *one-half* of the earth's post-Rapture population will be killed during the Seal and the Trumpet Judgments.

Chart 8-A

THE CHRONOLOGY OF <u>REVELATION</u> (CHAPTERS 4 - 22)

A.   The scene in *heaven* before the First Series of Tribulation Judgments

B.   The First Series of Judgments on *Earth*

C.   The scene in *heaven* before the Second Series of Tribulation Judgments

D.   The Second Series of Judgments on *Earth*

E.   The scene in *heaven* before the Third Series of Tribulation Judgments

F.   The Third Series of Judgments on *Earth*

G.   The scene in *heaven* before the Second Coming of Christ

H.   The Second Coming of Christ to the *Earth*

I.   The Battle of Armageddon—and Christ's Victory over All His Enemies

J.   The Millennial Kingdom on Earth (and the Binding of Satan)

K.   The Final Rebellion (and Defeat) of Satan

L.   The Second Resurrection; the Destruction of the Present Heavens and Earth; and the Great White Throne Judgment

M.   The Creation of the New Heavens and New Earth; and the Eternal Kingdom in Heaven

Chapter 9

THE BASIC END-TIMES CHRONOLOGY (PER <u>REVELATION</u>)

Through careful examination of the chronological passages in the book of Revelation, the student of the end times can readily grasp the basic sequence of events. The sequence is presented as follows in Revelation (and is laid out visually in Chart 9-A):

1. the Rapture of the Church

2. the seven-year Tribulation period

3. the Second Coming of Jesus Christ to the earth

4. the Battle of Armageddon—and Christ's Victory over All His Enemies (including the binding of Satan)

5. the Millennial Kingdom on earth (and the binding of Satan)

6. the release, final rebellion, and defeat of Satan

7. the Second Resurrection

8. the destruction of the present heavens and earth

9. the Great White Throne Judgment

10. the creation of the new heaven and new earth

11. the Eternal Kingdom in Heaven

Though God reveals the broad pattern of end-times events in the book of Revelation, the vast majority of Christians remain unaware of the future God has already foretold. No Christian, however, need be ignorant of these events.

Chart 9-A

THE END-TIMES SEQUENCE OF EVENTS (PER <u>REVELATION</u>)

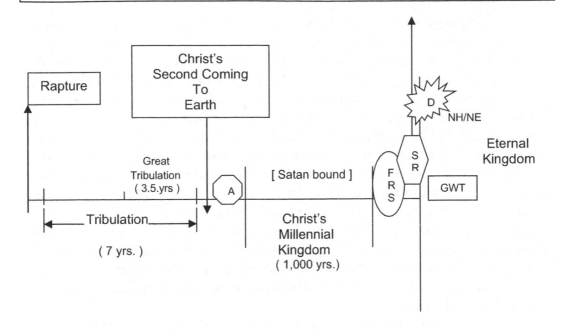

 = THE BATTLE OF ARMAGEDDON—AND CHRIST'S VICTORY OVER ALL HIS ENEMIES

= THE FINAL REBELLION (AND DEFEAT) OF SATAN

= THE SECOND RESURRECTION

= THE DESTRUCTION OF THE PRESENT HEAVENS AND EARTH

GWT = THE GREAT WHITE THRONE JUDGMENT

NH / NE = THE CREATION OF THE NEW HEAVENS AND NEW EARTH

THE OLIVET DISCOURSE

In Chapters 24 and 25 of Matthew's Gospel—chapters known as the Olivet Discourse—Christ gives today's Christian an extensive look at major parts of the end-times scenario. Shocked by the Lord's comment that the Jerusalem temple would one day be destroyed (and shocked by His previous revelation that He would be leaving them shortly, only to return in the future), the disciples ask Christ three questions (in Matt. 24:3): When will these things be (i.e., the destruction of the temple); what will be the sign of the end of the age; and what will be the sign of Your coming? Jesus answers each of these questions in the first half of the Discourse. After answering these questions Jesus then introduces the disciples (and us) to *additional* information about the end-times events—answering, if you will, the questions the disciples *didn't* ask. Three of the additional disclosures are particularly noteworthy: (1) Christ's revelation of a *pre-tribulation* coming for His Bride (at the Rapture), (2) Christ's revelation that He will be gone for a long period of time, and (3) Christ's revelation that, when He finally does return to the earth, He will judge the earth's remaining inhabitants before He establishes His Millennial reign over the earth.

Once again (as was the case in the book of Revelation) it is imperative for the student of the end times to identify which passages in the Olivet Discourse are **chronological** in nature and which ones are **parenthetical** in nature. The Olivet Discourse is in fact a mixture of (1) the future sequence of human events and (2) parenthetical exhortations, descriptions, promises, and warnings which relate in some way to this future sequence of events—*but which do not advance the sequence of events*. Jesus presents four chronological vignettes in the Discourse and seven parenthetical vignettes. This writer's outline of the Olivet Discourse is given in Chart 10-A.

The chronological passages depict the following major events: the Church Age (the period of time between the Day of Pentecost and a pre-tribulation Rapture); the seven-year Tribulation period; the Second Coming of Christ to the earth; and Christ's judgment of the earth's remaining nations after His return. Augmenting these four chronological passages (but having nothing to do with the *timing* of the events) are seven parenthetical passages which, among other things, exhort those living in Jerusalem (and Israel) during the Tribulation period to flee the Abomination of Desolation; describe the severity of the second half of the Tribulation; exhort Christians to avoid false Christs while Christ Himself is away; and exhort Christians to be alert for an unannounced, any-moment Rapture.

A.   The doctrinal significance of the Discourse today

Jesus describes *two* very different comings of the Son of Man in the Olivet Discourse. These comings not only are two separate events, but they are *mutually exclusive* events (i.e., an event cannot be both unannounced and announced at the same time; an event cannot simultaneously be unexpected and expected). In addition, these two events are necessarily separated in time while the human condition deteriorates from the one described in Matthew 24:37-38 to the one described parenthetically in Matthew 24:15-22.

One coming is *unannounced* (like a thief in the night), unexpected, and occurs when the human condition is one of "eating, drinking, and marrying." Scoffers in fact will have been asking: *"Where is the sign of His coming? For ever since the fathers fell asleep, all continues just as it was from the beginning of creation"* (II Pet. 3:4). This previously undisclosed coming of the Son of Man (introduced and explained parenthetically by Christ in Matthew 24:36-44 and Matthew 25:1-13) is the *pre-tribulation* **Rapture of the Church**—Christ's sudden, unannounced, unexpected, instantaneous coming in the air for His own. To be sure, Jesus provides significant information about the Rapture in the Olivet Discourse. First, He describes the *human condition* prior to the Rapture—people will be eating and drinking, and marrying and giving in marriage. In the vernacular of our day, it will be "business as usual" on earth at the time of this unexpected coming. Second, He describes *what happens* at the Rapture—some will be taken and others will be left behind. Third, He teaches *who* will be taken into heaven at the Rapture—born again believers in Jesus Christ (those having indwelling Holy Spirit)—and *who* will be left behind on earth to face judgment—counterfeit "Christians" (those not having the indwelling Holy Spirit) and all other unbelievers. Fourth, He explains that the Rapture will occur *before* the Tribulation judgments. [Note: It is Paul who later adds that the Rapture will be instantaneous ("in the twinkling of an eye"); that the dead in Christ will be raised first and the living in Christ will then be translated; that the raptured will meet Christ in the air; that the raptured will be given eternal, imperishable bodies; and so on.]

The other coming is *announced* (by signs in the sky), expected (thirty days after the end of the Tribulation period), and takes place immediately after the final three-and-a-half years of the Tribulation period—a period filled with death, horror, terror, panic, and fright. It will *not* be "business as usual" on earth prior to the Lord's bodily return. This particular coming of the Son of Man (presented chronologically by Christ in Matthew 24:29-31) is the **Second Coming of Jesus Christ**—the bodily return of Christ to the earth *with* His own, the entirety of His elect (including resurrected Old Testament saints, resurrected Church Age saints, and resurrected Tribulation saints), in order to save Israel from annihilation, to judge the earth's remaining nations, and to set up His long-awaited Messianic (Millennial) Kingdom.

Summary of Christ's Olivet Discourse teaching:

- Christ presents a four-fold chronology of future events in the Olivet:
  (1) the Church Age (24:4-8)
  (2) the Tribulation period (24:9-14)
  (3) the Second Coming of Christ to the earth (24:29-31)
  (4) the Judgment of the earth's remaining nations by Christ before He begins His Millennial reign over the earth (25:31-46)

- Christ teaches that the Church Age will be characterized by the following phenomena (Matt. 24:4-8):
  (1) many will come in Christ's name, claiming to be Christ
  (2) many will be misled by these claims
  (3) there will be wars and rumors of wars
  (4) nation will rise against nation, and kingdom will rise against kingdom
  (5) there will be earthquakes in various places
  (6) there will be famines in various places

- Christ teaches that the Church Age will last for a long time and that His return will not take place for a long time (Matt. 24:48; 25:5; 25:19)

- Christ confirms, by referring the disciples to Daniel 9:24-27, that the Tribulation period will last for seven years

- Christ teaches that the seven-year Tribulation period will be characterized by the following phenomena (Matt. 24:9-14):
  (1) Many Tribulation Christians (i.e., those who by faith turn to Christ for salvation after the Rapture) will be killed
  (2) Tribulation Christians will be hated by all nations because of Christ
  (3) many so-called "Christians" will fall away, will hate Tribulation Christians, and will deliver up Tribulation Christians to be killed
  (4) many false prophets will arise—and will mislead many
  (5) lawlessness will increase
  (6) most people's love will grow cold
  (7) Tribulation Christians who endure to the end will enter the Millennial Kingdom
  (8) the gospel of the kingdom will be preached in the whole world for a witness to all nations

- Christ teaches that the second half of the Tribulation will be a time of unimaginable horror on earth—and that "unless those days be cut short no life would survive" (Matt. 24:19-22)

- Christ teaches that His bodily return to the earth will be "announced" by four signs in the sky—the sun will be darkened; the moon will not give off its light; the stars will move out of their customary positions in the sky; and the celestial laws which govern the solar systems and galaxies will be altered—and then by *the* sign of His return (Matt. 24:29-30)

- Christ introduces the disciples to the doctrine of the pre-tribulation Rapture of the Church in two parenthetical passages: Matthew 24:36-44 and 25:1-13. Unlike the Second Coming of Christ to the earth, which will be announced by signs in the sky, the Rapture will be *unannounced* and will occur *unexpectedly*

- Christ teaches in four separate verses that the born-again Christian is to be ever-expectant and always ready for this any moment Rapture (Matt. 24:42; 24:43-44; 24:50; 25:13)

- Christ teaches that those within Christendom who are born-again believers will be taken from the earth at the time of the Rapture—and that the Rapture will occur *before* the Tribulation judgments (Matt. 24:36-44; 25:1-13)

- Christ teaches that those within Christendom who are not born-again believers will be left behind on earth at the time of the Rapture—and will not be able to escape the Tribulation judgments even if some of them want to turn to Christ after the Rapture (Matt. 24:36-44; 25:1-13)

- Christ teaches that the born-again Christian, even though he cannot know the day or the hour of the Rapture, can nevertheless discern when the Lord's return is near: Just as a person knows that summer is near when the leaves begin to burst forth in the spring, so too a person can know that Christ's return is near when the "leaves" of world events begin to burst forth in ways which could allow for a literal fulfillment of the end-times prophecies (Matt. 24:32-35)

- Christ teaches that all persons who survive the horrors of the Tribulation will be judged by Jesus Himself after His return. Those who have put their faith in Him will be allowed to enter the Millennial Kingdom. Those who have not put their faith in Him will be slain (Matt. 25:31-46)

- Christ points out that most persons during the Church Age—including persons today—will pay no attention to God's pronouncement of impending judgment, just as humans paid no attention to God's pronouncement of impending judgment in Noah's day (Matt. 24:36-39)

- Christ teaches that virtually all of Christendom—including His own children (those indwelled with the Holy Spirit)—will be drowsy and asleep (i.e., not alert) when He comes unexpectedly at the Rapture (Matt. 25:1-13)

- Christ exhorts today's believer to set his heart on doing the Lord's work and to be a faithful, sensible servant of the Lord while He is away (Matt. 24:45-51)

- Christ teaches that all who name the name of Christ (i.e., both the "wheat" and the "tares) will one day give an accounting of their lives to Christ. Those who are born again will enter into the joy of their Master; those who are not born again will be cast into Hell (Matt. 25:14-30)

- Christ teaches that faithfulness with however much or little the Lord gifts each born-again believer is all that Christ asks of His children and that equal faithfulness will be rewarded equally (Matt. 25:14-29)

- Christ teaches that Hell will be a place of utter separation from God (and from God's people) and will be a place of weeping and gnashing of teeth (Matt. 25:30)

Chart 10-A

THE OLIVET DISCOURSE -- MATTHEW 24-25

I.   CHRIST'S PROPHECY ABOUT THE JERUSALEM TEMPLE
       (24:1-2)

II.   THE DISCIPLES' QUESTIONS ABOUT THIS PROPHECY
       (24:3)

III.   CHRIST'S ANSWERS TO THE DISCIPLES' QUESTIONS AND
       CHRIST'S EXPLANATION OF THE END-TIMES EVENTS
       (24:4 - 25:46)

   A.   THE CHURCH AGE (24:4-8)

   B.   THE TRIBULATION PERIOD (24:9-14)

   *PARENTHETICAL: CHRIST'S EXHORTATION TO FLEE THE
   ABOMINATION OF DESOLATION, AND CHRIST'S PRONOUNCEMENT OF
   THE SEVERITY OF THE 2ND HALF OF THE TRIBULATION (24:15-22)*

   *PARENTHETICAL: CHRIST'S EXHORTATION TO AVOID FALSE
   CHRISTS WHILE HE IS AWAY (24:23-28)*

   C.   THE SECOND COMING OF CHRIST TO THE EARTH (24:29-31)

   *PARENTHETICAL: THE PARABLE OF THE FIG TREE—AND THE SIGN
   OF THE END OF THE AGE (24:32-35)*

   *PARENTHETICAL: CHRIST'S FIRST TEACHING ON THE RAPTURE AND
   HIS EXHORTATION TO BE ALERT FOR IT AT ALL TIMES (24:36-44)*

   *PARENTHETICAL: CHRIST'S PROMISE OF BLESSING AND REWARD
   FOR FAITHFUL, SENSIBLE SERVANTHOOD WHILE HE IS AWAY
   (24:45-51)*

   *PARENTHETICAL: THE PARABLE OF THE TEN VIRGINS—THE
   PICTURE OF CHRIST'S COMING FOR HIS OWN AT THE RAPTURE
   (25:1-13)*

Chart 10-A

PARENTHETICAL: THE PARABLE OF THE TALENTS (25:14-30)

D.   THE JUDGMENT OF THE REMAINING NATIONS BY CHRIST (25:31-46)

Chart 10-B

THE TWO COMINGS OF THE SON OF MAN IN THE OLIVET DISCOURSE

THE RAPTURE:

BEFORE THE TRIBULATION
"just like the days of Noah . ."
(Matt. 24:37-39)

RETURNS FOR HIS SAINTS
(Matt. 24:36-41; 25:1-10)

UNANNOUNCED (LIKE THIEF . .)
(Matt. 24:43-44)

UNEXPECTED
(Matt. 24:43-44; 24:50; 25:5-6)

UNKNOWN DAY OR HOUR
(Matt. 24:36; 24:42; 24:50; 25:13)

CONDITION ON EARTH PRIOR:
"business as usual"
 eating & drinking
 marrying & giving in marriage
(Matt. 24:37-39)

INVISIBLE RETURN [2]

A CATCHING UP [3]

UP INTO HEAVEN
(Matt. 25:6-12)

FOR DELIVERANCE
(Matt. 24:37-42)

THE SECOND COMING:

AFTER THE TRIBULATION
"immediately after the tribulation . ."
(Matt. 24:29-30)

RETURNS WITH HIS SAINTS
(Matt. 24:31)

ANNOUNCED (SIGNS IN THE SKY)
(Matt. 24:29-30)

EXPECTED
(Matt. 24:29-30)

KNOWN DAY [1]

CONDITION ON EARTH PRIOR:
not "business as usual"
 woe to those with child . .
 unless those days be cut short . .
(Matt. 24:19-22)

VISIBLE RETURN (WILL SEE . .)
(Matt. 24:30)

A COMING DOWN
(Matt. 24:29-30)

DOWN TO THE EARTH
(Matt. 25:31-32a)

FOR JUDGMENT
(Matt. 25:14-19,24-30; 25:31-46)

---

[1] Dan. 12:11-12
[2] I Cor. 15:50-52; I Thess. 4:15-18
[3] I Thess. 4:15-18; I Cor. 15:50-52

A MORE DETAILED END-TIMES CHRONOLOGY

Through careful examination of other prophetic passages of Scripture, the student of the End Times can readily augment the basic sequence of events presented in Chapter 9. This more detailed sequence of end-times events is laid out in Chart 11-A. From Revelation and other references, we can discern the following order of events:

1. the Rapture of born-again believers

2. the seven-year Tribulation period
   (including the Great Tribulation after the mid-point)

3. the sacking of Jerusalem

4. the signs in the sky announcing the Lord's return

5. the Second Coming of Jesus Christ to the earth

6. the Battle of Armageddon—and Christ's victory over all His enemies

7. Christ's judgment of the earth's remaining Jews and Gentiles

8. Christ's Millennial Kingdom on earth (and the binding of Satan for 1,000 years)

9. the final rebellion (and defeat) of Satan

10. the Second Resurrection

11. the destruction of the present heavens and earth

12. the Great White Throne Judgment

13. the creation of the new heaven and new earth

14. the Eternal Kingdom in Heaven

An unspecified period of time takes place between the Rapture and the beginning of the seven-year Tribulation. During this interval the Antichrist rises to power, and God sends a deluding influence upon all who refuse to repent (II Thess. 2:7-11). The Great Tribulation begins at the mid-point of the Tribulation period, when the Antichrist, according to Daniel 9:27 and II Thessalonians 2:4, enters the Jerusalem temple, sets up an idol of himself, and declares himself to be God. The second half of the Tribulation will be a time of unparalleled horror and bloodshed. Says Jesus of this period: *". . . there will be great tribulation, such as has not occurred since the beginning of the world until now, nor ever shall again. And except those days be cut short, no life would be saved" (Matt. 24:21-22).* How severe will the results be? The book of Revelation explains that one-half of the earth's post-Rapture population will die during the Seal and Trumpet judgments. Moreover, due to the symmetry of the Seal and Trumpet death tolls, it is likely that the Bowl judgments will kill another one-fourth of the earth's initial post-Rapture population. Thus, *three-fourths* of the earth's post-Rapture population will be killed during the Tribulation (with most of this toll taking place during the Great Tribulation). Tragically, today's unbeliever has no comprehension of the magnitude of the judgments which lie ahead.

Zechariah 12 and 14 picture the sacking of Jerusalem after the end of the Tribulation. It is this sacking of Jerusalem at the hands of the world's remaining armies which prompts the Lord's return to the earth to save Israel from annihilation. Matthew 24:29 in turn describes the signs in the sky which precede and announce Christ's bodily return to the earth. Daniel 12:11-12 provides the Christian with a truly remarkable prophecy which gives the exact timing of the Lord's bodily return to the earth as well as the exact timing of the beginning of Christ's Millennial Kingdom. According to Daniel 12:11, Christ will return to the earth 1,290 days after the Antichrist desecrates the Jerusalem temple. According to Daniel 12:12, Christ will begin His Millennial reign over the earth exactly 1,335 days after the desecration of the temple. Finally, Matthew 25:31-46 explains that, between the Lord's bodily return and the commencement of His Millennial reign, Christ will judge, after Armageddon, all remaining persons on earth. Those who have put their faith in Him after the Rapture (whether Jew or Gentile)—and who have survived to this point— will enter the Millennial Kingdom. Those who have refused to put their faith in Him will be slain. [Note: It is the writer's belief that only one to two percent of the earth's initial post-Rapture population will survive (1) the Tribulation judgments, (2) the Battle of Armageddon, and (3) Christ's post-return judgment of the earth's remaining inhabitants. Thus, the number of persons entering the Millennial Kingdom could be as little as sixty million. See Isaiah 24:3-6; Daniel 7:21-22.]

Chart 11-A

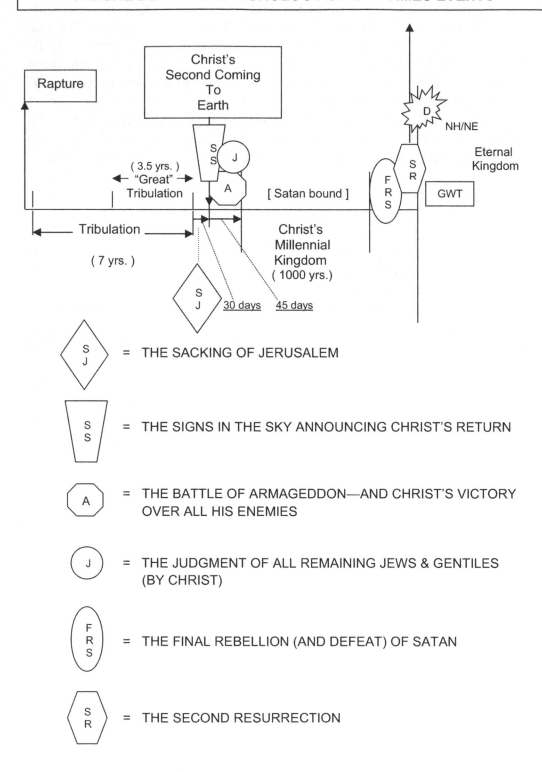

A MORE DETAILED CHRONOLOGY OF END-TIMES EVENTS

Rapture

Christ's
Second Coming
To
Earth

(3.5 yrs.)
← "Great" →
Tribulation

[Satan bound]

NH/NE

Eternal
Kingdom

GWT

Tribulation

(7 yrs.)

Christ's
Millennial
Kingdom
(1000 yrs.)

30 days   45 days

= THE SACKING OF JERUSALEM

= THE SIGNS IN THE SKY ANNOUNCING CHRIST'S RETURN

= THE BATTLE OF ARMAGEDDON—AND CHRIST'S VICTORY
  OVER ALL HIS ENEMIES

= THE JUDGMENT OF ALL REMAINING JEWS & GENTILES
  (BY CHRIST)

= THE FINAL REBELLION (AND DEFEAT) OF SATAN

= THE SECOND RESURRECTION

Chart 11-A

D = THE DESTRUCTION OF THE PRESENT HEAVENS AND EARTH

GWT = THE GREAT WHITE THRONE JUDGMENT

NH / NE = THE CREATION OF THE NEW HEAVENS AND NEW EARTH

THE FIRST INSTANCE OF UNIVERSAL JUDGMENT

Unregenerate mankind, both separated from God and ignorant of His absolute holiness and hatred of sin, has difficulty accepting the notion that God will one day pummel the earth with calamitous judgment. Most unbelievers seem to have it in their subconscious thoughts that God is a "loving" God and ultimately will not judge anyone. Scripture, however, does not teach this view of God. While God indeed is love (I John 4:8,16)—and showers His own with perfect love (I John 4:18)—He nevertheless is also righteous and just. God has made it overwhelmingly clear in His Word that a staggering, future, universal judgment awaits unregenerate mankind.

Such a judgment is not without precedent in human history. Approximately 4,500 years ago, God also brought forth a universal judgment on earth because of man's unrepentant heart. Listen to the account of this judgment in the book of Genesis:

> Then the Lord saw that the wickedness of man was great on the earth, and that every intent of the thoughts of his heart was only evil continually. And the Lord was sorry that He had made man on the earth, and He was grieved in His heart. And the Lord said, "I will blot out man whom I have created from the face of the land, from man to animals to creeping things and to birds of the sky; for I am sorry that I have made them."
>
> But Noah found favor in the eyes of the Lord. . . . Noah was a righteous man, blameless in his time; Noah walked with God. And Noah became the father of three sons: Shem, Ham, and Japheth.
>
> Now the earth was corrupt in the sight of God, and the earth was filled with violence. And God looked on the earth and, behold, it was corrupt, for all flesh had corrupted their way upon the earth.
>
> Then God said to Noah, "The end of all flesh has come before Me, for the earth is filled with violence because of them; and, behold, I am about to destroy them with the earth. Make for yourself an ark of gopher wood; you shall make the ark with rooms, and you shall cover it inside and out with pitch. . . . And behold, I, even I, am bringing a flood of water upon the earth to destroy all flesh in which is the breath of life. Everything that is on the earth shall perish. But I will establish My covenant with you; and you shall enter the ark—you and your sons and your wife and your sons' wives with you. (Gen. 6:5-17)

All mankind—with the exception of Noah—had turned its back on God. Because of this turning away, the wickedness of man was great, and the intentions of men were continually evil. With violence saturating the earth, God was even sorry that He had made man.

In due course, after striving with the human family for centuries, God brought judgment upon the entire race:

In the six hundredth year of Noah's life, in the second month, on the seventeenth day of the month, on the same day all the fountains of the great deep burst open, and the floodgates of the sky were opened. And the rain fell upon the earth for forty days and forty nights. . . . Then the flood came upon the earth for forty days; and the water increased and lifted up the ark, so that it rose above the earth. And the water prevailed and increased greatly upon the earth; and the ark floated on the surface of the water. And the water prevailed more and more upon the earth, so that all the high mountains everywhere under the heavens were covered. The water prevailed fifteen cubits [twenty-five feet] higher, and the mountains were covered. And all flesh that moved on the earth perished—birds and cattle and beasts and every swarming thing that swarms upon the earth, and all mankind. . . . Thus, He blotted out every living thing that was upon the face of the land, from man to animals to creeping things and to birds of the sky; and only Noah was left, together with those that were with him in the ark. (Gen. 7:11-23)

The Genesis account tells us that God not only caused it to rain for forty days and forty nights, but He also caused massive geological upheavals in the earth's ocean crust, which in turn rushed subterranean waters (Gen. 7:11) to an elevation of fifteen cubits (approximately twenty-five feet) above the highest place on earth. Thus, God drowned the entire human family, except the eight persons in the ark: Noah, his wife, their three sons (Shem, Ham, and Japheth), and the wives of the three sons. God also drowned all of the earth's animals, reptiles, and birds except those in the ark. Given pre-Flood human longevity, it is possible that the earth's population had reached one billion by this time. Nevertheless, God destroyed them because of their violence and wickedness. Only Noah walked with God—including the offering of atoning animal sacrifices for his personal sin (Gen. 8:20).

In short, God has already brought forth one universal judgment on earth, and He plans to bring forth another one in the future. This judgment has already been announced in the Word, has been impending for nearly 2,000 years, and is now imminent. At the moment of the Rapture, no person left on earth will be a believer in Jesus Christ. Though some will turn to Christ after the Rapture, most persons will refuse to do so. Ironically, the epitaph of those drowned in Genesis 6 will be the epitaph of the unrepentant during the End Times: *"and the wickedness of man was great on the earth, and every intent of his heart was only evil continually. . . . And the earth was corrupt in the sight of God, and the earth was filled with violence."*

[Note: in 1992, this writer created a computer model which utilized realistic birth rates/death rates and which began with three families (Ham, Shem, and Japheth). It placed the earth's population after 4,500 years at 5.5 billion, virtually identical with the earth's population at that time.]

THE REBELLION AT BABEL

After the Genesis Flood subsided, God gave Noah specific instructions: *"Go out of the ark, you and your wife and your sons and your sons' wives, and bring out with you every living thing of all flesh that is with you, birds and animals and every creeping thing so that they may breed abundantly on the earth. Moreover, be fruitful and multiply on the earth" (Gen. 8:17).* For emphasis, God repeated the instructions two more times, first in Genesis 9:1 (*"Be fruitful and multiply, and fill the earth"*) and then in Genesis 9:7 (*"Be fruitful and multiply; populate the earth abundantly and multiply in it"*). God's instructions to Noah and his sons were thus explicit: they were to be fruitful, to multiply, and to fill the earth.

When we pick up the story of the human family approximately a hundred years after the Flood, the fledgling family (birthing a fourth generation and now perhaps 10,000 in number) has already turned away from one of God's explicit instructions:

Now the whole earth used the same language and the same words. And it came about as they journeyed east that they found a plain in the land of Shinar [present-day Iraq] and settled there.

And they said to one another, "Come, let us make bricks and burn them thoroughly." And they used brick for stone, and they used tar for mortar. And they said, "Come, let us build for ourselves a city, and a tower whose top will reach into heaven, and let us make for ourselves a name, lest we be scattered abroad over the face of the whole earth." (Gen. 11:1-4)

Rather than spreading out over the earth as God had instructed, the post-Flood human family has disobeyed God and chosen instead to remain together as one unit in order to build a single grand city. Worse, their hearts have turned away from God toward self: *"Come, let us build for ourselves a city . . . and let us make a name for ourselves."* Their philosophy has become one of "man is to be exalted and glorified, not God." Man can make it on his own; man can be self-sufficient and self-determining. Man does not need to have a relationship with God; man need not follow the counsel and instruction of God. After all, what could God possibly know? The seeds of humanism have taken root in man's heart.

In addition, the post-Flood human family has not only turned away from God to self, but it has also turned away from God to Satan: *"Let us build a tower whose top will reach into heaven."* Noah built an altar on which to offer animal sacrifices (as prescribed by God) for atonement of personal sin; Noah's offspring now want to build a tower to "reach into heaven." Hence, we see post-Flood man either attempting to come to God on his own terms (by way of works and ritual) rather than on God's terms (faith and substitutionary atonement)—or simply casting off God altogether in favor of Satan worship. To be sure, much of the human family had again been seduced by Satan. [Note: archaeologists working in the Babel region have unearthed towers similar to the one built by the post-Flood family[1]; all of them contain occult symbols and evidence of occult worship practices.[2]] [Additional note: The Antichrist and the False Prophet will champion the same message expressed at Babel: "Come, let us build for ourselves a world empire ('Babylon the Great'), and let us make a name for ourselves (as 'global citizens'), and let us make a tower that will reach into 'heaven' so that we can be like gods."]

Listen to God's reaction to man's post-Flood rebellion:

> *And the Lord came down to see the city and the tower which the sons of men had built. And the Lord said, "Behold, they are one people, and they all have the same language. And this is what they began to do, and now nothing which they purpose to do will be impossible for them. Come, let Us go down and there confuse their language, that they may not understand one another's speech."*
>
> *So the Lord scattered them abroad from there over the face of the whole earth; and they stopped building the city. Therefore, its name was called Babel, because there the Lord confused the language of the whole earth; and from there the Lord scattered them abroad over the face of the whole earth. (Gen. 11:5-9)*

God judged mankind's rebellion at Babel in three specific ways: first, He confused man's language (i.e., He brought forth the different languages seen on earth today); second, He scattered the post-Flood family into different parts of the earth; and third, through the genetic makeup existing in every male and female, He brought forth the different "races" (i.e., the different human tribes or "people groups") now seen on earth. [Note: in truth there is just one race: the human race.]

Because post-Flood mankind refused to heed God's command to begin to spread out over the earth, God intervened supernaturally to execute His will. God took approximately seventy families (the number of separate family units living at the time), placed them in seventy separate locations ("lands") on earth, gave each of the seventy families a separate language (and, over time, the subsequent dialects seen today), and then began to bring forth the different racial distinctions seen on earth today (Gen. 10:1 - 11:9). Out of each of these seventy family-land-language units came the nations of the world: e.g., the Greeks, the Italians, the Spanish, the French, the Germans, the Russians, the Turks, the Egyptians, the Libyans, the Ethiopians, the Iranians, the Chinese, the Japanese, the Koreans, and so on.

God brought this form of judgment on the post-Flood family so that it would be difficult for mankind ever again to unite *en masse* against Him for the purpose of exalting man and Satan. During the end-times Tribulation period, however, mankind will attempt once again to do just that.

Chapter 14

THE PROPHETIC SIGNIFICANCE OF GOD'S JUDGMENT AT BABEL

God's removal of the human family out of Babel into approximately seventy different and distant locations (from where subsequent families likely migrated to other parts of the earth) was not a random dispersion. Based on evidence now known to linguists, anthropologists, and archaeologists, it appears that God dispersed the offspring of Noah's three sons as follows: the descendants of Japheth were dispersed to the north of the Mediterranean, the descendants of Shem were dispersed to the east of the Mediterranean, and the descendants of Ham were dispersed to the south of the Mediterranean. Anthropologist, for example, have determined that "Tarshish" is modern-day Spain; "Javan" is Greece; "Elam" is Iran; "Put" is Libya; "Mizraim" is Egypt; and "Cush" is Ethiopia. In conjunction with the "Table of Nations" given in Genesis 11, we can thus determine the geographic proximities of some of Shem, Ham, and Japheth's offspring (see charts on next two pages).

The prophetic significance of this pattern of dispersion is two-fold. First, we can conclude that the ancient Roman Empire was ruled by Japhethites. Italy, the core nation of the empire (and home to the Roman Caesars), was a Japhethite nation. Israel, on the other hand, was a Shemite nation (Gen. 11:10-26). At the time of Christ, the Roman Empire trod Israel underfoot. In anthropological terms, a Japhethite empire trod underfoot a Shemite nation. It was deliverance from this Japhethite bondage that many of the Jews in Jesus' time hoped Jesus would provide. During the second half of the end times Tribulation the Antichrist's *revived* Roman Empire (discussed in ensuing chapters) will likewise trod Israel underfoot, causing Tribulation Jews once again to long for the Davidic Kingdom of Messiah. In anthropological terms, "Japheth" will again trod "Shem" underfoot. Thus, when well-meaning Christians teach that the Antichrist's ten-nation core could be a coalition of ten Arab nations, they fail to recognize the anthropological contradiction of their position: the ten-nation core *cannot* be ten Arab nations, because Arabs are Shemites not Japhethites. Indeed, the results of the dispersion at Babel teach that the Antichrist's ten-nation core will be made up of Japethites (except, in the writer's view, likely member Japan and possible member Korea, both having been substantially Westernized).

Second, the Antichrist himself will be a Japhethite (Dan. 9:26). Stated in modern-day terms the Antichrist will be a Caucasian and a Westerner (i.e., a descendent of the bloodlines which once made up the north Mediterranean core of the ancient Roman Empire). It can be said unequivocally that the Antichrist will not be a Jew (as some commentators have put forth), nor will he be an Arab (as other commentators have put forth). In short, the Antichrist will come from the West, and the Antichrist will be a Japhethite, not a Shemite or a Hamite.

God's dispersal of Shem, Ham, and Japheth after Babel

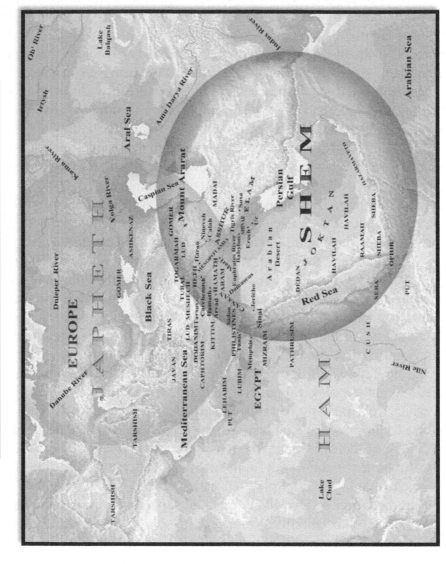

Microsoft Bing: map of shem ham and japheth

God's dispersal of Shem, Ham, and Japheth after Babel

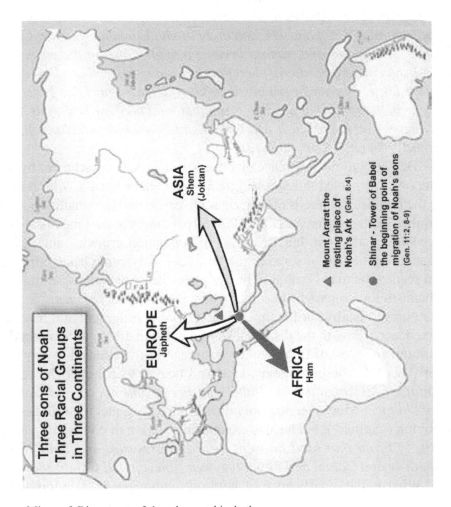

Three sons of Noah
Three Racial Groups
in Three Continents

ASIA
Shem
(Joktan)

EUROPE
Japheth

AFRICA
Ham

▲ Mount Ararat the
resting place of
Noah's Ark (Gen. 8:4)

● Shinar - Tower of Babel
the beginning point of
migration of Noah's sons
(Gen. 11:2, 8-9)

Microsoft Bing: map of shem ham and japheth

MANKIND'S FIRST EMPIRE

Approximately two hundred years after God's dispersal of the human family, a man named Nimrod—a grandson of Ham—migrated back to Babel, consolidated his power throughout Babylon, and became the world's first "emperor": *"And the sons of Ham were Cush and Mizraim and Put and Canaan. . . . Now Cush became the father of Nimrod; and Nimrod became a mighty one on the earth. He was a mighty hunter before the Lord; therefore it is said, 'Like Nimrod a mighty hunter before the Lord.' And the beginning of his kingdom was Babel and Erech and Accad and Calneh, in the land of Shinar. From that land he went forth into Assyria, and built Nineveh and Rehoboth-Ir and Calah, and Resen between Nineveh and Calah; that is the great city" (Gen. 10:6-12).*

Before Nimrod's entrance onto the scene, little encroachment by any family into the other dispersed families had likely taken place because of the distance between the families (hundreds of miles in some cases) and the smallish populations of the families (perhaps a maximum of 100-150 per family at the time of the dispersion). Now, however, after two hundred years of population growth—and probable land exploration on the part of some of the families—a dynamic leader emerges on the human scene: the man Nimrod. The Scriptures describe him as a "mighty hunter," a euphemism for a ruler who becomes a hunter (conqueror) of *men*.

Nimrod is alive at the time of God's Babel judgment and has likely been dispersed, according to the dispersal shown in Chart 14-A, several hundred miles to the south and west of Babylon. Over time, Nimrod makes his way back to the former place of rebellion against God and begins to conquer the region: *"the beginning of his kingdom was Babel and Erech and Accad and Calneh, in the land of Shinar."* Moreover, not only does Nimrod conquer the villages and towns in Babylon ("Shinar"), but he also expands his sphere of control into neighboring Assyria: *"From that land he went forth into Assyria, and built Nineveh and Rehoboth-Ir and Calah, and Resen between Nineveh and Calah; that is the great city."* What is the significance of Nimrod's conquest of Babylon and his later takeover of Assyria? It is this: for the first time since God's judgment at Babel approximately 250 years earlier, a political leader has appeared on the scene who attempts once again to unite parts of the world into one "empire"—in direct opposition to God's expressed will for mankind (Gen. 9:1).

Nimrod thus represents the first foreshadow of the end-times Antichrist, who himself will attempt to unite the world into one global family. Furthermore, Nimrod's empire represents the first forerunner of the Antichrist's Godless end-times Empire ("Babylon *the Great*"), which in turn will attempt to take over the entire earth (including an attempted annihilation of Israel). Nimrod's "Babylon" was a man-centered, Godless empire filled with immorality, idolatry, and wickedness. The Antichrist's end-times "Babylon the Great" (Rev. 18:2-3) will be the ultimate manifestation of Nimrod's Godless, man-centered, immoral, idolatrous, and wicked empire. "Babylon" commenced with Nimrod; "Babylon the Great" will commence with the Antichrist.

Significantly, it is out of Nimrod's pagan Babylon that God calls Abraham to begin the plan of redemption for mankind: *"Go forth from your country and from your relatives and from your father's house to the land which I will show you. And I will make you a great nation, and I will bless you and make your name great, and you shall be a blessing. And I will bless those who bless you, and I will curse those who curse you. And in you all the families of the earth will be blessed" (Gen. 12:1-3).* Through Abraham's seed would come Messiah, Jesus Christ—God the Son, the Son of God, the Lamb of God, who would take away the sins of the world.

THE SEVEN WORLD EMPIRES CONCURRENT WITH ISRAEL

According to Scripture, seven world empires will exist *concurrently* with Israel during her entire history. Six of these empires have now come and gone; the seventh and final empire has yet to come. While other empires have existed on earth at the time of the six presented in God's Word, these six are *contiguous* with Israel (or have occupied Israel) and *relate directly to the life of Israel* in some way: Jacob's family wound up in Egypt because of a severe famine in Canaan; Moses delivered the nation of Israel from Egyptian bondage; the ten northern tribes of Israel were carried off into captivity by the Assyrians; the two southern tribes of Israel were carried off into captivity by the Babylonians; Daniel received his "seventy weeks" prophecy while in Babylonian captivity; Zerubbabel led a remnant of Jews back to Jerusalem with the blessings of a Medo-Persian king; Nehemiah rebuilt the walls of Jerusalem during the days of the Medo-Persian Empire; Daniel 11:3-35 traces the history of the Grecian Empire and its forays through Israel, including the desecration of the Jerusalem temple by Antiochus Epiphanes in 167 B.C. (a foreshadow of the Antichrist's end-times desecration of the temple); and God the Son, Jesus Christ, became flesh and offered himself up for mankind's sins during the days of the Roman Empire.

The seven world empires which encompass Israel's entire history are as follows (and are listed in Charts 16-A, B, & C): the **Egyptian** Empire; the **Assyrian** Empire; the **Babylonian** Empire; the **Medo-Persian** Empire; the **Grecian** Empire; the **Roman** Empire; and the **revived Roman** Empire. Three passages of Scripture provide important information about these seven world empires: Revelation 13:1-10; Revelation 17:7-13; and Daniel 2:31-44. Revelation 17:7-13 will be discussed in this chapter and Daniel 2:31-44 will be discussed in the next.

Because the Antichrist's Empire is identified in all three, it is vitally important to understand each of the passages as we move toward an accurate understanding of the end times. Let us first examine Revelation 17:7-13:

> *And the angel said to me, "Why do you wonder? I will tell you the mystery of the woman and of the beast carrying her, the beast which has the seven heads and the ten horns. The beast that you saw was and is not, and is about to come up out of the abyss and to go to destruction. And those who dwell on the earth will wonder, those whose name has not been written in the book of life from the foundation of the world, when they see the beast, that he was and is not and will come. Here is the mind which has wisdom. The seven heads are seven mountains on which the woman sits, and they are seven kings; five have fallen, one is, the other has not yet come; and when he comes, he must remain a little while. And the beast which was and is not, is himself also an eighth, and is one of the seven, and he goes to destruction. And the ten horns which you saw are*

ten kings, who have not yet received a kingdom, but they receive authority as kings with the beast for one hour. These have one purpose and they give their power and authority to the beast" (Rev. 17:7-13).

When the Apostle John sees "a woman sitting on a scarlet beast" in Revelation 17:3, he momentarily becomes confused by the scene (*"the angel said to me, 'Why do you wonder?'"*). To be sure, John—having only a first century perspective (in which the simplicity of the gospel and the informal gatherings of Christians [typically in homes] prevailed)—has difficulty comprehending the enormity of, and the paradoxes within, the end-times Apostate Christendom he witnesses in this vision.

The angel then tells John that he will show him *"the mystery of the woman and of the beast carrying her."* The principal subject of the rest of the passage, however, is the "beast" and can be seen in the phrase, *"the beast which has the seven heads and the ten horns."* This phrase contains three key terms: (1) "beast," (2) "seven heads," and (3) "ten horns." In the book of Revelation the term "beast" has dual meaning. At times it pictures the Antichrist (e.g., Rev. 13:5-8; 17:11,16; 19:19-20), and at other times it pictures the Antichrist's Empire (e.g., Rev. 13:1-4; 17:10). At still other times it represents both (e.g., Rev. 13:3-4; 17:12-13).

The term "seven heads" also has dual meaning. First, the "seven heads" are *"seven mountains on which the woman sits."* The "woman" (according to Revelation 17:1-6) is Apostate Christendom. The "seven mountains" seemingly represents the geographic core (or headquarters) of Apostate Christendom—specifically, Rome. Says one noted commentator:

> The first key to the revelation is in the statement, 'The seven heads are seven mountains on which the woman sits.' Many expositors refer this to Rome. Seven hills formed the nucleus of the ancient city on the left bank of the Tiber. These hills received the names of Palatine, Aventine, Caelian, Esquiline, Viminal, Quirinal, and Capitoline. . . . Throughout its history Rome has been described as the city of seven hills as indicated in coins which refer to it in this way and in countless allusions in Roman literature. Victorinus, one of the first to write a commentary on the book of Revelation, identified the seven mountains as the city of Rome. [3]

Second, the "seven heads" are also *"seven kings: five have fallen, one is, the other has yet to come. And when he comes, he must remain a little while."* The "seven heads," therefore, represent seven historical kings and kingdoms. Five of these kings-kingdoms have fallen: the kings of Egypt, Assyria, Babylon, Medo-Persia, and Greece. One king and kingdom still exists (in 95 A.D. when John received these visions)—the king-kingdom of the Roman Empire during John's writing. One king-kingdom has not yet come—the king of the revived Roman Empire. Because the passage goes on to say that *"the beast is one of the seven and is himself also an eighth,"* we can likewise conclude the following: The "beast" is a literal king and in fact is the

Antichrist; the Antichrist will be the "king" (i.e., the political leader) over the revived Roman Empire and, in effect, will be one of the seven kings—i.e., the "seventh" king when, during the first three-and-one-half years of the Tribulation, he appears to be a man of peace. However, when he enters the Jerusalem temple and declares himself to be God (just as Antiochus Epiphanes did in 167 B.C.), he in effect becomes the "eighth" king. Thus, the Antichrist is both the seventh and the eighth kings: the seventh comes on the scene as a man of peace (Rev. 6:1,2); but the eighth turns into a man of destruction who, during the second half of the seven-year Tribulation period, reigns over a godless empire and leads to the death of one-half of the earth's population.

Finally, we also see that the "ten horns" are ten kings who, in 95 A.D., have not yet received their kingdoms but who, in the end times, will be heads-of-state of their ten respective nations (*"who will receive authority as kings with the beast for one hour"*). The phrase "one hour" represents the seven-year Tribulation period—the time during which the ten kings will be heads-of-state. These ten heads-of-state, however, will be puppets of the Antichrist because *"they have one purpose, and they give their power and authority to the beast."* (Alternatively, the phrase "one hour" represents the first three and one-half years of the Tribulation period, the time during which the Antichrist is given authority over the earth. Because Daniel 7:24 states that the Antichrist will at some point during the Tribulation "subdue" three of the ten end-times kings and because this "subduing" seems to best fit into treachery and bloodshed of the second half of the Tribulation, the "one hour" of authority granted to all ten kings would be limited to the length of time—three and one-half years—before the three are double-crossed.)

In short, the Antichrist's end-times Empire will be a revived Roman Empire having a ten-nation core. The heads-of-state of these ten nations will give their allegiance to the Antichrist as king of the world. As we will see in upcoming chapters, these ten nations will include the richest and strongest nations on earth. Moreover, the Antichrist, as we shall also see in upcoming chapters, will expand this ten-nation empire "peacefully" during the first half of the Tribulation—and then attempt to take over the entire earth during the second half of the Tribulation.

Chart 16-A

WORLD EMPIRES & THE NATION OF ISRAEL

[NIMROD'S "BABYLON"]

1.　　**EGYPTIAN**

2.　　**ASSYRIAN**

3.　　**BABYLONIAN**

4.　　**MEDO-PERSIAN**

5.　　**GRECIAN**

6.　　**ROMAN**

7.　　**REVIVED ROMAN　("BABYLON THE GREAT")**

Chart 16-B

THE TIMEFRAMES OF KEY FIGURES IN THE HISTORY OF ISRAEL

[NIMROD'S "BABYLON"] . . . *(Abraham)*

1.   EGYPTIAN . . . *(Moses)*

2.   ASSYRIAN

3.   BABYLONIAN . . . *(Daniel)*

4.   MEDO-PERSIAN

5.   GRECIAN

6.   ROMAN . . . *(Jesus Christ, at His 1st Coming)*

7.   REVIVED ROMAN ("BABYLON THE GREAT") . . .
            . . . *(Jesus Christ, at His 2nd Coming)*

Chart 16-C

THE TIMEFRAMES OF WORLD EMPIRES IN ISRAEL'S HISTORY

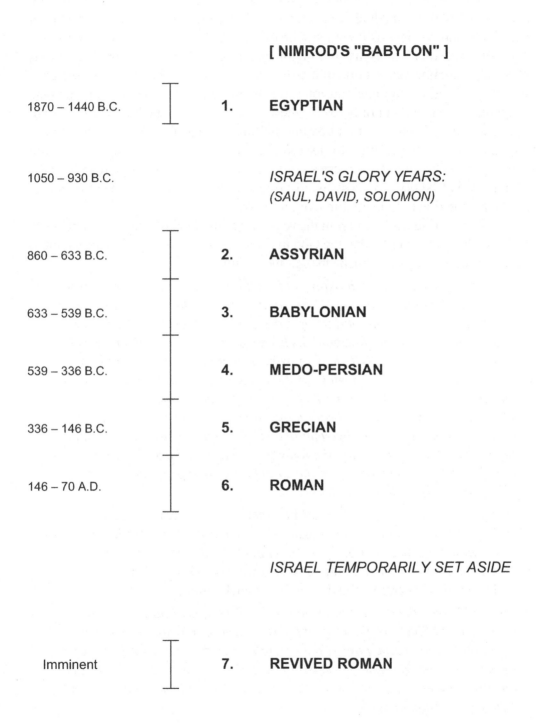

[NIMROD'S "BABYLON"]

1870 – 1440 B.C.	1.	**EGYPTIAN**
1050 – 930 B.C.		*ISRAEL'S GLORY YEARS:* *(SAUL, DAVID, SOLOMON)*
860 – 633 B.C.	2.	**ASSYRIAN**
633 – 539 B.C.	3.	**BABYLONIAN**
539 – 336 B.C.	4.	**MEDO-PERSIAN**
336 – 146 B.C.	5.	**GRECIAN**
146 – 70 A.D.	6.	**ROMAN**

ISRAEL TEMPORARILY SET ASIDE

Imminent	7.	**REVIVED ROMAN**

THE PROPHETIC SIGNIFICANCE OF NEBUCHADNEZZAR'S DREAM

The Jewish prophet Daniel, through a revelation from God approximately 600 years before the first advent of Christ, reveals the empires which will exist both concurrently and contiguously with the life of Israel after the Babylonian captivity.

During Israel's captivity in Babylon, the king of Babylon, Nebuchadnezzar, has a strange dream. When none of the Babylonian magicians, sorcerers, and conjurers in the king's entourage can interpret the dream, Nebuchadnezzar instructs the captain of his guard not only to slay these men but to slay the Hebrew wise men as well, including Daniel. Upon hearing the king's edict, Daniel asks the captain of the guard to grant him time to discern the dream and its meaning. When the captain agrees, Daniel fervently cries out to the Living God for the dream's interpretation so that Nebuchadnezzar would relent of the executions. That evening, God reveals the dream to Daniel in a night vision.

After pouring out his heart in thanksgiving to the God of heaven, Daniel goes to Nebuchadnezzar, explains that the God in heaven has revealed the interpretation to him, and proceeds to give Nebuchadnezzar the dream:

> *You, O king, were looking and, behold, there was a single great statue. That statue, which was large and of extraordinary splendor, was standing in front of you, and its appearance was awesome. The head of that statue was made of fine gold, its breast and its arms of silver, its belly and its thighs of bronze, its legs of iron, its feet partly of iron and partly of clay. You continued looking until a stone was cut out without hands, and it struck the statue on its feet of iron and clay, and crushed them. Then the iron, the clay, the bronze, the silver and the gold were crushed all at the same time, and became like chaff from the summer threshing floors; and the wind carried them away so that not a trace of them was found. But the stone that struck the statue became a great mountain and filled the whole earth (Dan. 2:31-35).*

According to Daniel, Nebuchadnezzar has seen a great statue in his dream. Not only is the statue made out of varied materials, but the statue is ultimately smashed by a stone which has been cut out of rock without the use of hands. Moreover, the stone then grows into a great mountain which fills the whole earth.

Daniel then interprets the dream for Nebuchadnezzar:

> *This was the dream; now we shall tell its interpretation before the king. You, O king, are the king of kings, to whom the God of heaven has given the kingdom, the power, the strength, and the glory; and wherever the sons of men dwell, or the beasts of the field, or the birds of the sky, He has given them into your hand and has caused you to rule over them all. You are the head of gold.*

> *And after you there will arise another kingdom inferior to you, then another third kingdom of bronze, which will rule over all the earth. Then there will be a fourth kingdom as strong as iron; inasmuch as iron crushes and shatters all things, so, like iron that breaks in pieces, it will crush and break all these in pieces. And in that you saw the feet and toes, partly of potter's clay and partly of iron, it will be a divided kingdom; but it will have in it the toughness of iron, inasmuch as you saw the iron mixed with common clay. And as the toes of the feet were partly of iron and partly of pottery, so some of the kingdom will be strong and part of it will be brittle. And in that you saw the iron mixed with common clay, they will combine with one another in the seed of men; but they will not adhere to one another, even as iron does not combine with pottery.*
>
> *And in the days of those kings the God of heaven will set up a kingdom which will never be destroyed, and that kingdom will not be left for another people; it will crush and put an end to all these kingdoms, but it will itself endure forever (Dan. 2:36-44).*

Daniel explains to the king that God has ordained five consecutive empires—contiguous with and encompassing the history of God's people Israel—before He establishes a kingdom which will cover the entire earth, which will never be defeated by another kingdom, and which will last forever. [Note: two antecedent world empires concurrent with Israel—the Egyptian Empire and the Assyrian Empire—have already come and gone by the time of Nebuchadnezzar's dream.]

These five empires are depicted as sections of the statue, the first empire being represented by the statue's head of gold. Much to Nebuchadnezzar's surprise, this part of the statue represents his very own Babylonian empire. Daniel explains, however, that, after the Babylonian empire, four increasingly weaker empires will emerge on the scene—weaker in the sense that they grow increasingly less homogeneous nationally and ethnically (*"they will combine with one another in the seed of men, but they will not adhere to one another"*), the final empire being made out of a non-cleaving mixture of iron and common clay. The five empires are as follows: the **Babylonian** Empire ("gold"); the **Medo-Persian** Empire ("silver"); the **Grecian** Empire ("bronze"); the **Roman** Empire ("iron"); and the **revived Roman** Empire ("iron and clay") (see Chart 17-A).

The identity of the revived Roman Empire is gleaned from several other passages of Scripture as well, including Revelation 17:8, in which the phrase *"the beast that you saw was, and is not, and is about to come up out of the abyss and to go to destruction"* seemingly alludes to the Roman Empire, which at one time "was" (until approximately 476 A.D.), and then "is not" (after 476 A.D.), and will one day come back to life ("and is about to come up out of the abyss") during the end times. Today's E.U. (European Union) and "Group of Seven" provide us with tantalizing foreshadows of a future revived Roman Empire. Much of the wealth of the world and much of its strategic military power are now in the hands of Europe and the United States (whose colonial ancestry was European).

Revelation 13:3 also seems to picture a revived Roman Empire in its description of the seven-headed beast (i.e., the seven world empires): *"And I saw one of his heads as if it had been slain, and his fatal wound was healed."* The key expression in Revelation 13:3 is the expression "as if." In its context, the verse appears to allude to the disintegration of the Roman Empire at some point in time and to its eventual reemergence during the end times. Such a conclusion seems to fit the imagery of Nebuchadnezzar's statue—with the revived Roman Empire being described as having the same basic element of iron as the ancient Roman Empire, but also as having the additional element of clay, making it difficult for this end-times empire truly to congeal. The existence of the "ten toes" likewise fits a picture of the Antichrist's revived Roman Empire, with the ten toes representing the ten core nations of the Antichrist's Empire (and perhaps even the ten heads-of-state who give their allegiance to the Antichrist). Finally, let us recall from our discussion of Daniel's "Seventy Weeks" prophecy in Chapter 2 that Daniel 9:26 unequivocally states that the Antichrist will descend from the people—the ancient Roman Empire—who destroyed Jerusalem in 70 A.D.

The import of Nebuchadnezzar's dream is that God has ordained five world empires from the time of Nebuchadnezzar's reign (and relative to God's people Israel) *before* He brings the reign of His Son, Jesus Christ, to earth—a reign covenanted three thousand years ago with Israel's greatest king, King David (II Sam. 7:8-29). The fifth and final world empire to appear on the human scene before the reign of Messiah over the earth will be a revived Roman Empire led by the Antichrist. Finally, Messiah's Kingdom will crush and put an end to this final man-centered kingdom (the Antichrist's Empire); will itself never be destroyed; will itself fill the whole earth; and will endure forever.

Chart 17-A

WORLD EMPIRES IN NEBUCHADNEZZAR'S DREAM

BABYLONIAN *("GOLD")*

MEDO-PERSIAN *("SILVER")*

GRECIAN *("BRONZE")*

ROMAN *("IRON")*

REVIVED ROMAN *("IRON AND CLAY")*

CHRIST'S MESSIANIC (MILLENNIAL) KINGDOM

> *("WILL NEVER BE DESTROYED; WILL CRUSH AND PUT AN END TO ALL THESE KINGDOMS; WILL ENDURE FOREVER")*

TWO KEY END-TIMES "KINGDOM OF HEAVEN" PARABLES

Jesus often presented parables to the multitudes who followed Him. In Matthew's Gospel, twelve of the Lord's parables (discussed earlier in Chapter 4) deal with the nature and substance of a spiritual kingdom (the "kingdom of heaven") He would bring forth on the earth between His two advents. Several of these parables in turn have particular relevance to the end times and help us arrive at an accurate understanding of the end-times events. For now, however, let us look at two of the key parables: the Parable of the Mustard Seed and the Parable of the Wheat & Tares.

A.　　The Parable of the Mustard Seed

Matthew 13:31-32 records the Lord's Parable of the Mustard Seed as follows: *"He presented another parable to them, saying, 'The kingdom of heaven is like a mustard seed which a man took and sowed in his field. And this seed is smaller than all other seeds; but when it is full grown, it is larger than the garden plants and becomes a tree, so that the birds of the air come and nest in its branches.'"* Christ states that His kingdom on earth between His two advents (Christianity or "Christendom") will begin as an inconsequential, hardly noticeable group at its genesis, but will grow to become the largest religion on earth prior to His return. Today, Christianity has become the largest of the earth's religions both numerically and geographically. Nearly 2.2 billion people claim to be Christians, and Christianity is the predominant religion in the entire Western Hemisphere, the British Isles, Scandinavia, Western Europe, Eastern Europe, Russia, Australia, and New Zealand. At this juncture in human history, the Mustard Seed has become the "full-grown tree" described in the parable.

The end-times significance of the Mustard Seed has to do with its geographic size at the time of Christ's revelation to the Apostle John on the island of Patmos in 95 A.D—*and its geographic size today.* By 95 A.D., Christianity (the "mustard seed") had taken root throughout the ancient Roman Empire. Thus, when John received his end-times visions from Christ, the size of Christendom had grown so swiftly that it equaled the size of the ancient Roman Empire. Indeed, for Christians living in 95 A.D., the Roman Empire—destroyer of Jerusalem in 70 A.D. and fervent persecutor of Christians—was akin to the Antichrist's Empire. In other words, not only did Christendom equal the size of the ancient Roman Empire but it equaled the size of what to them was the Antichrist's Empire! The mustard seed, however, in 95 A.D. had not yet become the largest of the world's religions, and the mustard seed, to be sure, has continued to *grow* during the past nineteen centuries (its size no longer limited to the Mediterranean basin and Western Europe). This growth phenomenon will be analyzed at length in Chapters 19 and

20—and will provide us with the precise geographic size of the Antichrist's Empire at the mid-point of the Tribulation.

B.   The Parable of the Wheat & Tares

The second key end-times parable is the Parable of the Wheat and Tares, a parable recorded in Matthew 13:24-30. Christ explains its meaning in Matthew 13:36-43:

> *Then He left the multitudes, and went into the house. And His disciples came to Him, saying, "Explain to us the parable of the tares of the field." And He answered and said, "The one who sows the good seed is the Son of Man, and the field is the world; and as for the good seed, these are the sons of the kingdom; and the tares are the sons of the evil one; and the enemy who sowed them is the devil, and the harvest is the end of the age; and the reapers are angels. Therefore, just as the tares are gathered up and burned with fire, so shall it be at the end of the age. The Son of Man will send forth His angels, and they will gather out of His kingdom all stumbling blocks, and those who commit lawlessness, and will cast them into the furnace of fire; in that place there shall be weeping and gnashing of teeth. Then the righteous will shine forth as the sun in the kingdom of their Father. He who has ears, let him hear."*

Christ tells His disciples that, in heaven's kingdom on earth ("Christendom") between His advents, two kinds of "Christians" will exist. He likens them to "wheat" and "tares." Wheat is the real item, while a tare is a counterfeit: the tare looks like wheat, but in reality is a worthless weed. Soberingly, Christ states that, although He Himself has sown the wheat (the true Christians), Satan has sown the tares (the counterfeit "Christians"). Thus, though twenty-first century Christianity is the world's largest religion both numerically and geographically, Christendom today contains both wheat and tares—those who are born-again and those who are not. In short, the wheat have put their faith in the finished work of Jesus Christ for their sin problem; the tares have not. The wheat are indwelled with the Holy Spirit; the tares are not. The wheat have come to Christ on the basis of a grace-faith belief system; the tares are trying to come to Christ on the basis of a law-works belief system. Charts 18-A, B, & C highlight the contrasts between the wheat and the tares.

The end-times significance of this parable lies in the fact that the "wheat" represents the "Bride" of Christ (Christians indwelled with the Holy Spirit). The Bride will be removed instantaneously from the earth into heaven at the Rapture. The "tares," on the other hand, represent the "Harlot" of the Tribulation period ("Christians" not indwelled with the Holy Spirit). The tares will be that part of Christianity left behind on earth at the Rapture (*"Truly I say to you, I do not know you"*—Matt. *25:12*). Although some of the tares left behind will likely turn to Christ after the Rapture, most of them will reject Christ and will instead become part of the Tribulation period's Great Harlot—a grand, apostate, ecumenical brand of Christianity consisting of Roman Catholic, Eastern Orthodox, and liberal Protestant churches.

Today's liberal Protestants mirror the Sadducees of Christ's day—denying the essentials of the faith, including the inerrancy of Scripture, the miracles of Christ, the deity of Christ, the resurrection of Christ, and a literal Second Coming of Christ. The Catholics and Orthodoxes in turn mirror the Pharisees of Christ's day, having surrounded themselves with man-made ritual and a salvation system based on a law-works gospel rather than the grace-faith gospel of the New Testament. In short, although Christianity is the largest religion on earth today, it nevertheless contains both true adherents and counterfeit adherents. [Note: By God's grace, some Catholics and liberal Protestants are coming to Christ after hearing the true gospel—often through evangelism crusades, parachurch ministries, or friend-to-friend evangelism—and are acknowledging the necessity of the new birth as taught by Jesus in John 3:1-8.]

Sadly, the percentage of counterfeit Christians in the Western world far outweighs the number of true Christians. In Protestant Great Britain, for example, eighty-five percent of the population is Anglican. Only ten percent of the population actually attends church, and only four to five percent is born-again. In France, ninety percent of the population is Catholic. Only two percent of the population attends church, and less than one-half of one percent is born-again. Thus, virtually all of France's "Christians" are tares. In Greece, ninety-eight percent of the population is Greek Orthodox, yet less than one percent of the population is born-again. The Anglican, Catholic, and Orthodox churches baptize infants into the church, contending that such infants are "justified" (saved) in the sight of God at that moment. Yet the New Testament teaches that *"faith comes from hearing, and hearing by the Word of God"* (Romans 10:17). How can an infant hear and understand the gospel message? Jesus instead teaches that each person much consciously choose to invite Him into his or her life (Rev. 3:20). To Nicodemus, a seeking Pharisee, Jesus said: *"Truly, truly, I say to you, unless one is born-again, he cannot see the kingdom of God" (John 3:3).* Though some Catholics and Orthodoxes *are* born-again (Rev. 3:4), most are spiritually dead (Rev. 3:2).

If you call yourself a Christian, are you "wheat" or a "tare"? How do you stack up against the descriptions given in Charts 18-A & B? Have you consciously turned your heart to God and put your faith in Jesus Christ's finished work for you, or are you trusting in your infant baptism or church membership or good works for salvation? Do you understand Christianity to be a supernatural regeneration through the new birth (John 3:3-8), or do you understand it to be nothing more than a package of ethical principles to live by? Have your ever consciously opened up your heart to invite Christ into your life as Savior, or do you think that you're acceptable to God because you belong to a socially prominent church or because you're a "good" person? If it's the latter, then God will one day say to you, *"Depart from Me, accursed ones, into the eternal fire which has been prepared for the devil and his angels" (Matt. 25:41).*

Chart 18-A

THE MAKE-UP OF CHRISTENDOM TODAY

"WHEAT"	"TARES"
TRUE CHRISTIANS	COUNTERFEIT CHRISTIANS
SOWN BY CHRIST	SOWN BY SATAN
BORN-AGAIN	NOT BORN-AGAIN
INDWELLED W/THE H.S.	NOT INDWELLED W/THE H.S.
SAVED	NOT SAVED
EMPOWERED BY THE H.S.	EMPOWERED BY THE FLESH
BEAR AUTHENTIC FRUIT	BEAR COUNTERFEIT FRUIT
PRUNED	CUT-OFF
"THE BRIDE"	"THE HARLOT"
WILL BE RAPTURED	WILL NOT BE RAPTURED
GRACE-FAITH DOCTRINE	LAW-WORKS DOCTRINE

Chart 18-B

THE MAKE-UP OF CHRISTENDOM TODAY
---

1. **"WHEAT" (BORN-AGAIN CHRISTIANS)**

    . . . HAVE RECEIVED CHRIST AS THEIR SAVIOR

    . . . ARE INDWELLED WITH THE HOLY SPIRIT

    . . . COMPRISE THE TRUE CHURCH TODAY

    . . . ARE THE "BRIDE" OF CHRIST

    . . . WILL LEAVE THE EARTH AT THE RAPTURE

2. **"TARES" (CHRISTIANS IN NAME ONLY)**

    . . . HAVE NOT RECEIVED CHRIST AS THEIR SAVIOR

    . . . ARE NOT INDWELLED WITH THE HOLY SPIRIT

    . . . COMPRISE THE APOSTATE CHURCH TODAY

    . . . ARE THE "GREAT HARLOT"

    . . . WILL BE LEFT ON EARTH AT THE RAPTURE

Chart 18-C

JOHN 15:1-6

"VINEDRESSER" = GOD THE FATHER

"VINE" = JESUS CHRIST

"BRANCHES" = CHRISTENDOM → **"WHEAT" (PRUNED)**

→ **"TARES" (CUT OFF)**

THE GROWTH OF THE "MUSTARD SEED" (CHRISTENDOM)

By tracing the long-term growth of the "Mustard Seed" (Christ's kingdom on earth between His two advents), we can determine geographic size of the Antichrist's end-times Empire. Thus, let us examine the growth of Christendom over the centuries and then draw some conclusions with regard to the magnitude of the Antichrist's Empire—conclusions which in turn maintain the prophetic integrity of the visions given to the Apostle John on the island of Patmos in 95 A.D.

A.   The Germination of the Mustard Seed

The Mustard Seed began its growth on the Day of Pentecost in 30 A.D. when 3,000 Jews in Jerusalem, upon hearing the gospel message from the Apostle Peter, put their faith in Jesus Christ for salvation and eternal life. Several weeks later, the Mustard Seed continued its first steps of growth when another 5,000 Jews put their faith in Christ after again hearing Peter preach the gospel (See Chart 19-A).

B.   The Early Growth of the Mustard Seed

Approximately a year after the initial germination of the Mustard Seed, a convert named Stephen was stoned to death in Jerusalem. Stephen's stoning precipitated an intense persecution of the growing number of Christians in Jerusalem, causing much of the Christian community to flee into Judea and Samaria. Though Jerusalem's unbelieving Jews meant to rid the area of this new phenomenon, the dispersed Christians began to share the good news of Jesus Christ with their Jewish brethren in these areas—and the Mustard Seed began to grow beyond the boundaries of Jerusalem. Several years later, Peter, while in Caesarea, shared the gospel with a Gentile named Cornelius, and the Mustard Seed had its first Gentile convert. About a dozen years after the germination of the Mustard Seed, Jewish Christians in the Syrian town of Antioch began to preach the gospel to Antioch's Gentiles, and large numbers of Gentiles put their faith in Jesus Christ. The Mustard Seed was continuing its inexorable growth.

In 44 A.D., the Apostle Paul (converted on the Damascus Road a dozen years earlier) and Barnabas took the gospel to the southern part of present-day Turkey, and hundreds of people turned their hearts to Christ. Six years later, Paul returned to his first converts in southern Turkey and rejoiced to find that the Mustard Seed was continuing its growth in the area. Paul then took the gospel to modern day Greece, and hundreds more came to faith in Christ. During this same timeframe, still other Christians were taking the gospel to Egypt, Libya, Ethiopia, and Rome. In 54 A.D., Paul began his third missionary journey and, after visiting his first churches in southern Turkey, moved on to Ephesus in western Turkey, where he led hundreds more to faith in Christ. Shortly thereafter, the Ephesus church became the hub from which much of western Turkey was evangelized.

C.   The Mustard Seed by 95 A.D.—and the Mustard Seed Clue

By 95 A.D., the gospel of Jesus Christ, having been shared by Christians traveling the Mediterranean basin on the extensive network of Roman roads, had taken root throughout the Roman Empire. Local churches had sprung up in every region of the empire and in virtually every major city. Consequently, at this point in the history of Christendom, the geographic scope of the Mustard Seed had expanded to a size which *equaled the geographic scope of the ancient Roman Empire—and vice versa* (See Chart 19-B). Simultaneous with this phenomenon, the Resurrected Christ in 95 A.D., by way of three visions to His most beloved earthly friend, the Apostle John, presented the entire panorama of end-times events to the Apostle. These visions were written down by John, were circulated to seven local churches in Asia Minor (western Turkey), and eventually became the book of Revelation.

Furthermore, Christ, through these visions to John, also gave the Church a "snapshot" of the world scene in 95 A.D. which He would *replicate* prior to His second advent: In 95 A.D., a "Japhethite" empire—the ancient Roman Empire— ruled the region of the world contiguous with Israel. During the end-times Tribulation, a Japhethite empire—the revived Roman Empire of the Antichrist— will once again rule the region of the world contiguous with Israel. By 95 A.D., Israel had been made desolate by the Roman Empire. After the mid-point of the Tribulation period, Israel will again be made desolate by the revived Roman Empire. The ancient Roman Empire was fiercely anti-Semitic, leading to the destruction of Jerusalem in 70 A.D. The revived Roman Empire of the Antichrist will likewise be fiercely anti-Semitic after the mid-point of the Tribulation period, leading to the attempted annihilation of Israel. In addition, the ancient Roman Empire was *anti-Christian*—and mercilessly persecuted Christians during the last half of the first century. The revived Roman Empire of the Antichrist will also be *anti-Christian*—and will countenance the merciless persecution and martyrdom of post-Rapture Christians during the second half of the Tribulation.

What's more, because the Mustard Seed has continued to grow since 95 A.D., Christ has given the Church today a wonderful clue with regard to the *geographic size* of the Antichrist's Empire. The clue is this: By the time the Apostle John received his visions on Patmos from the resurrected Christ in approximately 95 A.D., the "mustard seed" had grown throughout most of the then Roman Empire. Thus, in 95 A.D., Christendom (which included both "wheat" and "tares") equaled, roughly speaking, the geographic size of the Roman Empire—and vice versa. Today, however, and this is a detail which Bible commentators universally seem to miss, the Mustard Seed (Christendom) is no longer limited geographically to the Mediterranean basin. In fact, the

Mustard Seed has now grown to include Canada, the United States, Mexico, Central America, South America, Great Britain, Scandinavia, Eastern Europe, Russia, Australia, New Zealand, and much of southern Africa—taken to these countries, it should be noted, by explorers (e.g., Columbus) whose ancestors once lived in the Ancient Roman Empire.

The point is this: it is no longer necessary for 21st Century commentators to limit the ten core nations of the Antichrist's Empire to ten Western European nations (the most popular view), nor is it necessary for commentators to limit the Antichrist's end-times Empire to Western Europe or a "Mediterranean Confederacy"—because the Lord's Mustard Seed parable is designed to give the Church a picture of an *expanding* sphere of Christendom at any point in time between His first and second advents. Indeed, only one scenario maintains the prophetic integrity of John's vision: just as Christendom equaled the size of the ancient Roman Empire in 95 A.D. (and vice versa), *Christendom during the end times should equal the geographic scope of the revived Roman Empire (and vice versa).* Thus, we can say with a high degree of certainty that the Antichrist's Empire, after the "peaceful" expansion beyond its ten-nation core during the first Seal judgment (the first three and a half years of the Tribulation period), will include (as mentioned above) all nations and regions whose principal religion is Christianity: Canada, the United States, Mexico, Central America, South America, Scandinavia, Great Britain, Western Europe, Eastern Europe, Russia, Australia, New Zealand, and much of southern Africa (See Chart 19-D). *Of major note, the Parable of the Mustard Seed and the mustard seed clue allow us to look at the United States and Russia as possible members of the Antichrist's Empire as well.* Chapters 22 & 23 will examine this contention more extensively.

D. The Mustard Seed by the Fourteenth Century

See Chart 19-C.

E. The Mustard Seed by the Twentieth Century—and the Clue

See Chart 19-D.

Chart 19-A

Christendom in 30 A.D.

Chart 19-C

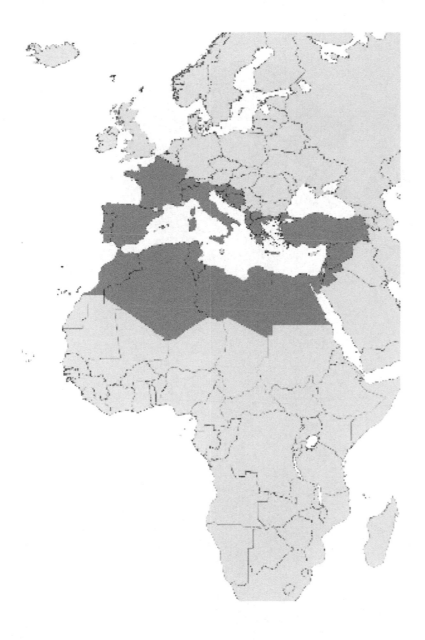

Christendom in 95 A.D.
(mostly "wheat"; some "tares")

the geographic scope of Christendom
equals
the geographic scope of the Ancient Roman Empire

Chart 19-C

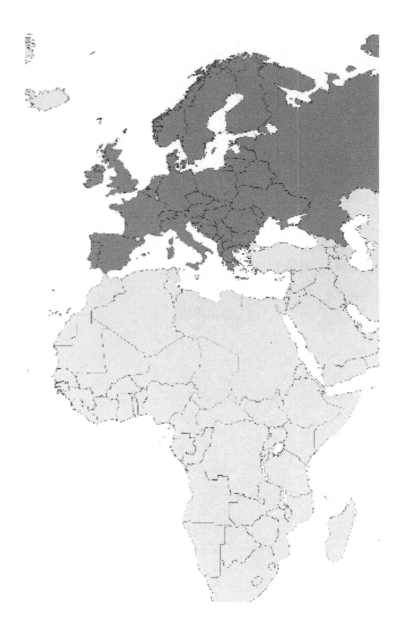

Christendom in 1420 A.D.

(includes "wheat" and "tares")

Chart 19-D

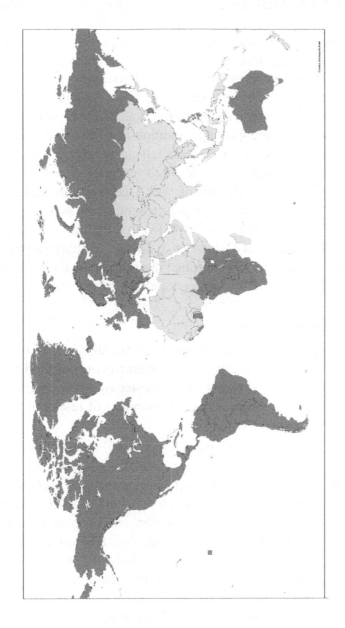

Christendom in 2020 A.D.

(includes "wheat" and "tares")

the geographic scope of Christendom
equals
the geographic scope of the Revived Roman Empire!

OTHER COMMENTS ABOUT THE MUSTARD SEED (CHRISTENDOM)

To most non-believers, Christianity is an enigmatic religion containing the extremes of genuine transformation, pious ritual, blatant politicization, and hypocritical huckstering. Why, however, does Christendom have such a mixed witness to the world? Jesus Himself gives us the answers in two other "kingdom" parables (the Parable of the Sower and the Parable of the Leaven) as well as Chapters 2 & 3 of Revelation where He describes the spiritual condition of Christendom at any point in time between His two advents. In short, Jesus tells us (1) that the gospel will be met with varying degrees of response, from heartfelt reception to outright rejection; (2) that portions of Christendom, while starting with receptive hearts and pure doctrine, will over time become infiltrated with poor teaching and false doctrine, thus producing a confusing witness to the world; and (3) that the local churches within Christendom will themselves, between Christ's two advents, display varying witness to the world, depending on their level of spiritual discernment and degree of gospel receptivity. Let us examine each of these three topics.

A.   The Parable of the Sower

In the Parable of the Sower, Jesus explains to His disciples that the gospel message—the good news of the Crucifixion and Resurrection of God the Son to provide atonement for mankind's sins and the guarantee of eternal life for all who will put their faith in Him—will experience a *continuum* of response from those who hear the message between His two advents.

> *Behold, the sower went out to sow; and as he sowed, some seeds fell beside the road, and the birds came and ate them up. And others fell upon the rocky places, where they did not have much soil; and immediately they sprang up, because they had no depth of soil. But when the sun had risen, they were scorched; and because they had no root, they withered away. And others fell among the thorns, and the thorns came up and choked them out. And others fell on the good soil, and yielded a crop, some a hundredfold, some sixty, and some thirty. He who has ears, let him hear (Matt. 13:3-9).*
>
> *Hear then the parable of the sower. When anyone hears the word of the kingdom and does not understand it, the evil one comes and snatches away what has been sown in his heart. This is the one on whom seed was sown beside the road. And the one on whom seed was sown on the rocky places, this is the man who hears the word and immediately receives it with joy; yet he has no firm root in himself, but is only temporary, and when affliction or persecution arises because of the word, immediately he falls away. And the one on whom seed was sown among the thorns, this is the man who hears the word, and the worry of the world*

and the deceitfulness of riches choke the word, and it becomes unfruitful. And the one on whom seed was sown on the good soil, this is the man who hears the word and understands it; who indeed bears fruit, and brings forth, some a hundredfold, some sixty, and some thirty (Matt. 13:18-23).

Jesus first warns that many who hear the gospel will not embrace it because their hearts are hard (like the hardened soil of first century roads). He then explains that others will respond excitedly to the gospel for a time but, having no root, will fall away when any type of persecution arises from the non-believing world. Jesus teaches that still others will receive the gospel into their hearts for salvation, but over time will allow the worries of the world and the deceitfulness of riches to suffocate much of the spiritual fruitfulness in their lives. And finally, Jesus confirms that some will respond to the gospel with willing and fertile hearts and, after receiving Christ, will grow in their relationship with Him and will bear significant spiritual fruit in their lives—the supernatural fruit of the Spirit (love, joy, peace, longsuffering, gentleness, goodness, faithfulness, meekness, and self-control—Gal. 5:21-22), fruit which was not present in their lives before they invited Christ into their hearts.

B.   The Parable of the Leaven

Commentators usually ascribe one of two interpretations to the Parable of the Leaven. The first interpretation suggests that Christ will cause His kingdom to grow inexorably between His two advents, just as leaven (or yeast) hidden in dough causes bread to rise inexorably before it is baked. The second interpretation suggests that Christ's kingdom between His two advents will become "leavened" with false teaching (e.g., Matt. 16:11-12). The term "leaven" in the Scriptures typically depicts sin, evil, or false teaching. Both interpretations seem plausible and both, in fact, have taken place since Christ's first advent. Let us focus on the latter interpretation for now.

Accordingly, in the Parable of the Leaven, Jesus warns His disciples that Christendom—His inter-advent spiritual kingdom on earth—will become infiltrated with error, false teaching (by "wolves in sheep's clothing"), false doctrine, and counterfeit Christians ("tares"). Just as leaven placed in a lump of dough comes to permeate much of the loaf of bread, so too the "leaven" of error and false teaching would come to permeate a good portion of Christendom by the time of the Lord's second advent.

During its first few years of existence, the Church had no "leaven" in its midst. It understood, and held to, the grace-faith belief system of the pure gospel. Unfortunately, by the time Paul revisited his first churches in southern Turkey (on his second missionary journey and perhaps twenty years after the Day of Pentecost), doctrinal error and false teaching had already begun to buffet these churches (Gal. 3:1-14): "Judaizers" were descending upon these churches and were trying to make salvation a matter of also keeping the Old Testament Law. Thus, instead of the pure gospel of "justification by faith alone," the Judaizers were teaching that salvation came by way of faith plus keeping the Law—a false gospel and an error which caused Paul to write the letter known as Galatians.

During the ensuing nineteen hundred years, other error and false teaching has found its way into parts of the Church so that, today, Christendom has liberal churches which deny the virgin birth of Christ, the sinless life of Christ, the Resurrection of Christ, the deity of Christ, and the necessity of the new birth—denials which "leaven" the Christian faith. Christendom has ritualistic churches which teach that a person is saved when he or she is baptized into that church as an infant—a teaching which is in direct opposition to John 3:3 and Romans 10:17. Christendom has ritualistic churches which teach that a person is infused with the grace of Christ when he or she partakes of the sacraments of that particular church—a teaching nowhere found in Scripture. Christendom has evangelical churches which deny the inerrancy of Scripture, evangelical churches which insist that the gospel amounts to keeping a list of "do's" and "don'ts," and evangelical churches which deny a future literal reign of Jesus Christ over the earth—beliefs which likewise leaven the Christian faith. Thus, just as Jesus prophesied nearly two thousand years ago, much of Christendom has become leavened with a wide range of poor and false teaching. As a result, non-Christians have a hard time distinguishing the true gospel of Jesus Christ and are left in the dark with regard to God's overall purposes in human history.

C.   The Seven Churches of Revelation 2 & 3

In Chapters 2 & 3 of Revelation, the resurrected Lord gives the Apostle John seven messages—one for each of seven designated churches in Asia Minor—which in turn detail the spiritual condition of Christendom near the end of the first century, approximately thirty-five to forty years after the founding of these churches. The seven churches are as follows: Ephesus, Smyrna, Pergamum, Thyatira, Sardis, Philadelphia, and Laodicea.

The messages typically contain five elements: (1) a figurative description of Christ, who in each message is also identified as the one addressing that particular church; (2) a commendation (if any) for the church being addressed; (3) a rebuke (if any) of the church being addressed; (4) an exhortation for the church being addressed; and (5) a promise from the Lord to believers (called "overcomers" in these messages). While many commentators contend that these seven messages also correspond to particular phases of Christendom during the period of time between the first and second advents of Christ, such will not be the position taken in this discussion. Rather, it is this writer's belief that the primary purpose of these messages is to describe the overall spiritual condition of Christendom at any point in time between the two advents of Christ and that the spiritual condition of twenty-first century Christendom can be readily seen in the strengths and weaknesses of these seven first century churches. Moreover, Chapters 2 and 3 of Revelation help explain, to both critics and adherents alike, why Christendom has generated such a wide spectrum of witness over the past nineteen centuries—from the genuinely transformed lives of some within its ranks to the naive, legalistic, hypocritical, or unchanged lives of others within its ranks.

Two of the seven churches received no rebuke from the Lord in 95 A.D. and picture faithful, believing evangelical churches today as well. The church at **Smyrna**, for example, was faithful to the Lord despite being the target of intense persecution from the world (and reminds us of today's underground church in China, whose faithfulness to the Lord resulted in explosive growth from 1949 to 1992 despite intense persecution). The church at **Philadelphia**, in turn, was a faithful, missionary-sending church (and reminds us of local churches today who are focused on reaching others with the gospel and making disciples of all nations). For the purpose of analyzing the "leaven" in present-day Christianity, however, let us highlight the five churches who received rebukes from the Lord—the churches at Ephesus, Pergamum, Thyatira, Sardis, and Laodicea.

The church at **Ephesus** was an outreach-minded, discerning, doctrinally-sound church, which nevertheless had "left its first love." Apparently, this church was no longer seeking intimacy with Christ above all else—and reminds us of evangelical churches today who have fallen into a pattern of self-sufficiency, prayerlessness, and perhaps even legalism. Such churches are likely operating in the power of the flesh rather than the Spirit—and the Holy Spirit, as a result, is being stifled or smothered

The church at **Pergamum** was a believing, steadfast church in the midst of persecution. Yet it had some in its midst who held to compromising, licentious, and syncretistic beliefs. The Pergamum church reminds us of evangelical churches today who are so accommodating to the world and so lacking in discernment that the world has infiltrated these churches rather than vice versa. Some in these churches are carnal—and are grieving the Holy Spirit. Others in these churches are attempting to marry the Word of God with the philosophies of men—and are quenching the Holy Spirit.

The church at **Thyatira** was a loving, persevering, serving church, which nevertheless tolerated a woman who called herself a prophetess, but was not. Her dangerously false teachings ("the deep things of Satan") were leading Christ's bondservants astray—and reminds us of Christian cults who have likewise allowed "prophets" and extra-Biblical revelation to lead the unsuspecting astray. Even today, some evangelical churches allow so-called "apostles" and "prophets" to proclaim supposed "revelation from God." Such churches are typically more enamored with extra-biblical revelation than with the living and active Word of God. These churches have a mixture of true Christians ("wheat") and counterfeit

Christians ("tares"). To their discredit, some of these churches even sanction occultic practices within their ranks.

The church at **Sardis** was an apostate unbelieving church, which thought itself to be spiritually alive, but in reality was dead. This church reminds us today of the Roman and Orthodox churches, who think themselves to be alive (with their ecclesiastical pomp and ritual), but who, in the main, are dead—with their false gospel of salvation by sacraments, good works, and church membership. Says Christ of this church: *"I know your deeds, that you have a name that you are alive, but you are dead. Wake up, and strengthen the things that remain, which are about to die, for I have not found your deeds completed in the sight of My God. . . . But you have a few people in Sardis who have not soiled their garments; and they will walk with Me in white, for they are worthy"* (Rev. 3:1-4). Such churches today are dead because the Holy Spirit does not indwell the persons in this church (with the exception of a few, v.4). Indeed, most "Christians" attending these churches are merely cultural Christians who have no personal relationship with Christ.

Finally, the church at **Laodicea** was an unbelieving, lukewarm church. It reminds us today of liberal Protestant churches around the world who, for the most part, deny the essentials of the faith—including the deity of Christ, the resurrection of Christ, and the necessity of the new birth. Says Christ of these churches: *"I know your deeds, that you are neither cold nor hot; I wish that you were one or the other. So, because you are lukewarm, and are neither hot nor cold, I will spew you out of My mouth."* (Rev. 3:15-16). Such churches attempt to have a relationship with Christ on their own terms rather than on God's. These churches are lukewarm because the Holy Spirit does not indwell those who attend these churches. Salvation in these churches is either works-based or universalism-based. As is the case with "Sardian" churches, many in today's "Laodicean" churches are merely "cultural Christians" who have no personal relationship with Christ. Laodicean churches usually feature feel-good social messages, and their ministry thrust typically involves a social gospel rather than the true gospel of Jesus Christ.

[Note 1: it is imperative that the reader of Chapters 2 and 3 of Revelation recognize that Christ is describing the spiritual condition of "Christendom" or "Christianity" as a whole in these seven messages. He is *not* simply describing the condition of the true Church (born-again believers in Jesus Christ). It is essential to understand that Christianity at the end of the first century contained both born-again Christians (the "wheat" of Matt. 13:37-38) and counterfeit Christians (the "tares" of Matt. 13:38-39). The same phenomenon holds true today: Christianity contains both born-again Christians and counterfeit Christians. The wheat at any given time in Christendom has been sown by Christ; the tares (i.e., those who call themselves "Christians" but who are not born again) have been sown by Satan.]

[Note 2: The end-times significance of the seven churches of Revelation 2 and 3 is found primarily in the churches at Sardis ("You have a name that you are alive, but you are dead") and Laodicea ("Because you are lukewarm, I will

spew you out of my mouth"). Today's "Sardian" and "Laodicean" churches—
the Roman Catholic, Eastern Orthodox and Liberal Protestant churches—(1) will
be the principal churches left behind on earth after the Rapture and (2) will unite
in a final grand ecumenical gesture to form the apostate "Harlot" church of the
Tribulation period.]

THE KEY PERSONAGES AND INSTITUTIONS OF THE END TIMES

The prophetic scriptures of the Old and New Testaments describe more than a dozen principal end-times personages and institutions. It is essential for the Christian to gain a basic knowledge of each. To this end, let us offer the following thumbnail sketches:

A.   The Antichrist

The Antichrist will be a charismatic world political leader who is a Japhethite (a Caucasian) and who comes from the Western world. He possibly will come from Italy (Dan. 9:26), but could also come from another European nation, Russia, Britain, Canada, or the United States (all predominantly Japhethite nations). The Antichrist will orchestrate a seven-year peace agreement between his ten core nations, Israel, and Israel's Islamic neighbors. The signing of this agreement will initiate the seven-year Tribulation period. During the first half of the Tribulation, the Antichrist will appear to the world as an "angel of light"—a man of peace. However, once he breaks his peace treaty with Israel, his true colors will unfold. After he desecrates the Jerusalem temple at the mid-point of the Tribulation, the Antichrist will overrun the Middle East (including Israel) (Dan. 11:36-43) and Africa in a military campaign which leads to the death of one-fourth of the earth's post-Rapture population (Rev. 6:3-8). Sometime thereafter, he will confront the "kings of the east" (the Asian nations) and Russia ("rumors from the north") (Dan. 11:44)—and one-third of the earth's remaining population will be killed in this conflagration (Rev. 9:13-18). Thus, the Antichrist will be responsible for the death of one-half of the earth's post-Rapture population.

B.   The Antichrist's Empire ("Babylon the Great")

The Antichrist's Empire will be a revived Roman Empire—i.e., a Western, predominantly Japhethite empire. At the beginning of the seven-year Tribulation, the empire will consist of ten wealthy, industrial nations who, backed by the most sophisticated armaments on earth, will begin to call the shots for the rest of the world (while protecting their own mutual interests). During the first half of the Tribulation, the Antichrist will expand his empire beyond its ten-nation core and will amass, by the mid-point of the Tribulation period, all nations in which Christianity currently represents the predominant religion. This expansion will take place peacefully, and the Antichrist will use the Pope and the Apostate Church to accomplish much of this objective. During the second half of the Tribulation, the Antichrist—through much bloodshed—will take over the Islamic Middle East and all of Africa. When accomplished, the Antichrist's Empire ("Babylon the Great") will be the largest empire ever to appear on the human scene.

C.   Apostate Christendom ("The Great Harlot")

Apostate Christendom—the Great Harlot—will be a sizable (perhaps a billion persons during the early stages of the Tribulation), ecumenical "Christian" entity consisting of Roman Catholic, Eastern Orthodox, and liberal Protestant churches. The Apostate Church is called a "harlot" in Scripture because it has been unfaithful to the Bridegroom, Jesus Christ—having rejected the true gospel for a false one. The Great Harlot will either deny some or all of the basic truths of the Word of God—the inherent sin nature of man, the deity of Christ, the Crucifixion of Christ for mankind's sins, the Resurrection of Christ, and the necessity of the new birth—or will reject the grace-faith belief system of the gospel in favor of the a law-works system. With the exception of a small remnant of believers within the Roman Catholic, Eastern Orthodox, and liberal Protestant movements of today (Rev. 3:4), most members of these churches are blind to, or ignorant of, the true gospel.

In line with her spiritual bankruptcy, the Harlot will persecute and martyr (during the first half of the Tribulation) many of those who come to saving faith in Christ after the Rapture (Rev. 17:6). In what amounts to the greatest irony of the entire Tribulation period, however, Apostate Christendom, which has allied itself with the Antichrist (naively thinking that it could expand its world social agenda through the Antichrist), will itself be utterly destroyed by the Antichrist after the mid-point of the Tribulation (Rev. 17:1-2, 16-17).

D.   The False Prophet

Whereas the Antichrist will be a political figure who rules over a vast empire, the False Prophet will be a religious figure who operates in the spiritual arena on behalf of the Antichrist. The False Prophet, however, will *not* be part of Apostate Christendom, but instead will be a proponent of a Hindu-metaphysical spiritual system which practices the occult and which rejects all of the foundational truths of Biblical Christianity. The religion of the False Prophet will be *anti*-Christian in every respect. One expert on the occult and the New Age/New Spirituality Movement suggests that the False Prophet will preach the following:

(1) Jesus was not and is not the only Christ, nor is He God; (2) "God" is impersonal, cosmic—a God of energy forces; (3) man is himself God, for he consists of and is the creator of "the forces"; man already exercises the powers inherent in his divinity and needs only to awaken to this fact; (4) man should seek and accept spiritual instruction and direction directly from the spirit world; (5) all religions and religious teachings lead to the same goal; all are equally of merit; (6) the "ancient wisdom" of Babylon, Egypt and Greece—not the Bible—is the basis of all truth; (7) sin and evil do not exist; peace and love are the ultimate realities.[4]

Biblical Christianity, on the other hand, teaches that (1) Jesus Christ is God the Son, who became flesh and dwelled among us; (2) God is personal and desires all men to be reconciled to Him in order to partake of His perfect shepherding; (3) man, because of Adam's sin, inherits a sin nature which separates him from sinless God; (4) the Bible is man's only authoritative source of God's word; (5) man has access to God solely on the basis of, and through faith in, the finished work of Jesus Christ; (6) the Bible alone is the repository of all truth; and (7) sin not only exists, but separates man from his maker.

Part of the False Prophet's ministry includes a counterfeit miracle-performing capability—empowered by Satan and done in the presence of the Antichrist—which enables the False Prophet to deceive earthlings to such a degree that he will convince many of them into making an image (an idol of some sort) of the Antichrist, which they in turn must worship (Rev. 13:12-14).

Still another part of the False Prophet's ministry enables him to cause men and women throughout the earth to receive the "mark" of the Antichrist on their forehead or right hand (Rev. 13:16). Because some persons will resist such a decree, the False Prophet will then decree that no one can buy or sell unless he has the "mark" on his forehead or right hand (Rev. 13:17). Thus, at some point during the Tribulation, probably just after its mid-point, no one on earth will be able to transact business within the Antichrist's Empire—or into and out of the Antichrist's Empire—unless he has the mark of the beast on his forehead or right hand.

Hence, the Antichrist will have devised a convenient way to rid the planet of post-Rapture Christians because true Christians will refuse his mark, and some of them will starve to death as a result. The Antichrist will also have devised a convenient way to put the Islamic nations "on the spot" because, unless they accept the Antichrist's mark (a mark which would probably symbolize and stand for a person's adherence to the principles of "global peace" and "global unity" within the framework of the Antichrist's "New World Order"), they will not be able to sell their wares (principally their oil) into the Antichrist's Western global empire. Much of the Islamic world will balk at the Antichrist's requirement of the mark (decreed by the False Prophet), and much of the carnage of the second and third Seal Judgments will unfold as a result.

E. The Ten Heads-of-State who Give Their Allegiance to the Antichrist

Revelation 17:12-13 informs us that ten heads-of-state will gather their nations into a ten-nation coalition and will give allegiance to the Antichrist (who will rule this empire): *"And the ten horns which you saw are ten kings, who have not yet received a kingdom, but they receive authority as kings with the beast for one hour. These have one purpose, and they give their power and authority to the beast."* After the Rapture, the present-day United Nations, highly cumbersome and ineffective in the minds of many in the elitist West, will be outflanked and rendered obsolete by a "Group of Ten" (to be discussed in Chapter 23)—who, because of their military and economic muscle, will dictate a self-serving agenda to the rest of the world. Because of the deluding influence sent by God after the Rapture upon those who refuse to believe the gospel (II Thess. 2:11), citizens in these ten nations will agree to subrogate the national sovereignty of their countries to this "new world order." Foreshadows of this eventual gathering of a "Group of Ten" exist today with the periodic meetings of heads-of-state at the Group of Seven, the Group of Eight, and the Group of Twenty.

F.   The Arab Nations ("The King of the North & the King of the South")

Most of the Islamic Middle East will fervently refuse to worship the Antichrist near the end of the first half of the Tribulation when the False Prophet decrees that each person make an image of the Antichrist to worship. When the Arabs and Jews refuse to worship the Antichrist, he will break his treaty with them and declare himself to be God. After the breaking of the treaty, the Antichrist will overrun Israel and use it as a staging ground to slaughter the Islamic Middle East and Islamic North Africa ("the king of the north and the king of the south") (Dan. 11:40-43).

G.   The Asian Nations ("The Kings of the East")

The "kings of the east" represent those nations (and kings) which lie east of the Tigres-Euphrates River (Rev. 16:12). These nations will do battle with the Antichrist during the Trumpet judgments (perhaps six years into the Tribulation period). Because the Eastern nations have more than one-half of the earth's population, these nations will represent a sizable military adversary to the West, even though much of their weaponry is low-tech compared with the sophisticated weaponry of the West (the Antichrist's Empire). During the sixth Trumpet (an apparent Sino-Western—or Sino-Russo-Western—nuclear holocaust), one-third of the earth's remaining population is killed, with much of the death toll likely being in the highly-populated East.

H.   Russia ("The Land of Magog")

Russia and parts of Eastern Europe ("Magog, Gomer, Beth-togarmah") are depicted extensively in Chapters 38 & 39 of Ezekiel. According to these prophecies, Russia and her allies will descend upon Israel at some point during the end times, only to be destroyed supernaturally by God. While much debate exists with regard to the timing of this northern descent into Israel, the context of the Ezekiel passages readily suggests a descent into Israel at the *end* of the Tribulation period (Ezek. 39:1-8, 17-20), in line with prophecies contained in both Daniel and Revelation about God's gathering of all the earth's remaining armies into northern Israel immediately before the Lord's bodily return for the Battle of Armageddon. Thus, with roughly half of present-day Russia favoring alignment with the West in a "New World Order" (the Gorbachev-Yeltsin position) and the other half of Russia favoring nationalism and a return to the U.S.S.R. (the Zhirinovsky-Putin position), it seems plausible that the former position will prevail for most of the Tribulation, until the apparent Sino-Western—or Sino-Russo-Western—conflagration of the Trumpet Judgments devastates the Antichrist's Empire (likely during the sixth year of the Tribulation). After this disaster (in which part of Russia is also perhaps destroyed), the nationalists could come to power and choose to descend upon Israel near the end of the Tribulation (as depicted in Ezekiel).

I.   Israel

The focal point of much of the Tribulation intrigue will be Israel. The Antichrist will engineer a Middle East peace treaty in order to satisfy Israel and surrounding Islam. To enforce the treaty the Antichrist's ten-nation core will likely station peacekeeping troops in Israel (and perhaps in selected neighboring countries) to enforce the peace, just as the 60,000 Western peacekeeping troops took up positions in Bosnia-Herzegovina after the United States brokered the Bosnian peace treaty in late 1995.

After the Antichrist's desecration of the Jerusalem temple and breaking of the Middle East peace treaty, Israel will be overrun and made desolate by the Antichrist's forces during early months of the second half of the Tribulation period. Israel will be blamed for all the world's ills during the second half of the Tribulation and will become the world's scapegoat by the end of the Tribulation. God will nevertheless select 144,000 Jewish witnesses to take the gospel message to the ends of the earth during the Tribulation (the 144,000 are the first persons saved after the Rapture (Rev. 14:4); and God will also place two witnesses in Jerusalem during the second half of the Tribulation to proclaim the imminence of Christ's return (Rev. 11:3,7) and to protect the inner court of the Jerusalem temple. Israel will ultimately recognize her Messiah after the end of the Tribulation: *"And I will pour out on the house of David and on the inhabitants of Jerusalem, the Spirit of grace and of supplication, so that they will look on Me whom they have pierced; and they will mourn for Him, as one mourns for an only son, and they will weep bitterly over Him, like the bitter weeping over a first-born" (Zech. 12:10).* One-third of the earth's post-Rapture Jews will come to faith in Jesus Christ and will subsequently enter Christ's Millennial Kingdom (Zech. 13:9).

J.   The New Age/New Spirituality Movement

Because the doctrine of today's New Age/New Spirituality movement is essentially the same as that of the Eastern religions (particularly Hinduism), and because it has no recognition of sin or a Creator God to whom man is accountable, the different false religions of the world will readily unite under the New Age banner as the one true "world" religion. As a result, the New Age/New Spirituality movement will be the religion of the Antichrist and the False Prophet.

The only religions which will oppose this one-world religion are Christianity, Judaism, and Islam. Each of these three religions believes in a transcendent God (as opposed to the "god within" of the Eastern religions and the New Age/New Spirituality movement), and each will be the target of the Antichrist's venom after he declares himself to be God at the mid-point of the Tribulation. The Antichrist will slaughter Apostate Christendom (Rev. 17:16). Post-Rapture Christians will be murdered (or left to live as utter outcasts, not being able to buy or sell). Islamic fundamentalists will be exterminated during the Antichrist's initial military adventurism (the second through fourth Seal judgments) after his breaking of the Middle East peace treaty. Jews who fail to heed Christ's Olivet Discourse admonition to flee to Israel's and Jordan's mountains (no doubt taught to them by the 144,000 Jewish evangelists) will be also be hunted down and killed by the Antichrist.

K.   Islam

Islam will stand in impassioned opposition to the Antichrist after the mid-point of the Tribulation period. They will be slaughtered as a result. Virtually all Arabs and the majority of Africans (particularly North Africans and East Africans) are Muslims; consequently, most Arabs and Islamic Africans will continue to worship Allah rather than the Antichrist. Moreover, not only will they refuse to worship the Antichrist, but they will, with Islamic fervor, likely attempt to rid the earth of this "Western infidel." Middle Eastern and North African Islam, however, will be no match for the Antichrist's high-tech weaponry, and perhaps a billion Arabs, Africans, and Islamic Indonesians will be killed in the bloodshed (Dan. 11:40-43; Rev. 6:3-8).

L.   Judaism

During the end-times Tribulation period, many in Israel will return to their Mosaic-Levitical worship roots and will rebuild a Jerusalem temple to accommodate this worship. The Antichrist will put a stop to this worship (Dan. 9:27) at the mid-point of the Tribulation when he enters the temple and declares himself to be God (Matt. 24:15; II Thess. 2:4).

M.   Post-Rapture Christians

After the Rapture, tens of millions of people throughout the world will turn their hearts to the living God and will put their faith in Jesus Christ for salvation and eternal life. Many of them will be hunted down and murdered by the Great Harlot (Rev. 17:6) during the first half of the Tribulation. Many more will be hunted down and murdered by the Antichrist's forces during the second half of the Tribulation (Rev. 12:17; 13:6,7). Some will be beheaded (Rev. 20:4), and those who escape to hiding places will have difficulty living normal lives because of the False Prophet's decree that no one can buy or sell without having the mark of the

Beast on their right hand or forehead. True post-Rapture Christians will refuse the Antichrist's mark.

N.   The 144,000 Jewish Evangelists

Jesus teaches that, during the end-times Tribulation period, *"this gospel of the kingdom will be preached in the whole world for a witness to all the nations, and then the end shall come"* (Matt. 24:9-14). Who, then, will be the human instruments God uses to take the gospel to all nations during the Tribulation? The Scriptures teach that God will call 144,000 Jews—12,000 from each of the twelve tribes of Israel—to salvation in Jesus Christ (Rev. 7:1-8) for the purpose of taking the gospel message to the ends of the earth (Rev. 14:1-7). According to Revelation 14:4, the 144,000 Jews are the first persons saved after the Rapture (*"as first fruits to God and to the Lamb"*) and apparently are virgin males (Rev. 14:4). They are also saved before the Tribulation period begins (Rev. 7:2-4)—perhaps, in this writer's view, within twenty-four to forty-eight hours after the Rapture. It is likely that the 144,000 will have "Damascus Road" conversions (Acts 9:1-22) and that God, in effect, will have 144,000 "Paul's" on earth, each having all of the "sign" gifts of the first century Apostles. In addition, we can conjecture that part of the "new song" learned by the 144,000 (Rev. 14:3) will be the ability to preach and teach the *whole counsel of God's Word*, not just the gospel message. Thus, the 144,000 will likely be anointed by God to understand the Scriptures from cover to cover instantly—or at least very quickly—including the end-times prophecies.

Here's the logic. The 144,000 will have been uniquely called by God to take God's Word and the gospel message to those peoples, nations, and tongues who have never heard the gospel. But because the Tribulation last only seven years and because the timeframe between the Rapture and the beginning of the Tribulation could be relatively short (perhaps no more than one to two years), then it seems logical that those whom God calls to lead the gospel effort after the Rapture will have to grow and mature spiritually *almost overnight*. In contrast, it is likely that all others who come to faith in Christ during the Tribulation will begin as spiritual babes and will grow more slowly (as is the case with born-again Christians today). This early calling of the 144,000 would likewise provide a maximum amount of time for them to take the gospel message throughout the world during the Tribulation. We can speculate, moreover, because of the fact that one-third of all Jews remaining on earth after the Rapture will be saved and will enter the Millennial Kingdom (Zech. 13:9), (1) that all or most of the earth's Jews will hear a clear presentation of the gospel and (2) that the 144,000's first order of business (perhaps even before the Antichrist rises to power) will be to take the gospel message into every synagogue on earth (following the Apostle Paul's missionary pattern of preaching the gospel in a city's synagogue before preaching it to the Gentiles—"to the Jew first and then to the Gentiles"). All 144,000 will survive the horrors of the Tribulation and will be in Jerusalem to greet the Lord Jesus upon His return to the Mount of Olives (Rev. 14:1).

O.   The Two Witnesses in Jerusalem

God will place two witnesses in Jerusalem (1) to proclaim the impending kingdom of God, (1) to prevent the inner court of the temple from being destroyed, and (3) to keep Israel from utter annihilation during the second half of the Tribulation. They will possess supernatural powers from God (Rev. 11:3-6) for the second three-and-a-half years of the Tribulation. The Antichrist will murder these two witnesses immediately after the end of the Tribulation. The Antichrist will refuse to allow them to be buried, but God will raise them from the dead three days later, to the astonishment and fear of God's enemies in Jerusalem (Rev. 11:1-13).

P.   Jesus Christ

In the twinkling of an eye and as unexpectedly as a thief entering a home at night, Jesus Christ will come in the air for His Bride—all dead and living born-again Christians from the Day of Pentecost until the Rapture. Christ's coming in the air for His bride will take place several months to many months before the seven-year Tribulation period begins, thus allowing time for God to send a deluding influence upon the earth (II Thess. 2:11-12) and time for the Antichrist to rise to power. Thirty days after the end of the seven-year Tribulation period (Dan. 12:11-12), Jesus Christ will return bodily to the earth to save Israel from annihilation at the hands of the world's remaining Gentile armies, to defeat these armies during the Battle of Armageddon, to judge the earth's remaining Jews and Gentiles, and to commence His Millennial reign on earth.

THE DEFINING CHARACTERISTICS OF THE ANTICHRIST'S EMPIRE

God's Word does not leave the Christian without clues when it comes to the identity of the Antichrist's Empire. In addition to giving Christians the Parable of the Mustard Seed (a wonderful clue which defines the geographic boundaries of the Antichrist's Empire by the time he breaks his Middle East peace treaty), God's Word also gives Christians three other substantive clues which help the discerning mind identify the nations that will likely belong to the Antichrist's ten-nation core. These three clues give us the defining characteristics of the Antichrist's Empire— and provide us with the "fingerprints" that identify the nations involved. Let us analyze what these fingerprints reveal.

A.   *"your merchants were the great men of the earth"*

The first fingerprint is found in Revelation 18:21-23:

> *And a strong angel took up a stone like a great millstone and threw it into the sea, saying, "Thus will Babylon, the great city, be thrown down with violence, and will not be found any longer. And the sound of harpists and musicians and flute-players and trumpeters will not be heard in you any longer; and no craftsman of any craft will be found in you any longer; and the sound of a mill will not be heard in you any longer; and the light of a lamp will not shine in you any longer; and the voice of the bridegroom and bride will not be heard in you any longer;* **for your merchants were the great men of the earth** *[emphasis added], because all the nations were deceived by your sorcery.*

The prophetic word of the Apostle John tells us that the Antichrist's end-times Empire (*"Babylon, the great city"*) will include the world's richest nations, whose "merchants" (corporate leaders and industrial giants) are considered to be the "great men of the earth (v.23)." We need only to read a *Fortune* magazine to recognize that most of the earth's wealthiest men live in the United States, Europe, and Japan. Moreover, the West's wealthy, for the most part, are the owners, financiers, or C.E.O.'s of the West's major corporations—persons who, in the main, are viewed throughout the world as being the most powerful men on earth (*"your merchants were the great men of the earth"*). More than sixty percent of the world's annual production of goods and services comes from *seven* nations: the United States, Canada, Great Britain, France, Germany, Italy, and Japan. These countries are synonymous with world-wide corporate power. Names such as Ford, General Motors, Tesla, Mercedes, Volkswagon, I.B.M., Microsoft, Intel, Apple, Google, Facebook, Amazon, Mitsubishi, Honda, Toyota, Sony, Canon, Fiat, Alfa-Romeo, Standard Oil, Mobil, Exxon, British Petroleum, Boeing, General Electric, Amazon, Walmart, Levi-Strauss, Johnson & Johnson, Proctor & Gamble, McDonald's,

Coca-Cola, PepsiCo, Anheiser Busch, American Airlines, British Airways, Air France, JAL, ABC, NBC, CBS, CNN, and the BBC are not only household names in the West but also icons of power throughout the world. Moreover, in view of the fact that the United States has the largest economy in the world (as well as the majority of the wealthiest men in the world), it is clear that the United States' fingerprints are all over this passage.

Equally important in this "fingerprint analysis" are the nations which must be eliminated from consideration when assessing which nations will form the Antichrist's ten-nation core. For example, it is hard to accept the position that ten *Arab* nations could make up the Antichrist's ten-nation core. Although it is true that Arab nations control up to forty percent of the earth's known oil reserves (and that more than a handful of Arab sheiks are extremely wealthy men), it is also true that the annual GNP's of the Arab oil-producing nations amount to just one-fifth of the leading (and far broader-based) economies in the West. In short, the "fingerprint" given to us in Revelation 18:21-23 corroborates the prophecy found in Daniel 2 (Nebuchadnezzar's dream): the core of the Antichrist's Empire will be the wealthy nations of the West—a revived Roman Empire.

B. *"who is like the Beast and who is able to wage war with him"*

The second clue is found in Revelation 13:4: *"And they worshipped the dragon, because he gave his authority to the beast; and they worshipped the beast, saying, "Who is like the beast, and who is able to wage war with him?" [emphasis added]*. The Apostle John tells us that the end-times Empire of the Antichrist will include the military powerhouses of the world, so powerful in fact that the world will muse, "who can possibly defeat him?"

In late 1989, a widely unforeseen (by commentators) and stunning new end-times possibility emerged as a result of the dismantling of the Berlin Wall and the subsequent efforts to reunify not only Germany but all of Western and Eastern Europe. The seeming "Achilles' heel" of every end-times scenario which limits the Antichrist's Empire solely to Western Europe is the fact that the United States and Russia, rather than Western Europe, currently possess, in terms of strategic arsenals and delivery capabilities, the military strength of the world. Consequently, the type of intrigue and destruction pictured in the Seal judgments of Revelation 6:3-8 appear to be only remotely possible from an empire made up of Western European nations alone. On the other hand, the magnitude of the intrigue would be readily possible if the United States is allied with Western Europe, and the magnitude of the intrigue would be overwhelmingly possible if both the United States and Russia are part of the Antichrist's ten-nation core. In view of the growing "democratization" of Eastern Europe and the Bush-Gorbachev summit in December 1989, it now seems possible (for the first time since Israel once again became a nation in 1948) that Eastern Europe and Russia could be part of the Antichrist's Empire. Should the United States and Russia become part of the Antichrist's core, the combined military strength of, let us say, the United States, Russia, Great Britain, Germany, Japan, France, Italy, Canada, and two others (to be discussed in Chapter 23) would be so staggering (the only buffer being China) that the world would readily say: *"Who is like the beast [i.e., the Antichrist and his Empire], and who is able to wage war with him?"* (Rev. 13:4).

As a footnote, it should be mentioned that the United States—because of the significant number of born-again Christians living within its borders—would be the most crippled of the Western nations by the sudden disappearance of true Christians at the Rapture. The economy of the United States could thus fall just enough from its position of world leadership that it would become significantly more interdependent with Western Europe. Japan, a substantially interdependent nation with the West today, would become still more interdependent when the economy of its principal export customer (the United States) becomes so jarred. In addition, Russia—because of the rapid emergence of China on the world scene— would probably find alliance with the West even more attractive in view of the growing Islamic and Chinese military threats to her south and southeast. In short, the Rapture could likely cause just enough balance-of-power shift in today's geo- political dynamic of Canada, the United States, Britain, France, Germany, Italy, Japan, and Russia that it would be the very catalyst behind a post-Rapture gathering together of a "Group of Ten."

C.   *"all the nations have drunk of the wine of her immorality"*

The third clue is found in Revelation 18:1-3:

> *After these things I saw another angel coming down from heaven, having great authority, and the earth was illumined with his glory. And he cried out with a mighty voice, saying, "Fallen, fallen is Babylon the great! And she has become a dwelling place of demons and a prison of every unclean spirit, and a prison of every unclean and hateful bird. **For all the nations have drunk of the wine of the passion of her immorality** [emphasis added], and the kings of the earth have committed acts of immorality with her, and the merchants of the earth have become rich by the wealth of her sensuality."*

The Apostle John explains prophetically that the Antichrist's end-times Empire (*"Babylon the great"*) will have a lifestyle desired and sought after by the whole world. This lifestyle will be worldly and seductive: *"for all the nations have drunk of the wine of the passion of her immorality. . . ."* Once again, the discerning eye can see that, on the world stage, it is the lifestyle of the West (particularly that of the United States) which the world (with the exception of fundamentalist Islam) seeks to emulate. Thus, in supposedly "communist" Shanghai, back-lit "Marlboro man" billboards line the downtown streets every five hundred yards. Coca-Cola is a desired drink in virtually every country on earth. Levi's are desired by the youth of virtually every country on earth. Hollywood's movies are desired and seen throughout much of the world. The West's god of "individual rights" is lusted after by the youngest generation in many Asian nations. In China, for example, three distinct generations now exist. The oldest generation largely clings to the 4,000-year traditions of China. The middle generation bridges the gap between the old China and the new China. But the youngest generation desires everything Western—from smart phones to tablets to personal computers to Western-style movies to CNN and ESPN. In short, the "fingerprint" described in Revelation 18:1-3—the West's lifestyle of mammon, power, pleasure, and sex—once again points to a Western core for the Antichrist's Empire.

What can we conclude about the United States after considering the three "fingerprints" above? It is this: we can say with absolute certainty that the United States (apart from national repentance) will be a member of the Antichrist's Empire at some point during the Tribulation Period; we can say with a high degree of certainty that the United States will be one of the ten nations which gives its allegiance to the Antichrist; and we can say with good reason that the United States might even be the leading nation in the Antichrist's Empire despite the economic uncertainties incurred by the U.S. at the Rapture (See Chart 22-A).

Chart 22-A

WHY THE U.S. COULD BE ONE OF THE ANTICHRIST'S TEN NATIONS

1.   The "Mustard Seed" has grown to include the United States.

2.   America was colonized by descendants of the ancient Roman Empire, and the majority of Americans emigrated from countries which were once in the ancient Roman Empire.

3.   The majority of the "rich" and "powerful" and "great merchants of the earth" live in the United States.

4.   The United States is the world's nuclear weapons superpower ("who is like the beast, and who can wage war with him?"). It is highly unlikely that the Antichrist would not want this arsenal in his Empire and under his control.

5.   The lifestyle of the United States is the most desired throughout the earth ("and the whole world followed after the beast . . . and the whole world has drunk of the wine of her immorality").

6.   The United States has much of the world's global communications capability.

7.   Most of America's corporate, political, media, and educational elites are now unabashed globalists

8.   The United States, because of its religious freedom and abundance of Christian resources, is the most accountable nation on earth with regard to a stewardship of the gospel. Therefore, will not the mockers and the indifferent in the United States be the targets of God's greatest judgments (Revelation 18)?

Chart 22-B

WHY RUSSIA COULD BE ONE OF THE ANTICHRIST'S TEN NATIONS

---

1.   The "Mustard Seed" has grown to include Russia

2.   The Russian Orthodox Church took root in Russia in the mid-10th century—and flourished before the Communist Revolution in 1917. The Russian Orthodox Church has once again emerged on the scene since the fall of Communism in 1989

3.   Lutheranism—mostly through German and Finnish immigrants—took root in certain parts of Russia after the Protestant Reformation

4.   Russia, during the 17th century, experienced a rapid process of Europeanization (or "Westernization") under Tsar Peter the Great. Peter himself developed St. Petersburg (Leningrad during the Soviet Union) into one of the most beautiful and progressive cities in all of Europe. Upon completion of construction, Peter called St. Petersburg the "Third Rome" (after Rome itself and Constantinople—the seats of Western and Eastern Christianity, respectively) and made St. Petersburg a symbol of the new Russia

5.   The word "Tsar" means "Caesar" in Russian

6.   The process of Russia's Westernization—catalyzed by Peter the Great, but put somewhat on hold during Russia's seventy years of Communism—was re-ignited under the regimes of Mikhail Gorbachev and Boris Yeltsin

7.   Most Russians under the age of fifty have been Westernized

8.   Russia is the world's #2 nuclear weapons superpower ("who is like the beast, and who can wage war with him?"). It has 7,200 nuclear warheads (3,800 strategic) and the missile capability of delivering them anywhere in the world. The Antichrist would want this strategic arsenal on his side of the net

---
THE ANTICHRIST'S TEN-NATION CORE

Among Christians who hold to a literal seven-year Tribulation period, four positions are typically put forth with regard to the identity of the ten nations which make up the core of the Antichrist's Empire: (1) ten Western European nations (the most prevalent view); (2) ten Mediterranean nations (a "Mediterranean Confederacy"); and (3) ten Arab/Islamic nations; and (4) ten regions of the world (the most recent view). Yet, how tenable are these positions? How do they stack up with the Scriptural evidence given so far? How do they stack up with Nebuchadnezzar's dream, Daniel 9:26, the Parable of the Mustard Seed, and the three clues or "fingerprints" just analyzed? As the reader will shortly see, each of these positions has difficulty measuring up to the Scriptural evidence. Consequently, a fifth position will be presented, one which the author believes lines up more closely with the Scripture. Finally, after developing the rationale behind this fifth position, we will see on a world map how the Antichrist's Empire will expand "peacefully" during the first three-and-a-half years of the Tribulation to become the largest and most daunting Empire ever seen on earth.

A. Ten Western European Nations

The most widely-held position with regard to the ten core nations of the Antichrist's Empire is one which contends that these nations will be Western European nations. To its credit, this position acknowledges the evidence of Scripture which points to the Antichrist's Empire being a revived Roman Empire (Dan. 2:1-45; 7:1-25). Moreover, the emergence of the twenty-seven country European Union in 1993, with its efforts to unify Europe into a grand trading alliance, has also fueled speculation that the ten nations of the End Times will be an "E.U. of ten." Nevertheless, this widely-held position—while compelling—has holes in it. For starters, the United States, not the E.U., is the strategic military superpower of the world. As well, the United States, not the E.U., is the one nation on earth still trusted by Israel to broker and enforce a Middle East peace treaty (though that trust has eroded somewhat since 2010).

Most Bible commentators have relegated the United States to either no role or an insignificant role in the end-times events—due to the widely-held interpretation (erroneous in this author's opinion) that the Antichrist's ten nations will be Western European nations. Let us not forget, however, that the United States has the largest economy in the world and, for many other reasons, is far too important on the world scene—economically, politically, financially, and militarily—to be relegated to second-class status if this is the final generation before the Lord's return. The United States and Russia—not the E.U.—have manned space programs. The United States and Russia—not the E.U.—have 10,000-plus nuclear warheads. The United States—not the E.U.—has the Global Positioning System satellites that were able to monitor Coalition troop movements at all times during the Persian Gulf War (and enable GPS-guided "smart bombs" to land within a foot or two of their target).

In short, if this truly is the final generation before the Lord's return, then the United States—apart from substantial national repentance (in which case most of the country would vanish at the Rapture)—*has* to be a major player in the Antichrist's Empire. To be sure, the United States could crush any ten Western European nations in thirty minutes if it chose to do so. The keys to understanding the place of the United States (and Russia) in the end-times scheme of things are (1) the Parable of the Mustard Seed and (2) the three Revelation "fingerprint" clues. In view of the arguments above, it appears that the United States will indeed be a player in the ten nations. Unfortunately, most Americans have little or no cognizance of such a possibility, and most American evangelicals simply do not want to hear it.

B. Ten Mediterranean Nations (A "Mediterranean Confederacy")

Other commentators contend that the Antichrist's ten-nation core will consist of ten Mediterranean nations—presumably such nations as Spain, France, Italy, Greece, Turkey, Syria, Lebanon, Jordan, Egypt, and Libya. Such a contention is likely held because of the correct conclusion that the Antichrist's Empire will be a revived Roman Empire and because of an assumed similarity in the geographical coverage of the ancient Roman Empire and a revived Roman Empire. Once again, however, how does such a position stack up against the Scriptural evidence?

Although France and Italy have substantial economies and substantial wealth, they can hardly be considered the economic powerhouses of the world, nor can any others in this so-called Mediterranean Confederacy. A fairly small percentage of the "great men of the earth" live in the ten nations listed. Moreover, France and Italy are military pygmies compared to the United States (let alone the United States and Russia combined). Once again, when we ask the question, "who is like the Mediterranean Confederacy, and who can wage war with them?", the answer is clear: the United States or Russia. Either of these nations could take out a "Mediterranean Confederacy" in thirty minutes with the missiles of a single Trident or Boomer submarine. In short, the so-called Mediterranean Confederacy also fails the test of Scripture.

C. Ten Islamic Nations

Some end-times commentators contend that the Antichrist's Empire will consist of ten Middle Eastern Arab-Islamic nations, perhaps because the book of Revelation calls the Antichrist's Empire "Babylon the Great." A few of these commentators also contend that "Babylon, the Great City" mentioned in Revelation is the rebuilt city of Babylon in modern-day Iraq. Though such a position looks plausible on the surface, a closer analysis of the Scriptural evidence refutes this view.

First and foremost, the Antichrist will be a "Japhethite" and will descend from the Ancient Roman Empire (Dan. 9:26). Arabs, on the other hand, are "Shemites." This fact alone rules out the possibility of the Antichrist's Empire being an empire of ten Arab nations. Next, "Babylon the Great" refers to the philosophic (rather than geographic) roots of the Antichrist's Empire—i.e., it is the final and largest offspring of man's first anti-God empire, Nimrod's Babylon. In addition, the Arab nations, while containing considerable wealth as a result of their oil revenues, nevertheless pale in comparison to the West when it comes to overall industrial might. And finally, as was so clearly evidenced in the Persian Gulf War, the Arab nations are no match to the West militarily. Unequivocally, it cannot be said of any ten Arab nations one wishes to choose: "who is like these ten Arab nations, and who can wage war with them?" The United States by itself could destroy any ten Arab nations in thirty minutes with a hundred Minuteman III missiles and a Trident submarine. The West—not the Arab community—is in possession of ICBMs, stealth technology, cruise missiles, Trident submarines, laser-guided bombs, and much, much more.

D.   Ten Regions of the World

In recent years a fourth view has surfaced with regard to the Antichrist's ten nations. This view suggests that the ten players are not nations but *regions* covering the entire world. These regions are as follows: (1) North America; (2) Latin America (Mexico, Central & South America); (3) Western Europe; (4) Eastern Europe & Russia; (5) North Africa, Palestine, Syria & Turkey; (6) the Main of Africa; (7) the South of Africa, Australia & New Zealand; (8) Japan; (9) South Asia; and (10) Central Asia. This view has major problems, however, for the following reasons:

First, if ten regions of the entire world are ruled by ten heads of state on behalf of the Antichrist, then there would be no need for the Antichrist to go out "conquering and to conquer" during the first Seal judgment (Rev. 6:1-2). The whole world would already be under his control.

Second, if ten regions of the entire world are ruled by ten heads of state on behalf of the Antichrist, then Revelation 13:4—*"who is like the Beast, and who is able to make war with him?"*—is rendered meaningless. There would be no wars to fight. However, both the Seal judgments and the Trumpet judgments picture widespread conflict on earth, to such a degree in fact that one-half of the earth's post-Rapture population is killed in these wars.

Third, if ten regions of the entire world are ruled over by ten heads of state, then Revelation 18:23—*"your merchants were the great men of the earth"*—would present a woeful contradiction. At least some of the ten regions suggested in this view (e.g., the African and South Asian regions) simply cannot be described as having merchants who are the "great men of the earth."

Fourth, if ten regions of the entire world are ruled over by ten heads of state, then Revelation 17:2—*"and those who dwell on the earth were made drunk by the wine of her immorality"*—is also rendered meaningless. The phrase "her immorality" implies that the rest of the world is becoming drunk with a immorality coming from a specific part of the world. It is the immorality of the Western world, of course, which the rest of the world lusts after.

Fifth, the "ten regions" view does correlate with Daniel's interpretation of Nebuchadnezzar's "great statue" dream in Daniel 2:25-47, because Nebuchadnezzar's dream and other prophetic Scriptures (Dan. 2:1-45; 7:1-25; 9:26; Rev. 17:3-13) make it clear that the core of the Antichrist's Empire is a revived *Roman* Empire, not a Anglo-Euro-Russo-Indo-Asian-Arab-African Empire. Yes, the Antichrist wants to take over all ten regions of the world. But, no, his Empire does not begin with him having control over the ten regions. Instead, his Empire starts with ten powerful nations, from where he will go out "conquering and to conquer" (Rev. 6:1-2) much of the earth.

E.   The "Group of Seven" becomes a "Group of Ten"

Where does the evidence of Scripture leave us with regard to the ten core nations of this Empire? It is as follows: the so-called "Group of Seven" (Canada, the United States, Great Britain, France, Germany, Italy, and Japan) rather than the E.U. should likely be the focus of prophetic attention. The G-7 (the seven largest industrial democracies on earth) currently produces 60% of the Gross National Product of the world. In 1991 Mikhail Gorbachev desperately wanted Russia to become the eighth member of the club. In 1992 Boris Yeltsin also stated his desire to become a member and was invited to be an observer in 1995. Certainly the "democratization" of Russia (and Eastern Europe) as well as Russia's current efforts to move toward a quasi "market economy" appear to be the forerunners to eventual Russian admission into the G-7. In short, it seems that the G-7 could soon become a G-8 (perhaps before the Rapture occurs). Russia, while struggling economically, still has a staggering arsenal of nuclear weapons and delivery capability. *Indeed, it should almost be self-evident that the Antichrist would want the massive nuclear arsenals of both the United States and Russia under his control.* Consequently, with the United States, Russia, and Western Europe on the same side of the military net, it is easy to see how the world would say: "who is like the Beast, and who can wage war with him?" These ten countries would produce 70% of the world's output and would control 95% of the nuclear arsenals on earth.

[Note: the paragraph above was written in 1995. In 1998, Russia officially joined the G-7—making it a "Group of Eight." However, Russia was suspended from the G-8 in 2014, following its annexation of Crimea; and in 2017, Russia announced its permanent withdrawal from the G-8. Nevertheless, because of Russia's prodigious nuclear arsenal, look for the globalist West to coax Russia back into the fold after the Rapture (again making a G-8) in order to protect the West's (and Russia's) interests from China. The United States and Russia were allies during World War II—and most Russians under the age of fifty have become thoroughly Westernized. As well, forty percent of American adults under thirty-five favor some form of socialism according to recent polls. Finally, two other countries (in 2022) could readily be mentioned as possible candidates for the final two spots in a Group of Ten: Australia (with its European roots, large land mass, and strategic location for the protection of southern shipping lanes); and South Korea (with its robust and leading-edge industrial and electronics manufacturing capabilities—and its rapid Westernization).]

[Additional Note: many commentators, because of Russia's role in Ezekiel 38-39, reject any suggestion that Russia could one of the Antichrist's ten core nations. It should be noted, however, that Scripture indicates that the Antichrist at some point during the Tribulation will "subdue" (kill) three of the ten kings (heads-of-state) allied with him (Dan. 7:24). Thus, it is possible (and this writer believes probable) that Russia will be one of the two military musclemen (along with the United States) in the Antichrist's ten-nation coalition, but will exit the coalition during the second half of the Tribulation—perhaps because of dissatisfaction over her role in the coalition or dissatisfaction with the land or plunder she is allowed to take (Daniel 11:36-39).]

Chart 23-A

THE FOUR POPULAR POSITIONS ON THE "10 NATIONS"

1. **10 WESTERN EUROPEAN NATIONS**

2. **10 MEDITERRANEAN NATIONS**
    (A "MEDITERRANEAN CONFEDERACY")

3. **10 ARAB NATIONS (& A REBUILT CITY OF BABYLON)**

4. **10 REGIONS OF THE WORLD**

Chart 23-B

THE FOUR POPULAR POSITIONS ON THE "10 NATIONS"

---

1. 10 WESTERN EUROPEAN NATIONS *[NO]*

2. 10 MEDITERRANEAN NATIONS *[NO]*
   (A "MEDITERRANEAN CONFEDERACY")

3. 10 ARAB NATIONS (& A REBUILT CITY OF BABYLON) *[NO]*

4. 10 REGIONS OF THE WORLD *[NO]*

A FIFTH POSITION ON THE "10 NATIONS"

---

4. THE "GROUP OF SEVEN" ⎯⎯⎯⎯⎯⟶ A "GROUP OF TEN"

[MOST LIKELY]

Chart 23-C

THE "GROUP OF SEVEN"   (THE G-7)

1.   **UNITED STATES**
2.   **CANADA**
3.   **GREAT BRITAIN**
4.   **FRANCE**
5.   **GERMANY**
6.   **ITALY**
7.   **JAPAN**

NOTE: THESE SEVEN NATIONS ARE THE SEVEN LARGEST "INDUSTRIAL DEMOCRACIES" ON EARTH

Chart 23-D

THE "GROUP OF EIGHT" (THE G-8)

1. **UNITED STATES**
2. **CANADA**
3. **GREAT BRITAIN**
4. **FRANCE**
5. **GERMANY**
6. **ITALY**
7. **JAPAN**
8. **RUSSIA**

THE ABOVE "GROUP OF EIGHT" RANKED IN TERMS OF MILITARY STRENGTH:

1. *UNITED STATES*
2. *RUSSIA*
3. *GREAT BRITAIN*
4. *FRANCE*
5. *GERMANY*
6. *JAPAN*
7. *ITALY*
8. *CANADA*

Chart 23-E

A POSSIBLE "GROUP OF TEN"

---

1. **UNITED STATES**
2. **CANADA**
3. **GREAT BRITAIN**
4. **FRANCE**
5. **GERMANY**
6. **ITALY**
7. **JAPAN**
8. **RUSSIA**
9. **??**
10. **??**

AUSTRALIA ? (large land mass; strategically located)

SOUTH KOREA ? (Samsung, Hyundai, Kia, LG Electronics)

THE TWO "BIG TOES" OF DANIEL 2:41-43

As previously discussed in Chapter 17, the Jewish prophet Daniel, through a revelation from God, revealed the world empires which would exist both concurrently and contiguously with the life of God's people, Israel, after the Babylonian captivity:

> *And after you there will arise another kingdom inferior to you, then another third kingdom of bronze, which will rule over all the earth. Then there will be a fourth kingdom as strong as iron; inasmuch as iron crushes and shatters all things, so, like iron that breaks in pieces, it will crush and break all these in pieces. And in that you saw the feet and toes, partly of potter's clay and partly of iron, it will be a divided kingdom; but it will have in it the toughness of iron, inasmuch as you saw the iron mixed with common clay. And as the toes of the feet were partly of iron and partly of pottery, so some of the kingdom will be strong and part of it will be brittle. And in that you saw the iron mixed with common clay, they will combine with one another in the seed of men; but they will not adhere to one another, even as iron does not combine with pottery (Dan. 2:39-43).*

Daniel explains to Nebuchadnezzar that after the Babylonian empire four increasingly weaker empires would emerge on the scene. These empires will be weaker because they grow increasingly less homogeneous nationally and ethnically (*"they will combine with one another in the seed of men, but they will not adhere to one another"*), the last of these weaker empires—the revived Roman Empire—being made out of a non-cleaving mixture of iron and common clay. Moreover, the existence of the "ten toes" in Daniel's presentation of the final world empire before the coming of Messiah's reign over the earth fits the picture of the Antichrist's revived Roman Empire given in the book of Revelation, with the toes representing the ten core nations of the Antichrist's Empire

Based on the evidence previously presented in Chapters 16, 17, 18, 19, 20, 22, and 23, it is reasonable to conclude that the two "big toes" in Daniel 2:41-43 are the United States and Russia: (1) the "mustard seed" (Christianity or Christendom) has now grown to include the United States and Russia; (2) the United States and Russia are the number one and number two nuclear superpowers in the world; and (3) the musing of Revelation 13:13 "who is like the beast, and who can wage war with him"—would not be possible unless both the United States and Russia are core members of the Antichrist's Empire at the outset of the Tribulation period. Let those skeptical of such an alliance recall that the United States and Russia were allies in World War II against a common adversary—Nazism and Adolf Hitler. [Note: In the year 2015, two unpredictable and inexorable threats face the United States and Russia: the rapidly-developing military of China and the reality of radical Islam. Because of these threats, the Antichrist—leader of the Western world—assuredly would want the militaries of the United States and Russia in his camp.]

Nevertheless, it is also important for students of prophecy to understand the significance of steady *reduction* in the size of the nuclear and conventional arsenals of both the United States and Russia since their peak strength in the early 1970s. This decline is depicted in the following "foot" illustrations. The import of the declines is this: In the early 1970s, the United States and Russia (then the U.S.S.R.) were so strong militarily that their respective "big toes" dwarfed the size of the "toes" of the other Western-world militaries. By 2015, however, the military strength of both countries had declined to such a degree that their respective big toes were more fitting of the Daniel 2:41-43 word-picture. Though both countries could still stage a calamitous nuclear war today, such a war would not be of the magnitude it could have been during the 1970s.

The overwhelming nuclear and conventional military might of both countries in 1970 is depicted in the first "foot" illustration below. Thus, relative to the other "toes" the United States and Russia were greatly over-sized "big toes." By 1980, due to arms limitations negotiations between the two countries, the nuclear arsenals of the United States and Russia had contracted to a degree. Accordingly, in the second illustration below, the big toes of the two countries are somewhat smaller in size. Then, with the fall of the Berlin Wall in 1989 and the dissolution of the U.S.S.R., Russia's big toe shrunk still further, while America's big toe remained oversized as the "winner" of the Cold War. However, with the Cold War now won, every U.S. President since 1990 has systematically reduced the size and strength of the U.S. military, both in terms of nuclear and conventional capability. Today, the United States can no longer fight a two-theatre war. Hence, in the fourth illustration, the big toe of the United States has now contracted to a more proportional level with that of Russia—though the *nuclear* capabilities of the two powers are still staggeringly formidable (enough for the world to muse, "who is like the beast, and who can wage war with him").

1970

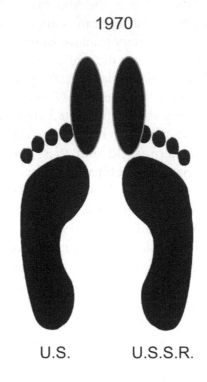

U.S.   U.S.S.R.

1980

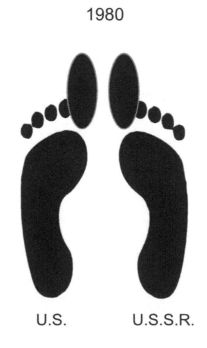

U.S.   U.S.S.R.

1990

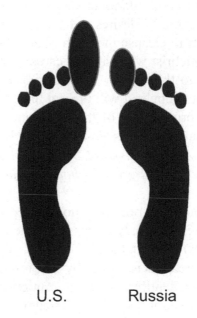

U.S.   Russia

2020

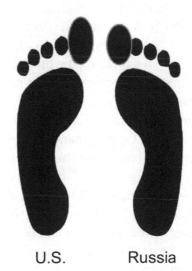

U.S.   Russia

THE GROWTH OF THE CORE DURING THE 1ST HALF OF THE TRIB.

It is important to understand the motives of the Antichrist. First, he desires to rule the world. Second, he desires to have the whole world worship him (Rev. 13:4). Third, he wants to cleanse the earth of all who refuse to worship him. The Satan-empowered Antichrist will play his cards shrewdly and will only gradually unfold these motives to the world. Thus, during the first half of the Tribulation period, the charismatic Antichrist will present himself as a messenger of peace and prosperity—and will bring much of the world into his Empire. This "peaceful" expansion of his Empire beyond its ten-nation core is pictured in Revelation 6:2, the first Seal judgment: *"And I looked and, behold, a white horse; and he who sat on it had a bow; and a crown was given to him; and he went out conquering, and to conquer."*

The word-picture of a rider on a horse often represents a battle metaphor in Scripture. In this case (Rev. 6:2) it represents the preparedness of one nation (or coalition of ten nations) to overtake other nations. The fact that the rider has a bow indicates that his preparedness is backed by the presence of military power. The fact that he is given a crown identifies him as the Antichrist, who, according to parenthetical description in Revelation 13:1-8, is granted widespread authority over the earth for the forty-two months of the Tribulation (the first Seal judgment). The Antichrist uses this authority to conquer. The color of the horse in each of the first four Seal judgments depicts the general tone or character of each of these judgments. The color white, in the context of the first Seal judgment, connotes "peace" or "peaceful conquest." It also connotes—in view of the fact that the color white elsewhere in Revelation depicts the righteousness and spotlessness of Christ—the *counterfeit* nature of the Antichrist's character and claims. Just as Satan comes as "an angel of light" (II Cor. 11:14) to deceive as many men as possible, so also will the Antichrist come as an "angel of light." In reality, of course, the Antichrist will prove to be the darkest political leader ever to appear on the human scene. Revelation 6:2, the first Seal judgment (and the first of the end-times judgments), thus depicts a panorama of world political peace engineered by the Antichrist, who, nevertheless, through the leverage of his economic muscle and military might, gathers (*"he went out conquering, and to conquer"*) into his Empire many nations "peacefully" (apparently with minimal bloodshed) and who consolidates his power into a vast sphere of control (*"a crown was given him"*) covering much of the earth.

Which nations will fall into the Antichrist's Empire during this peaceful conquest? Scripture—particularly Christ's Parable of the Mustard Seed—gives us some wonderful clues. Let us reiterate what has already been said about the Mustard Seed in Chapters 18 and 19. Jesus states in this parable that His inter-advent kingdom (Christianity or "Christendom") will start out as an insignificant religion but will expand to become the largest of the earth's religions before His return. In 30 A.D., the "mustard seed" was limited to Jerusalem. Two years later it began to grow into Judea and Samaria. About ten years later it had moved up into Syria. The Apostle Paul then took the gospel to Asia Minor and Greece. By the time the Apostle John received his visions on Patmos from the resurrected Christ in approximately 95 A.D., the "mustard seed" had grown throughout most of the then Roman Empire. Thus, in 95 A.D., Christendom (which included both "wheat" and "tares") equaled, roughly speaking, the geographic size of the ancient Roman Empire—*and vice versa.*

Today, however, the "mustard seed" (Christendom) is no longer limited geographically to the Mediterranean basin and the ancient Roman Empire. The mustard seed has continued to grow over the centuries and, as analyzed in Chapter 19 now includes Canada, the United States, Mexico, Central America, South America, Great Britain, Scandinavia, Western Europe, Eastern Europe, Russia, Australia, New Zealand, and much of southern Africa. Hence, it is not necessary for twenty-first century commentators to limit the ten core nations of the Antichrist's Empire to ten Western European nations, nor is it necessary for commentators to limit the Antichrist's Empire to Western Europe or a Mediterranean Confederacy. Instead, the Lord's parable is designed to give us a picture of a *growing* and *expanding* Christian religion at any point in time between His first and second advents.

In short, only one scenario maintains the prophetic integrity of John's vision. It is this: just as Christendom equaled the size of the Ancient Roman Empire in 95 A.D., Christendom during the end times should approximate the geographic scope of the *revived* Roman Empire—the Antichrist's Empire. Thus, we can say with a high degree of certainty that the Antichrist's Empire, after the "peaceful" expansion beyond its ten-nation core (during the first three and a half years of the Tribulation period) will include all nations and regions whose principal religion is *Christianity.* (See Map 2.) Consequently, at the mid-point of the Tribulation period, when the Antichrist's Empire covers a substantial geographic reach and possesses most of the world's nuclear arsenal, the prophetic statement in Revelation 13:3-5 will have come true: *"And the whole earth was amazed and followed after the beast [the Antichrist]; and they worshipped the dragon [Satan], because he gave authority to the beast; and they worshipped the beast, saying: 'Who is like the beast, and who is able to wage war with him?'"*

How will the Antichrist expand his Empire so easily during the first half of the Tribulation? It seems that four factors will enable him to do so: (1) the economic pragmatism of being aligned with the ten-nation economic juggernaut which makes up the core of his Empire; (2) the military benefits of being protected by the ten-nation core (specifically, its nuclear and high-tech weaponry); (3) the endorsement and cooperation of Apostate Church which allows the Antichrist to sell his agenda in those nations whose principal religion is Christianity; and (4) the deluding influence sent by God upon unbelievers (especially the unbelievers in those countries where Christianity is currently the predominant religion), thus causing these unbelievers to embrace the Antichrist's agenda.

The economic strength of the Antichrist's ten-nation core will be staggering. For sake of illustration, let us postulate that the Antichrist's ten core nations—based on an overall mixture of economic strength, military power, worldly sophistication, and geographic location—will be the United States, Russia, Great Britain, Germany, Japan, France, Italy, Canada, Australia, and South Korea. In terms of economic strength, the combined Gross National Product of these ten nations would represent 70% of the world's output. Seven of these ten nations were strong enough militarily seventy years ago to be the principal combatants in World War II. Today, all seven of these nations remain strong economically, militarily, and technologically—and two of the seven (the United States and Russia) are the military, nuclear, and space superpowers of the world. Geographically, these ten nations would control the Mediterranean, North, and Baltic Seas, as well as the Atlantic and Pacific Oceans. Virtually all of the world's strategic shipping lanes would fall under the protective umbrella of these ten nations. (See Map 1.)

Although the Apostate Church will sincerely believe that it is using the Antichrist to promote its social agenda throughout the Antichrist's expanding Empire (Rev. 17:3), in reality the Antichrist will be using the Apostate Church to further *his* agenda. *Specifically, the Antichrist will use the Apostate Church to cause all of present-day Christendom to align itself with and pledge allegiance to his grand, world Empire* (Rev. 6:1-2). After the Antichrist has completed this objective, he will then double-cross and slaughter the Apostate Church (Rev. 17:16). Why? Though the Apostate Church believes and teaches a false gospel, it nevertheless believes in a transcendent creator God. Consequently, at least some in the Apostate Church, including much of its leadership, will refuse to worship the Antichrist when he declares himself to be God at the mid-point of the Tribulation.

To be sure, such a collection of nations—the Antichrist's ten-nation core along with the "Christian" nations allied with that core —would cover approximately one-half of the world's inhabitable surface, would enjoy approximately 80% of its wealth, and would represent the most massive world empire to date. At the mid-point of the Tribulation, when he has "peacefully" expanded his Empire throughout all of present-day Christendom, the Antichrist will then covet the natural resources of defenseless Africa and the only indispensable natural resource he does not yet control entirely: Middle East oil. He will go after these during the second half of the Tribulation.

[Note: Soon after the mid-point of the Tribulation period, it can be deduced that the False Prophet will continue to "tighten the noose" on behalf of the Antichrist, particularly in the world's affluent nations, by decreeing that men and women throughout the world must receive the Antichrist's mark in order to buy and sell goods in the Antichrist's Empire. Thus, the executive in Chicago must put the mark of the beast on his right hand or forehead in order to buy the Mercedes he wants. The young married couple in Los Angeles will have to acquiesce to the mark of the beast in order to buy a Honda Civic and a Samsung flat screen television. The businessman in Paris will have to agree to the mark in order to purchase a Windows operating system from Microsoft. Pemex in Mexico will have to agree to the mark in order to sell its oil into Europe. Columbian coffee growers will have to agree to the mark in order to export their coffee into the United States. It is easy to see how the False Prophet will use this form of economic extortion in his effort to get every person on earth to worship the Antichrist and to become part of the Antichrist's Empire.]

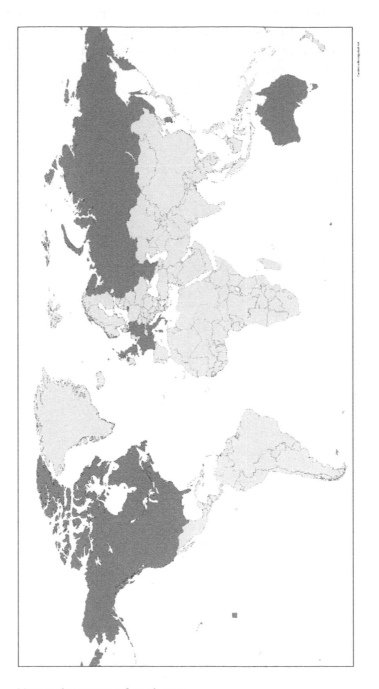

The Antichrist's Empire at the beginning of the Tribulation

Map template courtesy of mapchart.net

The Antichrist's Empire near the mid-point of the Tribulation

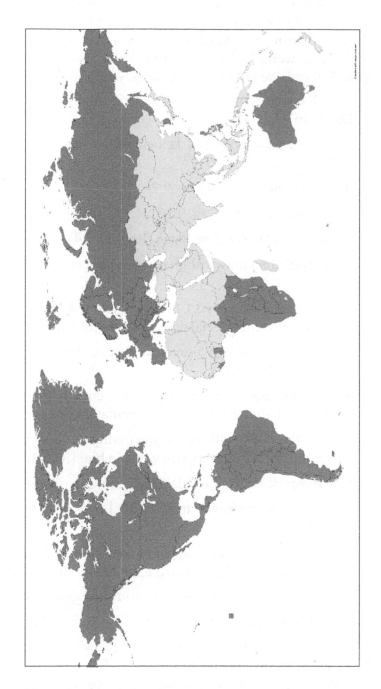

Map template courtesy of mapchart.net

THE NATURE AND CHARACTER OF THE ANTICHRIST

After the Rapture of born-again Christians and the gathering together of ten powerful nations into a coalition designed to advance and protect its mutual collective interests, a charismatic statesman—a person known in Scripture as the Antichrist—will rise to world political power (II Thess. 2:3,8-10). Based on assorted verses in God's Word, the following description of the Antichrist can be compiled:

- he will come from the revived Roman Empire (Dan. 2:31-33,36,43; Dan.9:26)

- he will be an offspring of Japheth rather than Ham or Shem (Dan. 9:26)

- he will not be an Arab (Dan. 9:26)

- he will not be a Jew (Dan. 9:26)

- he will be empowered by Satan (Rev. 13:2,4)

- ten powerful nations will give their allegiance to him (Rev. 17:12-13)

- as an "angel of light" (II Cor. 11:14), he will offer believable solutions to the world's social and political problems

- he will broker and sign a seven-year peace treaty with Israel and her neighbors (Dan. 9:27)

- he will rule largely unrestrained over a good portion of the earth for the first forty-two months of the Tribulation (Rev. 13:5)

- most of the world will follow him during the first half of the Tribulation, and all unbelievers will worship him (Rev. 13:8)

- he will speak arrogant words (Rev. 13:5)

- he will break his peace treaty with Israel after forty-two months (Dan. 9:27)

- he will enter the rebuilt temple in Jerusalem at the mid-point of the Tribulation and declare himself to be God (II Thess. 2:4)

- he will exalt himself above every so-called god (II Thess. 2:4)

- he will speak blasphemies against God (Rev. 13:5)

- he will murder Jews in Israel (and elsewhere) after he breaks his peace treaty with them, but Jews who flee immediately to the mountains of Israel and Jordan will be protected supernaturally (Rev. 12:13-16).

- he will persecute and murder post-Rapture Christians (Rev. 12:17)

- he will double-cross and destroy Apostate Christendom (the "harlot") (Rev. 17:16) when he has finished using the apostate false Church for his subjugation purposes

Due to the widespread scope of global telecommunications today, including the increasing availability of smart phones throughout Asia and much of the Third World, it is no longer difficult to see how a world political figure could emerge on the scene. The mediums of television and the internet have prodigious worldwide influence today and could easily catapult a charismatic figure to world power. In 1992, for example, Ross Perot, a political novice, went from nonexistence on the American presidential scene to a serious presidential contender in two months. Former U.S. President Donald Trump used the power of social media to spread his message throughout America and the world. Such is the overwhelming sway of these media platforms today. Thus, coming as he does as an "angel of light," the Antichrist will offer what seem to be believable and workable solutions to the world's major problems. Because of this—and in conjunction with his mastery of television and social media—much of the world will rally behind him.

Chapter 27

THE NATURE AND CHARACTER OF THE FALSE PROPHET

Coinciding with the rise of the Antichrist to power, a world spiritual figure—a person known in Scripture as the False Prophet—will rise to world prominence as well. The False Prophet will be a New Age adherent (and likely occultist) and will both reject and blaspheme all the basic tenets of Christianity. Instead, he will teach the inherent divinity of man. His teaching will attempt to unite all the world's religions. Many in post-Rapture Christendom will succumb to his deceptions. Most of post-Rapture Islam, however, will reject his deceptions (remaining loyal to "Allah"), will refuse the mark of the beast, and will subsequently be killed (likely in the 2nd through 4th Seal judgments). Like the Antichrist, he will derive his power from Satan. Scripture describes the False Prophet as follows:

- he will come as an angel of light (II Cor. 11:14; Rev. 13:11)

- his doctrine will be Satanic (Rev. 13:11)

- he will serve as the Antichrist's spiritual advisor (Rev. 13:12)

- he will cause much of the world to worship the Antichrist (Rev. 13:12)

- he will perform counterfeit miracles (Rev. 13:13)

- he will deceive millions of people with his counterfeit miracles (Rev. 13:14)

- he will tell earthlings to make an image (an idol) of the Antichrist and to worship the image (Rev. 13:14)

- he will control "ventriloquist" demons in these idols (Rev. 13:15)

- he will cause men and women throughout the earth to receive the "mark of the beast" on their right hand or forehead (Rev. 13:16)

- he will decree that no one on earth can buy or sell goods unless that person has the mark of the beast on their right hand or forehead (Rev. 13:17)

THE RELIGION OF THE ANTICHRIST AND THE FALSE PROPHET

One area of considerable confusion in the study of the End Times rests in the assumption by many commentators that the "Great Harlot" portrayed in the book of Revelation is the grand, one-world religion of the end times. This, however, is not the case.

In reality, three large-scale, competing false religious systems inhabit the end times. The first is the Great Harlot. The Harlot, as discussed in previous chapters, represents Apostate Christianity—those "Christians" who remain on earth after the Rapture of born-again Christians. These apostate Christians considered themselves to be a "Christian," but they never—by faith alone—invited Jesus Christ into their lives. Instead, they opted for a salvation system based on such things as membership in a particular church or sacraments or good works or universalism.

The second major end-times religious system is Islam. Like Christianity, Islam believes in a transcendent, creator God—whom it calls Allah (although Islam's "Allah" is actually a pagan moon god, not the living God of the universe).

The third large-scale religious system of the end times—the one that *will* be the true "one-world" religion (and the one embraced by the Antichrist and the False Prophet)—is today's so-called New Age Movement. The New Age/New Spirituality religious system essentially blends Eastern mysticism, Hinduism, and the occult, then presents them in attractive Western phraseology. Its beliefs are sufficiently inclusive to appeal to all other world religions and belief systems except Judaism, Christianity, and Islam.

This New Age-Metaphysical-Hindu-occultic religion of the Antichrist and False Prophet differs from Biblical Christianity in every essential doctrine and is anti-Christian in every respect. As explained in Chapter 21, the New Age-Metaphysical-Hindu-occult "global" religion of the Antichrist will preach the following message to the world: (1) Jesus was not and is not the only Christ, nor is he God; (2) "God" is impersonal and cosmic—a God of energy forces; (3) man is himself God; indeed, man already exercises the powers inherent in his divinity and he needs only to awaken to this fact; (4) man should seek and accept spiritual instruction and direction directly from the spirit world; (5) all religions and religious teachings lead to the same goal; all are equally of merit; (6) the "ancient wisdom" of Babylon, Egypt and Greece is the basis of all truth; and (7) sin and evil do not exist; peace and love are the ultimate realities.

In short, the New Age religion of the Antichrist and his False Prophet—rather than Apostate Christianity—will be the "politically correct" global religion of the end times. Perhaps two-thirds of the world's population will eventually embrace this belief system, including a small percentage of Muslims and a large percentage of apostate Christians who convert to the Antichrist's New Spirituality religion. In contrast, only a small percentage of the world's population will likely continue to embrace Apostate Christianity's beliefs after the False Prophet decrees that all persons must have the mark of the beast on their right hand or forehead in order to buy and sell goods (Rev. 13:16-17).

Chart 27-A provides a sampling of New Age magazines which reflect this accelerating infiltration of the occult into the Western mind-set. These magazines talk about "Western *inner* traditions" (alluding to the New Age doctrine of the "god" or "goddess" within every person) and "shamans" (persons who call up the devil or his demons and who believe in an unseen world of gods, demons, and ancestral spirits responsive only to him). In the Old Testament Law, God strictly forbids all forms of shamanism and instructs the Israelites to stone to death anyone practicing such acts (Exo. 22:18; Lev. 20:7). God, in fact, tells His people:

When you enter the land which the Lord your God gives you, you shall not learn to imitate the detestable things of those nations. There shall not be found among you anyone who makes his son or his daughter pass through the fire, one who uses divination, one who practices witchcraft, or one who interprets omens, or a sorcerer, or one who casts a spell, or a medium, or a spiritist, or one who calls up the dead. For whoever does these things is detestable to the Lord; and because of these detestable things the Lord your God will drive them out before you. You shall be blameless before the Lord your God. For those nations, which you shall dispossess, listen to those who practice witchcraft and to diviners, but as for you, the Lord your God has not allowed you to do so (Deut. 18:9-14).

God clearly states that the person who practices these things is detestable to Him; yet Western-world television routinely offers advertisements for psychic hotlines, and Western-world tabloids are filled with advertisements promoting every type of occult practice.

God also spells out His punishment of those who practice the occult: *"As for the person who turns to mediums and to spiritists, to play the harlot after them, I will also set My face against that person and will cut him off from among his people" (Lev. 20:6).* Thus, the living God of the universe will set Himself against the person who turns to the occult.

The whole realm of the "mystical" and the "metaphysical" and the "inner journey" is pouring into the West today. Fortune 500 companies, for example, routinely send their employees to seminars laced with New Age doctrine. Leading universities throughout the United States and Europe subscribe to and teach the metaphysical—but find the Bible to be wholly objectionable. Because of this infiltration, the historic Judeo-Christian beliefs of the West are being overtaken by Eastern mysticism and the occult. No wonder the book of Revelation describes the Antichrist's Empire (the West) as follows: *"Fallen, fallen is Babylon the Great [the Antichrist's Empire]. And she has become the dwelling place of demons and a prison of every unclean spirit" (Rev. 18:2).* The West today, through the New Age Movement (and its metaphysical, Eastern traditions), is being prepared by Satan for the end-times occultic religion of the Antichrist— and few Westerners have any idea what is happening.

Chart 28-A

MAGAZINES WHICH PROMOTE THE OCCULT

Pagan Oawm

Creation Spirituality: Earthly Wisdom for an Evolving Planet

Yoga Journal

Tantra

Sage Woman: Celebrating the Goddess in Every Woman

Mother Earth News

Nexus

Holistic Health

Light of Consciousness

New Age Journal

New Moon Rising: Journal of Magick & Wicca

Shambala Sun

Green Egg: A Journal of the Awakening Earth

Internal Arts

Gnosis: A Journal of the Western Internal Arts

Shaman's Drum: A Journal in Experiential Shamanism

Magical Blend: a Transformative Journey

Chart 28-B

"NEW AGE" / "DELUDING INFLUENCE" BUMPER STICKERS

---

1. **"THINK GLOBALLY, ACT LOCALLY"**

2. **"PRACTICE RANDOM KINDNESS AND SENSELESS ACTS OF BEAUTY"**

3. **"MINDS ARE LIKE PARACHUTES: THEY ONLY FUNCTION WHEN OPEN"**

4. **"ALL BIBLES ARE MAN-MADE (THOMAS EDISON)"**

5. **"THE GODDESS IS ALIVE AND MAGIC IS AFOOT"**

6. **"MAGIC HAPPENS"**

7. **"BACK OFF: I'M A GODDESS"**

8. **"WALK IN BALANCE ON THE MOTHER EARTH"**

9. **"SUBVERT THE DOMINANT PARADIGM"**

10. **"NATURE IS MY CHURCH"**

SOCIO-POLITICAL-ECONOMIC TRENDS AND THE END TIMES

Five major socio-political-economic trends are taking place in the world today which are setting the stage for an eventual attempt by the end-times Antichrist to subdue and rule the entire earth. Unregenerate political leaders and elite sociologists in the Western world recognize that some semblance of common ground must be developed among the diverse cultures of the world for unity to be achieved and for world peace to become a reality. Consequently, five major areas of common ground are being pushed upon the world by the power brokers of the West. This push attempts to create the following infrastructure: a world political system, a world economic system, a world sociological philosophy, a world religion, and a world language. These five areas of "common ground" are being touted continuously in the Western world as (1) the best way for the diverse cultures of the world govern themselves; (2) the best way for the diverse cultures to trade goods and services; (3) the best way for the diverse peoples of the world to get along with one another on a day-to-day basis; (4) the best way for the various cultures of the world to have a mutually-acceptable universal "god"; and (5) the best way for the political, educational, and business leaders of the different nations and cultures of the world to communicate with one another. The five major trends are as follows:

A. The Move toward a Universal Political System: "Democracy" or "Democratic Socialism"

The 1989 demise of communism in Eastern Europe and the former Soviet Union provided an enormous leap forward for those who dream of world government and world peace. To be sure, the only type of government deemed by the powerful, industrialized nations of the West to be acceptable for an eventual unification of the world is some form of democracy. Totalitarianism is unacceptable to the Western nations pulling the world's political strings. Thus, the "price tag" for any nation who wants to play in the affluent West's economic and military playground is a move toward freely-elected democracies. The visionary Mikhail Gorbachev readily understood this price tag and courageously took his empire into the brave new world of "democracy." Gorbachev saw his nation's future best served by partnership with the West—not only for economic reasons but also for military reasons (specifically, to thwart the Islamic threat from the south and any future Chinese threat from the southeast). In 1994, the price tag for Western aid to Haiti was democracy (the democracy headed by Jean-Bertrand Aristide). The price tag for any Cuban reconciliation with the West will likewise be democracy. Even in China, the groundwork is being laid for a German-style democratic socialism after the death of Premier Deng Xiaoping.

Those who choose not to play by these rules during the end-times Tribulation will ultimately by targeted by the Antichrist for destruction (e.g., the warlord government of Somalia). Thus, democracy is deemed by the world political power brokers of the West to be the only acceptable global political system.

[Note: by 2022, the push by Western elites toward the 1990's goal of national "democracies" had shifted rather dramatically toward the goal of widespread "democratic socialism." Ominously (and ironically), this shift reflects (1) the more authoritarian bent of Western-world nations (with power being hijacked by the political class and the bureaucratic state) and (2) academia's call for more economic and social "equity" in government policy.]

B. The Move toward a Universal Economic System: Free Markets and World Trade

Next, the West's power brokers have deemed "free market economies" to be the only acceptable global economic system. Why? Because countries who trade together will not likely go to war with one another. Again, Mikhail Gorbachev understood the "price of admission" into the West's playground, and he steered the Soviet monolith onto a course-heading which said "free market economies." Though such a radical change from a command economy to a market economy has not been easy for Russia—and will likely take years to fine-tune—a "market economy" die has nevertheless been cast in the three core nations of the former Soviet Union: Russia, Belarus, and the Ukraine. In China, the move toward a partial market economy (for pragmatic economic and trade reasons) has been even swifter. Today, the Western visitor to major cities in mainland China will find more construction activity in China than perhaps in any other country of the world. As of this writing (1996), the unwritten economic objective in Shanghai is to outtrade the market-economy bastion of Hong Kong by the year 2010.

C. The Move toward a Universal Sociological Philosophy: Pluralistic Tolerance and Unity in Diversity

With persons immigrating to the United States from every part of the world, America has become the melting pot of the world. So how can people with such diverse backgrounds rub shoulders together on a day-to-day basis without living at odds with one another? To unregenerate globalists the answer lies in "pluralism"— a sociological philosophy which states that each person, regardless of his neighbor's culture or ideological background, must not only tolerate that person's belief system, values, opinions, and lifestyle, but must also hold them to be just as acceptable as his own. Coinciding with sociological pluralism is the related belief that no moral absolutes exist in the world. Instead, everything is relative. Thus, "pluralistic tolerance," in the minds of Western sociologists, becomes the societal glue which will unite people from the widely varying cultures on earth into a one-world living arrangement.

Because the Western world finds itself being swept into a pluralistic mindset and being told that each person can do whatever he wants (as long as he allows others to do what they want), the societal condition of the West is rapidly approaching the same condition which grieved God in Israel's early history: *"and everyone did what is right in their own eyes"* (Judges 21:25b). Nowhere in the mantra of pluralism does anyone talk about the need for the diverse persons of the world to do what is right in *God's* eyes. Finally, the hypocrisy of contemporary pluralism should be obvious to Christians: for all its talk about tolerance of the beliefs, values, opinions, and lifestyles of others—it is intolerant of Judaism and Christianity because of their belief in personal sin, moral absolutes, and a transcendent God. Thus, in terms of "acceptable" religious beliefs, contemporary pluralism will only tolerate religions which teach that each person is himself a god or can become a god. It is the devil's lie of Genesis 3:1-7 all over again.

D. The Move toward a Universal Religion: The New Age/New Spirituality Movement

For utopian elites in the West the best way to unite the two-thirds of the world's population not espousing Judaism, Christianity, or Islam is to supply it with a religion universal enough for the various cultures of the world to embrace. The religion which best fits the bill is the so-called New Age Movement—the occultic-Hindu-Metaphysical package of doctrines infiltrating the West today. The two core doctrines of this religious system are (1) reincarnation and (2) the inherent or potential deity of man. All Eastern religions are comfortable with these two doctrines, and a sizeable portion of the West now embraces them as well. The only religions *not* comfortable with these two great lies are Judaism, Christianity, and Islam. Accordingly, these three religions will become the focus of the Antichrist's (and the world's) venom during the second half of the Tribulation. [Note: Much of Apostate Christianity, because of its nominal adherence, will fall away from Christianity during the Tribulation and will embrace the Antichrist's New Age religion instead.]

E. The Move toward a Universal Language: English

The final major socio-political-economic trend of the past seventy years is the dramatic move toward English as the world's language of government and commerce. Throughout the world, persons from every nation learn English in order to lead and trade in today's global economy. English is the tower-to-aircraft language of communication for all international airline flights. Multitudes of English speakers teach "English as a second language" in numerous countries around the globe. Hundreds of thousands of international students attend America's colleges and universities each year—sitting in classes being taught in English. In short, for the first time since God's confusion of mankind's language 4,400 years ago at the tower of Babel, man is coming remarkably close to being able once again to communicate in one universal language: English.

Chart 29-A

FIVE MAJOR "ONE-WORLD" TRENDS

---

1. A UNIVERSAL POLITICAL SYSTEM: DEMOCRACY OR DEMOCRATIC SOCIALISM

2. A UNIVERSAL ECONOMIC SYSTEM: FREE MARKETS AND WORLD TRADE

3. A UNIVERSAL SOCIOLOGICAL PHILOSOPHY: PLURALISTIC TOLERANCE AND UNITY IN DIVERSITY

4. A UNIVERSAL RELIGION: THE NEW AGE MOVEMENT

5. A UNIVERSAL LANGUAGE: ENGLISH

CURRENT SOCIETAL TRENDS IN THE WEST

Nine other societal trends exist in the West today which are subtly preparing the way for the coming of the Antichrist. Tragically, most people are oblivious to the significance of these trends.

A. The Inexorable March of "Globalism"

While the march toward a grand, one-world scheme has had growing impetus from many directions during the last half of the twentieth century, perhaps the most stunning impetus came from the famous "earthrise" photograph taken by America's Apollo VIII astronauts on mankind's first visit to the moon in December, 1968. Once and for all, the earth seemed to be but a speck in the larger scheme of the universe, and man consciously or subconsciously began to look upon the earth as "spaceship earth" and a "global village"—needing not only world peace but man's utmost care. Today, when measured in terms of political correctness and media sound bites, the word "global" heads the list. Dozens of times a day, the average Westerner either hears or sees the message of "globalism," be it "global warming" or "global communications" or "global economy" or "global investing" or global whatever. Today, the issues are not national or even international, but "global." To the hardcore globalist, national sovereignty must be subrogated to the higher principle of globalism. Phrases such as the "New World Order" have their roots in this inexorable march toward the humanist dream of a global government, a global economy, a global religion, and a global people—in short, a grand one-world global village.

B. The Exaltation of Individual Rights

Seemingly nothing is more sacred in the West than the doctrine of "individual rights." The rights of society have taken a back seat to the rights of the individual. The list of individual rights is endless: human rights, women's rights, worker rights, minority rights, students' rights, children's rights, prisoners' rights, gay rights, animal rights, and on and on. Is such a phenomenon dangerous to a society? What could possibly be wrong with this exaltation of "individual rights"?

The danger of this phenomenon is two-fold. First, the zealous demanding of one's own rights overturns, or runs counter to, the basic structure of order that God has established for the common good of mankind. For example, God, in His Word, has put forth certain basic guidelines for society: husband-wife guidelines; parent-child guidelines; employer-employee guidelines; and government-citizen guidelines. When society practices these Biblical guidelines, a much higher degree of harmony exists in these institutions. Indeed, when an employee (Christian or non-Christian) works heartily for his employer—rather than demanding his own rights as an employee—he gains favor in the eyes of the employer and is esteemed by the employer.

On the other hand, when an employee (Christian or non-Christian) is a contentious employee and continually demands his own rights, he becomes a "thorn" to his employer—and terminations typically ensue. Second, the zealous demanding of one's own rights runs counter to the second greatest commandment in God's economy: to love *others* as much as yourself. The person who is absorbed in demanding his own rights by definition has a difficult time unselfishly loving others.

C.   The Elevation of Creation (Rather than Creator)

"Mother Earth" has reached nearly god-like status in the West today. Cries go out to "save the earth" and to "protect your Mother." In contrast, the gospel message—the message which can save a man's *soul*—is largely mocked or ignored. In addition, man himself (though created) is being exalted in the West as being capable of accomplishing anything, not unlike what happened at the Tower of Babel 4,400 years ago when God said of the post-Flood human family: "*Behold, they are one people, and they all have the same language, . . . and now nothing which they purpose is impossible for them*" *(Gen. 11:6)*. Because of man's technological triumphs, today's humanist increasingly believes that he, with no help from the Living God, can determine his own fate.

Even animals are being exalted in the West. For example, many Western humanists argue that man should not eat animals (presumably to protect the "rights" of that animal). God's Word, on the other hand, states just the opposite: "*But the Spirit explicitly says that in later times some will fall away from the faith, paying attention to deceitful spirits and doctrines of demons, by means of the hypocrisy of liars seared in their own conscience as with a branding iron, men who forbid marriage and advocate abstaining from foods, which God has created to be gratefully shared in by those who believe and know the truth. For everything created by God is good, and nothing is to be rejected, if it is received with gratitude*" *(I Tim. 4:1-4)*.

D.   The Declining Influence of the Judeo-Christian Ethic

Not only is the Christian gospel being attacked from the outside and being subverted from within, but the historic Judeo-Christian ethic—an ethic which encompasses such things as "put in a good day's work, respect your employer, honor your leaders, do unto others as you would have them do unto you, abstain from stealing, remain faithful to one's spouse, and refuse to murder"—is giving way to situation ethics and doing what is right in one's own eyes rather than what is right in God's eyes.

E.   The Increasing Acceptability of the Occult

Western corporations—in an effort to enhance worker productivity and corporate results—at times offer seminars which embrace occultic practices. Western universities offer courses in the occult, yet refuse to have anything to do with the gospel. Western science sometimes dabbles in the occult rather than fleeing from it. Television infomercials offer psychic hotlines. Newsstand tabloids are filled with advertisements for the occult: personal psychics, tarot readings, messages from the dead, and personal horoscopes—practices which derive their power from Satan and which are forbidden by God. Hollywood celebrities openly talk about "channeling" (the occultic practice of communicating with demons) and having a "spirit guide" (a demon masquerading as a mystical messenger). All of these practices are conditioning the West to embrace the Antichrist and the False Prophet (the latter being a master occultist).

F.   The Growing Momentum of the Peace Movement

The peace movement of the sixties in the United States is now "back by popular demand" according to the nineties' bumper sticker. The peace movement has also spread into Europe, where the Bosnian conflict has highlighted the savagery of war for the post-Vietnam generation of Europeans. Increasingly in the West the doctrine and dogma of foreign policy is becoming the following: world peace at any cost.

History has proven, of course, that man-made political peace nearly always proves to be ephemeral, because apart from the Prince of Peace—Jesus Christ—residing in the human heart, the various nations and tongues and tribes of the human family can never have lasting peace. The indwelling Jesus Christ is the only true peacemaker available to man.

G.   The Rise of New Geopolitical Fears

Until 1990, the West's number one fear was the "evil empire" of the Soviet Union. Due to the dramatic turn of events in the late 1980s, that fear has diminished substantially. New fears, however, have emerged, which in turn have become preeminent in the minds of the West's power-brokers. Three principal threats dominate: Islamic terrorism, nuclear proliferation, and over-population of the earth.

Islamic terrorism now represents a significant threat to the West. The 9/11 attack on the World Trade Center at the hands of Islamic terrorists sent a new chill into the geopolitical thinking of the West: How can the West protect itself (and its global interests) from such fanaticism? The second major threat to the West is nuclear proliferation: How can the West ensure that the world's arsenal of nuclear warheads stays in safe hands? What if a nuclear weapon should fall into the hands of Islamic terrorists? For example, what if the 1993 World Trade Center bomb had been *nuclear*? The third new geopolitical threat to the West is longer-term: the supposed problem of an over-crowded, over-taxed earth. How can the West prevent such a crisis from happening? Should not the earth have *fewer* people? If so, *who* should be eliminated?

[Note: the rapid economic growth of China during the first two decades of the twenty-first century—with China's increasingly voracious appetite for oil and raw materials—has now become the fourth geopolitical threat to the West. Even more ominous, China is not only expanding the size of its military, but it is also expanding the size and sophistication of its nuclear arsenal and long-range ballistic missile capability.]

H.   The Prodigious Influence of the Media

Two hundred years ago, when the United States was still largely a rural society and the influence of the printing press was just beginning to be felt, most of the values received by a child or teenager were imparted by his parents. Today, few of the values received by a teenager are implanted by his parents or single parent. Instead, they are imparted by the various forms of media: the internet, social media, radio, television, streaming videos, movies, magazines, and billboards. Television's beer commercials subtly or not-so-subtly persuade the young person to "go for the gusto." Many of Hollywood's movies send the message of money, hedonism, materialism, power, pre-marital sex, adultery, and murder. The more anti-establishment the hero, the "cooler" he is deemed to be by today's youth. In short, the frontal and subliminal media messages being offered in the West today stand in stark contrast to the Apostle Paul's *"whatsoever things are honorable, whatsoever things are pure, whatsoever things are lovely"* exhortation of Philippians 4:8.

I.   The Deterioration in Morality: The Casting Off of Restraint

The Bible states that God has grief stored up for those who turn evil into good and good into evil (Isa. 5:20), yet it is now "politically correct" in the humanist West to do just that: Homosexuals have come out of the closet and in some cities flaunt their lifestyle. "Safe sex" is considered a *virtue* rather than blatant fornication. To "question authority" is considered chic. Government buildings are bombed by disenchanted citizens, with no apparent concern for the innocent victims. Drive-by shootings on the part of street-gangs routinely snuff out lives, with no apparent check of the human conscience let alone fear of any significant retribution from the judicial system. Because so many people in the West are casting off God, He in turn is giving them over to the degrading passions of their flesh (Rom. 1:26-32). The fruits of this casting off of restraint make the headlines daily.

ADDITIONAL COMMENTS

Two other topics have significance with regard to the end-times events and warrant brief comment as well: the Persian Gulf War and the current condition of sub-Saharan Africa.

A.   The Significance of the Persian Gulf War

The combatants of the Persian Gulf War closely mirrored the future combatants of Daniel 11:40-43. The West (the core of the Antichrist's future empire) was represented by a coalition of nations headed by the premier military nation on earth, the United States. The target of the West's military response in the Middle East was Islamic Iraq, who wanted to drive Israel into the Mediterranean and who frequently called for "Jihad" (holy war) against the Western satans.

During the Persian Gulf conflict, ominous new terms became household words in the West—terms like the "New World Order" and the "coalition of nations" and the "protection of our mutual collective interests." The world saw for the first time, on worldwide television, the startling new high-tech weapons of the West: laser-guided bombs (which provided precision, surgical military strikes); stand-off cruise missiles (which, using satellite-generated, terrain-mapped guidance systems, struck their designated targets from 500 miles away); stealth bombers (which launched their air strikes virtually undetected by enemy radar); Patriot missiles (which knocked down the majority of Iraq's Scud missiles). To the non-Western world, the military performance by the Western coalition during the Persian Gulf War comes very close to the Biblical prophecy describing the Antichrist's end-times capabilities: *"Who is like the beast, and who can wage war with him?" (Rev. 13:4).*

The only feature of the Persian Gulf War which will not be duplicated during the Antichrist's end-times Middle East takeover is the 1990-1991 alliance of several important Islamic nations with the West. When the Antichrist invades Israel immediately after the midpoint of the Tribulation, he will demand worship from the entire world—and most of the Islamic Middle East will reject such a decree as blasphemy. Thus, during the *end-times* "Persian Gulf War" (Daniel 11:40-43), the Antichrist's Western "coalition of nations" (including his ten core nations) will target *all* of the Islamic Middle East for destruction. Moreover, unlike the Persian Gulf War of 1991, the coalition will not stop before it gets to Baghdad and the coalition will not limit itself to conventional weapons (Rev. 6:3-8).

B.   The Vulnerability of Africa

The second topic needing additional comment is the current vulnerability of Africa in the face of the West's global agenda, worldly sophistication, and military muscle. During the first sixty years of the twentieth century, Africa lived under the yoke of European colonialism. Britain, Germany, France, Belgium, Holland, Spain, and Portugal essentially took over Africa, divvying it up for themselves. The colonialists made reasonable progress developing European-style infrastructures in countries which previously had lived virtually hand-to-mouth. During the 1960's the great African independence movement gained momentum, freeing most of Africa from the yoke of colonialism. Nevertheless, though free from this yoke, many African nations soon found themselves falling into decay.

Today, political corruption, fragile infrastructures, widespread poverty, and venomous tribal wars characterize much of post-colonial Africa. AIDS has devoured several African nations and famine is a regular visitor to various parts of the continent. Militarily, Africa is defenseless against the West, should the West ever choose strategic military aggression. Economically, Africa has the world's richest harvest of natural resources—resources which the post-Rapture West will covet. With the twentieth century colonial movement being a foreshadow, Africa is the likely candidate to be "parceled out for a price" by the Antichrist (Dan. 11:39). Worse, much of Africa will likely be slaughtered in the process (Rev. 6:3-8).

THE CLASH OF CIVILIZATIONS

In the summer of 1993, *Foreign Affairs* magazine published a highly-acclaimed article entitled, "The Clash of Civilizations?" by strategic policy expert, Samuel P. Huntington (from the John M. Olin Institute at Harvard University). Huntington argues the following:

It is my hypothesis that the fundamental source of conflict in the new world will not be primarily ideological or primarily economic. The great divisions among humankind and the dominating source of conflict will be cultural. Nation states will remain the most powerful actors in world affairs, but the principal conflicts of global politics will occur between nations and groups of different civilizations. The clash of civilizations will dominate global politics. The fault lines between civilizations will be the battle lines of the future.[5]

In addition, Huntington identifies which civilizations could clash and explains why they will likely clash:

Civilization identity will increasingly be important in the future, and the world will be shaped in large measure by the interactions among seven or eight major civilizations. These include Western, Confucian, Japanese, Islamic, Hindu, Slavic-Orthodox, Latin American and possibly African civilization. The most important conflicts of the future will occur along the cultural fault lines separating these civilizations from one another.

Why will this be the case?

First, differences among civilizations are not only real; they are basic. Civilizations are differentiated from each other by history, language, culture, tradition and, most important, religion. The people of different civilizations have different views on the relations between God and man, the individual and the group, the citizen and the state, parents and children, husband and wife, as well as differing views of the relative importance of rights and responsibilities, liberty and authority, equality and hierarchy. These differences are the product of centuries. They will not soon disappear. They are far more fundamental than differences among political ideologies and political regimes. Differences do not necessarily mean conflict, and conflict does not necessarily mean violence. Over the centuries, however, differences among civilizations have generated the most prolonged and the most violent conflicts.

Second, the world is becoming a smaller place. The interactions between peoples of different civilizations are increasing; these increasing interactions intensify civilization consciousness and awareness of differences between civilizations and commonalities within civilizations. North African immigration to France generates hostility among Frenchmen and at the same time increased receptivity to immigration by "good" European Catholic Poles. Americans react far more negatively to Japanese investment than to larger investments from Canada and European countries. . . . The interactions among peoples of different civilizations enhance the civilization-consciousness of people that, in turn, invigorates differences and animosities stretching or thought to stretch back deep into history.

Third, the processes of economic modernization and social change throughout the world are separating people from longstanding local identities. They also weaken the nation state as a source of identity. In much of the world, religion has moved in to fill this gap, often in the form of movements which are labeled "fundamentalist." Such movements are found in Western Christianity, Judaism, Buddhism and Hinduism, as well as Islam. . . . The "unsecularization of the world," George Weigel has remarked, "is one of the dominant social facts of life in the late twentieth century." The revival of religion . . . provides a basis for identity and commitment that transcends national boundaries and unites civilizations.

Fourth, the growth of civilization-consciousness is enhanced by the dual role of the West. On the one hand, the West is at a peak of power. At the same time, however, and perhaps as a result, a return to the roots phenomenon is occurring among non-Western civilizations. Increasingly one hears references to trends toward a turning inward and "Asianization" in Japan, the end of the Nehru legacy and the "Hinduization" of India, the failure of Western ideas of socialism and nationalism and hence the "re-Islamization" of the Middle East, and now a debate over Westernization versus Russianization in Boris Yeltsin's country. A West at the peak of its power confronts non-Wests that increasingly have the desire, the will and the resources to shape the world in non-Western ways.[6]

Though the article does not state whether Huntington is an evangelical Christian, his hypothesis is virtually identical with the realities of the prophesied end-times Tribulation conflicts.

As just cited, Huntington contends that seven or eight civilizations are likely to clash in the future: The West, China ("Confucian"), Japan, the Middle East ("Islamic"), India ("Hindu"), Russia-Eastern Europe ("Slavic-Orthodox"), Latin America, and possibly Africa. God's Word, on the other hand, tells us that *six* civilizations will clash during the end-times Tribulation horrors: the West, the Islamic Middle East, defenseless Africa, Russia-Eastern Europe, the "Kings of the East" (the nations east of the Tigres-Euphrates rivers), and Israel. Huntington thus (and probably unknowingly) comes remarkably close to identifying the civilizations which will clash during the end-times Tribulation period; more importantly, he identifies precisely *why* the prophesied Tribulation conflagrations will take place: the inherent cultural differences between several major civilizations on earth.

The West's relationship with China, for example, is presently frayed over such issues as "human rights" and "copyright laws." The West exalts individual rights while China elevates societal rights. Consequently, when the United States chastises China for what it deems to be an abysmal human rights record, China retorts with such arguments as "the murder rate in the United States is one hundred times as great as the one in China, and the United States can't even guarantee that the citizens of its largest cities can walk safely at night!" In the United States it is the inalienable right for every American to own a gun, even if he happens to be an eighteen-year-old belonging to a Los Angeles street gang; in China private citizens cannot own or possess guns. In the West, copyright laws are guarded fiercely and infringement of such copyrights can be remedied in a court of law; in China Western copyrights are routinely pirated under the guise of flattery: "You should be *honored* that we think enough of your work to translate it into our own language."

The gulf between the West and Middle East Islam is even greater. The West views the Islamic Middle East's treatment of women as barbaric, and the West equates Islamic Fundamentalism with Middle Eastern terrorism. The Islamic Middle East, on the other hand, views the West as decadent and "the great Satan." A December 17, 1979, essay in *Time* magazine reveals the inherent religious differences and historic distrust between the more fundamentalist Arab tribes and the West:

> The West and the world of Islam sometimes resemble two different centuries banging through the night on parallel courses. In full raucous cultural panoply, they keep each other awake. They make each other nervous. At times, as now, they veer together and collide: up and down the processions, threats are exchanged, pack animals and zealots bray, bales of ideological baggage spill onto the road. Embassies get burned, hostages taken. Songs of revenge in the throat.
>
> Are these collisions inevitable? The mutual misunderstandings of the West and the Islamic world have a rich patina of history.... From the time of the Muslim conquests and the Crusades, West and Islam have confronted each other by turns in attitudes of incomprehension, greed, fanaticism, prurient interest, fear and loathing. The drama has lost none of its historic tension in the stagecraft of the Ayatollah Khomeini. "This is not a struggle between the United States and Iran," he has told the faithful. "It is a struggle between Islam and the infidel."

A.   The End-Times Clash of Civilizations

How will the clash of these civilizations play out during the Tribulation period? Huntington's "Latin American" civilization is largely ruled by descendants of Europe—principally the Spanish and the Portuguese. This civilization will readily fall into the West's umbrella during the first half of the Tribulation, when the Antichrist uses the Apostate Church to bring Latin America (about 90% Roman Catholic) into the Antichrist's grand, revived Roman Empire.

The Islamic Middle East (including North Africa) and defenseless sub-Saharan Africa, according to Daniel 11:40-43, will apparently be slaughtered by the West during the initial stages of the second half of the Tribulation (the 2nd through 4th Seal judgments).

Japan, because of its current importance to the world economy, will likely be allied with the West during the first half of the Tribulation—but also could be one of the three kings "subdued" by the Western Antichrist during the second half of the Tribulation (Dan. 7:23-24). If so, Japan will then return to its Asian roots (during the latter stages of the Tribulation) as a "king of the east." Huntington's "Confucian" and "Hindu" civilizations are similar enough in terms of religion (reincarnation and the evolution toward the "godhood" of men) to unite (as the "kings of the east") against the West during the latter stages of the second half of the Tribulation.

Russia and Eastern Europe will likely ally themselves with the West during much of the Tribulation. However, after the devastation (most likely nuclear) heaped upon the West at the beginning of the seventh year of the Tribulation (the 6th Trumpet Judgment), Russia and Eastern Europe could either break ranks with the West (they are pictured by the prophet Ezekiel as descending upon Israel at the end of the Tribulation period—Ezekiel 38:18-20) or will represent the only significant fighting force left in the region after the conflagration of the sixth Trumpet (and will then descend upon Israel during the final month of the Tribulation).

Finally, Israel is the most crucial civilization of all (God having made a number of irrevocable promises to her) and will be the target of the world's universal venom during the second half of the Tribulation. Fortunately for Israel (and unfortunately for the rest of the world), God—through the bodily return of Jesus Christ to the earth—will intervene on behalf of Israel thirty days after the end of the Tribulation (Dan. 12:11-12) and will destroy the Gentile armies who have gathered against her. After destroying these armies (during the battle called "Armageddon"), Christ will then gather every remaining person on earth to Jerusalem for final judgment. All surviving Tribulation believers will be allowed to enter the Millennial Kingdom, while all surviving unbelievers will be slain. Once Christ completes this judgment, He will begin His Millennial reign over the earth. At the commencement of His reign, only believers in Jesus Christ will reside on planet earth.

Chart 32-A

CIVILIZATIONS WHICH WILL CLASH DURING THE TRIBULATION

---

1.   **THE WEST**
     (WESTERN EUROPE, SCANDINAVIA, & THE WESTERN HEMISPHERE)

2.   **ISLAM [I.E, THE MIDDLE EAST AND N. AFRICA]**

3.   **SUB-SAHARAN AFRICA**

4.   **THE EAST**
     (CHINA & THE ORIENT)

5.   **THE NORTH**
     (RUSSIA & EASTERN EUROPE)

6.   **ISRAEL**

ARE WE CLOSE?

Because of His hatred of sin, our long-suffering God has ordained the horrors of the end-times Tribulation period in order to bring judgment upon the earth's unrepentant, who refuse to believe the truth so as to be saved (II Thess. 2:7-10). These judgments have been impending for the past nineteen hundred years. But are they now *imminent*? After all, God's Word categorically states that no man or angel—not even Christ Himself—knows the date of the Rapture; only God Himself knows (Matt. 24:36). Yet, despite the fact that no man knows the date of the Rapture, God's Word also tells Christ's followers that two signs will be forerunners of His return. Let us thus examine these signs in order to discern the stunning imminency of the Rapture.

A.   "Peace and Safety"

The first century church in Thessalonica at one point during its early existence was being buffeted by teachers who argued that the Rapture had already occurred and that the Church was presently in the Tribulation period. When Paul heard of this teaching, he wrote I Thessalonians to correct the error. In this highly eschatological letter, not only did Paul inform the Thessalonians that the Rapture had not yet occurred, but he also explained to them one of the signs that would alert the discerning Christian to the nearness of the Rapture:

> *But we do not want you to be uninformed, brethren, about those who are asleep, that you may not grieve, as do the rest who have no hope. For if we believe that Jesus died and rose again, even so God will bring with Him those who have fallen asleep in Jesus. For this we say to you by the word of the Lord, that we who are alive, and who remain until the coming of the Lord, shall not precede those who have fallen asleep. For the Lord Himself will descend from heaven with a shout, with the voice of the archangel and with the trumpet of God, and the dead in Christ shall rise first. Then we who are alive and remain shall be caught up together with them in the clouds to meet the Lord in the air, and thus we shall always be with the Lord. Therefore, comfort one another with these words (I Thess. 4:13-18).*
>
> *Now as to the times and the epochs, brethren, you have no need of anything to be written to you. For you yourselves know full well that the day of the Lord will come just like a thief in the night. While they are saying, "Peace and safety!" then destruction will come upon them suddenly like birth pangs upon a woman with child, and they shall not escape (I Thess. 5:1-3).*

Paul tells the Thessalonians (and the modern-day Church as well) that the Rapture will occur suddenly (*"like a thief in the night"*) when mankind is saying *"Peace and safety!"*—in fact when mankind is clamoring for peace and safety. Until the twentieth century, man routinely clamored for war. Seventy years ago, however, one event changed the tenor of that clamor forever: Hiroshima. For the first time in human history man had developed a way to exterminate himself. Then, as scientists in the United States and the former Soviet Union developed land-based (and then submarine-based) intercontinental ballistic missiles which could deliver 15,000 Hiroshimas anywhere on the earth in less than thirty minutes, the cry for "peace and safety" became louder and louder throughout the civilized world. Today, because of existing nuclear arsenals (as well as potential nuclear proliferation), the call for "peace and safety" reaches every level of American and European citizenry (see Chart 32-A).

Let us again hear the words of Paul: *"While they are saying, 'Peace and safety!' then destruction will come upon them suddenly like the birth pangs upon a woman with child, and they shall not escape."* Once the Rapture occurs, it will be too late for those who have not put their faith in Jesus Christ. They will be left behind on earth to face the horrors of the Tribulation—horrors which will increase in frequency and intensity as the seven-year Tribulation unfolds.

Are we close to the Rapture? According to Paul's admonition in I Thessalonians, and because of the world's clamor for peace and safety, every born-again Christian should be wide awake for the imminent return of Jesus Christ for His Bride at the Rapture.

B. "Leaves Bursting Forth"

Does still more evidence exist that the Lord's return is imminent? The answer is yes. Jesus Himself gives the Church today a sign which points to the nearness of His return. Specifically, in Matthew 24:3 the disciples ask the Lord about His return: *"Tell us, what will be the sign of the end of the age?"* Jesus answers their question in Matthew 24:32-36:

> *Now learn the parable from the fig tree: when its branch has already become tender and puts forth its leaves, you know that summer is near; even so you, too, when you see all these things, recognize that He is near—right at the door. Truly I say to you, this generation [i.e., the generation that sees the 'leaves' burst forth] will not pass away until all these things take place. Heaven and earth will pass away, but My words shall not pass away. But of that day and hour no one knows, not even the angels of heaven, nor the Son, but the Father alone (Matt. 24:32-36).*

Jesus tells His disciples that, even though no one but the Father knows the day or hour of the Rapture, His unannounced return for His Bride (born-again believers) will nevertheless be preceded by "leaves bursting forth"—by world events which have such end-times significance that they serve to "announce," just as the leaves of the spring announce the coming of summer, the imminency of the end of the age.

Do such world events seem to be taking place? Again the answer is yes. The rebirth of Israel in 1948 represents the largest and most obvious "leaf" of all. But dozens of other "leaves" are bursting forth as well—including the staggering and sobering nuclear weapons capabilities of the United States and Russia. Chart 33-B (not an all-inclusive list) highlights these "leaves" and shows us that "summer" is indeed very near.

Chart 33-A

"PEACE AND SAFETY" BUMPER STICKERS

---

1. "VISUALIZE WORLD PEACE"

2. "BACK BY POPULAR DEMAND"

3. "WAGE PEACE, NOT WAR"

4. "MAKE LOVE, NOT WAR"

5. "A NUCLEAR BOMB CAN RUIN YOUR DAY"

6. "YOU CANNOT SIMULTANEOUSLY PREVENT AND PREPARE
   FOR WAR"

7. "IF YOU WANT PEACE, WORK FOR JUSTICE"

8. "WAR IS COSTLY, PEACE IS PRICELESS"

9. "TEACH PEACE"

10. "SOW THE SEEDS OF PEACE AND JUSTICE"

Chart 33-B

"LEAVES" BURSTING FORTH (1940s - 50s - 60s)

---

the birth of the atomic bomb

the rebirth of Israel as a nation

the birth of the hydrogen bomb

the strategic air forces of the U.S. & the U.S.S.R.

the "multinational corporation" phenomenon in the West

<u>Playboy</u> magazine and the acceptability of the playboy mentality

the ease of intercontinental travel via commercial jets

the deployment of land-based ICBM's by the U.S. & the U.S.S.R.

the deployment of submarine-based ICBM's by the U.S. & the U.S.S.R.

the drug culture of the 60's

the sexual revolution in the U.S. and the West (facilitated by the "pill")

the recapture and possession of Jerusalem by the Jews in 1967

Apollo 8's "earthrise" photograph (December, 1968)

Chart 33-B

"LEAVES" BURSTING FORTH (1970s)

spy satellites

legalized abortion

widespread fornication

the removal of prayer from the schools

the breakdown of the family unit

the declining influence of the Judeo-Christian ethic in the West

the increasing dependence of the West upon Middle East oil

the feminist movement (chafing under God's ordained role for women)

the "self" movement ("look out for #1")

Chart 33-B

"LEAVES" BURSTING FORTH (1980s)

---

widespread pornography

homosexuality and lesbianism: out of the closet (an "alternative lifestyle")

the out-of-control drug problem

the increasing litigiousness of society

the AIDS epidemic

global communications

the global economy

the New Age movement

the increase in the acceptability of psychics and the occult

the increasing belief in UFO's and ET's

the decline in respect for elected officials

the increase in television worldliness

the increase in motion picture violence, nudity, and vulgarity

the increasing acceptability and spread of legalized gambling

heavy metal rock

Chart 33-B

"LEAVES" BURSTING FORTH (1990s)
---

the "politically correct" phenomenon

the ever-growing momentum of the "save the planet" movement

cruise missiles

laser-guided weapons

stealth technology

the spread of gang violence throughout the U.S.

the "safe sex" campaign

microchip technology implanted into animals

Islamic terrorism

the threat of Islamic nuclear proliferation

the concern over weapons of mass destruction

the reemergence of the peace movement

global satellite TV

the "victim" mentality of society (rather than personal responsibility)

the Internet (and its facilitation of global communication)

Chart 33-B

"LEAVES" BURSTING FORTH (2000s)

the revelation that China has eleven nuclear missiles aimed at the U.S.

the proliferation of the New Age teaching through the media

the efforts of Iran to develop weapons-grade plutonium

the efforts of North Korea to develop ICBM's which can reach the U.S.

the increasing popularity of the occult in motion pictures and television

the embracing of Eastern mystical practices in public education

the sobering reality of radical Islam

the worldwide proliferation of smart phones: instant communication

Chart 33-B

"LEAVES" BURSTING FORTH (2010s)

the reality of near world-wide cell phone coverage

the reality of instant global communication through smart phones

the legalization of same-sex marriage in the U.S.

the LBGTQ movement

the cry for a world without borders

the rise of gender identity confusion

the divisiveness of identity politics

the birth of the "cancel" culture

the power of big tech censorship

Chart 33-B

"LEAVES" BURSTING FORTH (2020s)

---

the increased authoritarianism in the West (facilitated by the Covid-19 pandemic)

PUTTING IT ALL TOGETHER

TEN MAJOR PHASES OF POST-RAPTURE EVENTS:

PHASE 1:

After the Rapture, but before the peace treaty between the Antichrist, Israel and Islam is signed (the event which starts the clock on the seven-year Tribulation period), ten powerful nations will form a cooperative, strategic empire (based on a "new world order"), and the ten respective heads-of-state will give their allegiance to a charismatic, world political figure—the Antichrist. The Antichrist and the powerful heads-of-state who ally with him will then attempt to establish a one-world "global village" (patterned after their own wishes) once and for all. The ten-nation coalition will provide for the collective security of its mutual global interests. This "new world order" will exalt man and exclude God. [**Note**: This rebellion against God will be identical to the rebellion of mankind against God at the Tower of Babel, approximately 100 years after the Genesis Flood, when men (1) attempted to unite *en masse* "to make a name for themselves" rather than to disperse throughout the earth as God had commanded them to do and (2) resumed their worship of creation—specifically, the "gods" of Satan—rather than the Creator, the Living God.] According to current economic and military realities, and should the end-times events begin within the next dozen years, the ten nations which join together under the Antichrist could readily be the United States, Russia, Great Britain, Germany, Japan, France, Italy, and Canada (the current Group of Eight) as well as two other Westernized nations. **See Map 1**. (Rev. 17:9-13; Dan. 7:19-26; 9:27)

PHASE 2:

The Antichrist and his ten-nation coalition will devise a creative solution to the political problems of the Middle East. After assuaging the fears of both the Arab world and Israel, the Antichrist will sign a peace treaty with Israel and her surrounding neighbors—a treaty guaranteeing (most likely) (1) religious freedom for Israel and (2) military protection for Israel against the Islamic nations which surround her. **See Map 4**. The seven-year Tribulation Period begins on the day this treaty is signed.

PHASE 3:

The first Seal judgment takes place, during which time the Antichrist—empowered by Satan—will expand his Empire "peacefully" for a period of three and a half years. The Antichrist will use the Apostate Church to further his political agenda in the Western Hemisphere and will likely use economic incentives (and occasional military threats) to expand his Empire elsewhere. Many persons who put their faith in Jesus Christ after the Rapture will be murdered by the Great Harlot (Apostate Christendom) during this forty-two-month timeframe (Rev. 17:6). By the end of the first half of the Tribulation period, virtually all of the nations which comprise present-day Christendom will have allied themselves with the Antichrist and his Empire. When the Antichrist enters the rebuilt temple in Jerusalem 1,260 days after he signs the treaty with Israel, the Antichrist's Empire, in addition to its ten core nations, will include Western Europe, Eastern Europe, Scandinavia, Australia, New Zealand, much of southern Africa, and all of the Western Hemisphere. **See Map 2**. (Rev. 6:1-2; Dan. 9:27; Rev. 17)

PHASE 4:

After the Antichrist's breaking of the Middle East peace treaty at the mid-point of the seven-year Tribulation, the second and third Seal judgments take place, during which time the Antichrist will overrun the Middle East and Africa (both perhaps "parceled out for a price," in accordance with Daniel 11:39) and will kill one-fourth of the earth's post-Rapture population in the process. Included in this death toll will be all persons within Apostate Christendom who refuse to renounce their nominal Christianity in favor of the Antichrist's New Age "world" religion. After the first four Seal judgments have ended (approximately five and a half years into the Tribulation period), the boundaries of the Antichrist's Empire will have expanded to cover much of the earth and will now also include the Middle East and all of Africa. At this point in the Tribulation period, the Antichrist will be at the height of his power and his Empire will have reached its maximum size. **See Map 3**. (Rev. 6:3-8; Dan. 11:36-43)

PHASE 5:

The fifth and sixth Trumpet judgments take place, approximately sixty-six months and seventy-two months into the Tribulation, respectively. The fifth Trumpet judgment will bring widespread demonic activity throughout the earth for five months (Rev. 9:1-11), and the sixth Trumpet judgment will take the form of a Sino-Western (or Sino-Russo-Western) nuclear holocaust. Much of the East as well as parts of the Antichrist's Empire will be destroyed at this time (Rev. 18:9-20). The death toll from the sixth Trumpet judgment amounts to one-third of the earth's remaining post-Rapture population (thus bringing the Tribulation death toll to one-half of the earth's population). It also seems that the Antichrist "subdues" (double-crosses or murders) three of the ten heads-of-state just before this holocaust begins (Rev. 9:13-21; Dan. 11:44; Ezekiel 38:1 - 39:6).

[Note: in this writer's view the first through fourth Trumpet judgments (in an unusual literary prefigurement) describe the collateral damage and the after-effects of the sixth Trumpet judgment (the nuclear holocaust): specifically, one-third of the earth is burned up (Rev. 8:7); one-third of the trees are burned up (Rev. 8:7); one-third of the green grass is burned up (Rev. 8:7); one-third of the sea becomes blood (Rev. 8:8-9); one-third of the oceans' sea creatures die (Rev. 8:8-9); one-third of the earth's ships are destroyed (Rev. 8:8-9); one-third of the earth's fresh water rivers, lakes, streams, and ponds become contaminated (because of radioactive fallout) and many men die as a result (Rev. 8:10-11); and one-third of the earth will not be able to see the sun, moon, and stars (because of the atmospheric pall throughout the northern hemisphere caused by the mushroom clouds of perhaps a 1,000 to 2,000 nuclear explosions) (Rev. 8:12).]

PHASE 6:

The first six Bowl judgments (Rev. 16:2-16) are poured out on mankind (beginning, in this writer's view, approximately six months before the end of the Tribulation and taking place a month apart from one another). The first Bowl sends malignant sores upon all persons who have the mark of the beast on their right hand or forehead. The second Bowl turns the earth's oceans into blood and causes every sea creature to die. The third Bowl turns the earth's fresh water supply into blood. The fourth Bowl elevates the earth's temperature to scorching levels. The fifth Bowl brings forth excruciating pain on all unbelievers in the Antichrist's Empire. The sixth Bowl (most likely during the entire final month of the Tribulation period) gathers the world's remaining armies into northern Israel for their eventual slaughter by Christ (at the Battle of Armageddon) upon His return.

PHASE 7:

The seventh Bowl judgment takes place on the final day of the Tribulation period (the 2,520th day after the signing of the peace treaty), at which time God destroys every village, town, and city on earth with the most massive earthquake in human history (Rev. 16:17-18; Ezek. 38:20). Every island on earth slides into the oceans (Rev. 16:20), and every mountain melts like wax and disappears (Rev. 16:20; Ps. 46:2; Ps. 97:5). The Antichrist's Empire then breaks into three parts and falls to the bottom of the ocean—never to be found again (Rev. 16:19). Based on the symmetry of the death tolls recorded in the Seal and Trumpet judgments, it is likely that the Tribulation death toll reaches *three-fourths* of the earth's post-Rapture population after this final Bowl judgment.

PHASE 8:

Thirty days after the end of the Tribulation period, Jesus Christ returns to the Mount of Olives in Jerusalem and soon slays all who have gathered against Him (and against Israel) in the Valley of Megiddo (the battle being called "Armageddon"). After this victory, Christ consigns Satan and his demons to an imprisonment of 1,000 years in a place called the Abyss. Forty-five days after His return to the earth, Jesus begins His Millennial reign. (Rev. 19:11-21; Dan. 12:8-12)

PHASE 9:

Jesus Christ reigns over the earth from Jerusalem in fulfillment of God's covenant promises to Israel. Israel will be preeminent among the nations. Peace and righteousness fill the earth throughout Christ's reign. After Christ's 1,000-year reign, God releases Satan from the Abyss for a brief period of time in order to tempt and deceive earthlings living at the end of the Millennial Kingdom. Tragically, millions of people will turn their hearts away from Christ and follow Satan. Ultimately, Christ puts an end to this rebellion and casts Satan into the Lake of Fire ("Hell") forever.

PHASE 10:

The Second Resurrection takes place at which time God raises all pre-Rapture unbelievers and all dead and living post-Rapture believers and unbelievers for judgment at the Great White Throne. God then destroys the present heavens and earth, and creates a New Heaven and a New Earth—in which no sin or stain of sin exists. God places believers from every Age onto the New Earth (where they will live with God forever), and God casts all unbelievers from every Age into the Lake of Fire (where they will live in everlasting torment away from the presence of God).

[Note: the author's book, *The End-Times Events*, describes in detail the events summarized above]

Map 1

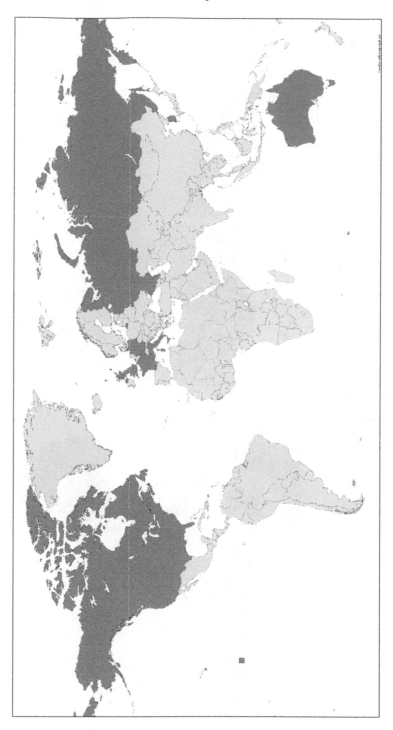

The Antichrist's Empire at the beginning of the Tribulation

Map template courtesy of mapchart.net

Map 2

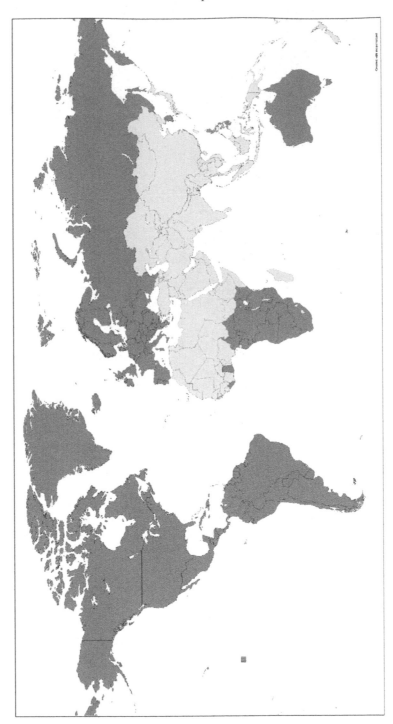

The Antichrist's Empire near the mid-point of the Tribulation

Map template courtesy of mapchart.net

Map 3

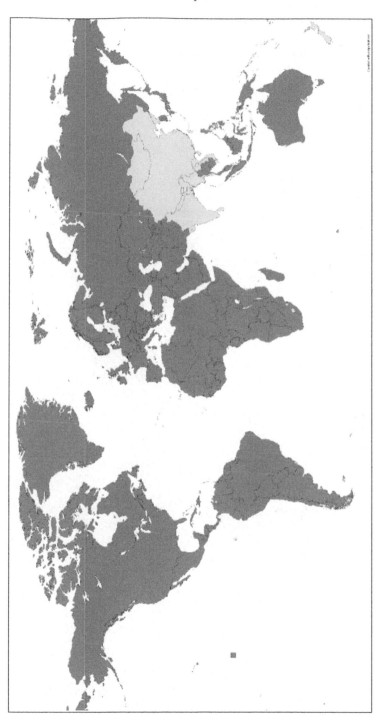

The Antichrist's Empire 5½ years into the Tribulation

Map template courtesy of mapchart.net

Map 4

The Islamic Conference

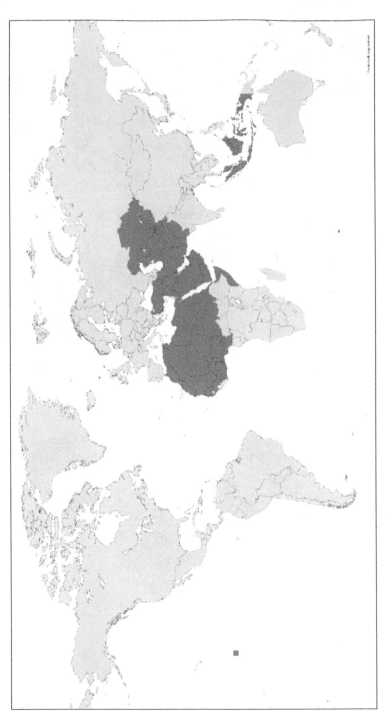

Map template courtesy of mapchart.net

EPILOGUE

John's New Testament Gospel gives mankind a beautiful summary of the essence and character of its Savior: *"And the Word became flesh and dwelt among us, and we beheld His glory, glory as of the only begotten from the Father, full of grace and truth. . . . For of His fulness we have all received, and grace upon grace. For the Law was given through Moses; grace and truth were realized through Jesus Christ" (John 1:14-17).* Not only did God the Son, Jesus Christ, become flesh and dwell among us, but He was full of grace and truth. The grace of God—God's gift of His only begotten Son on Calvary's Cross to atone for your sins and mine—represents the core essence of the gospel of Jesus Christ: *"For I delivered to you as of first importance what I also received, that Christ died for our sins according to the Scriptures, and that He was buried, and that He was raised on the third day according to the Scriptures, and that He appeared to Cephas, then to the twelve. After that He appeared to more than five hundred brethren at one time" (I Cor. 15:3-6).*

The true gospel is a grace-faith system (Eph. 2:9-10): All men—including you the reader—have sinned and have fallen short of the glory of God (Romans 3:23), but God has graciously provided the one provision of reconciliation which is acceptable to Him—the shed blood of His Son on Calvary's Cross (I Cor. 15:3-4). A person is saved for all eternity (reconciled and restored to God) when he puts his faith in God's provision. This faith is not mere intellectual assent but is a conscious turning of one's heart to God (repentance) and a conscious receiving of the salvation gift which God freely offers through Christ. A gift must be received by the recipient (rather than refused) for it to be of any benefit: *"but as many as received Him, to them He gave the right to become children of God, even to those who believe in His name" (John 1:12).* This acceptance or receiving of Christ involves inviting Jesus Christ into one's heart: *"Behold, I [Jesus Christ] stand at the door and knock. If anyone hears My voice and opens the door, I will come in to him, and will dine with him, and he with Me" (Rev. 3:20).*

Man typically imagines that he must *do* something in order to find favor with God. The disciples themselves reflected this attitude at one point in their travels with Christ: *"They therefore said to Him, 'what must we do that we may work the works of God?' Jesus answered and said to them: 'This is the work of God, that you believe in Him whom He has sent'" (John 6:28).* Tragically, the unbelieving world—and even parts of Christendom—are still trying to *do*, are still trying to find favor with God by human effort (and hence are still being condemned by the Old Covenant of Law rather than being liberated by New Covenant of Grace). God's purpose for every human is to be transformed into the image of Christ (Romans 8:29)—to be filled with grace and truth. As we conclude our study of the end-times events (and the sobering realities of the impending Tribulation judgments), let us therefore examine the topic of "grace and truth" in light of three categories of people: unbelievers; unbelievers who call themselves "Christians"; and born-again Christians. Every person reading this book falls into one of these categories.

A. Non-Christians

If you, the reader, are not a believer in Jesus Christ, then the horrors of the end-times Tribulation period as well as eternal separation from God—no matter how repugnant such words might sound to you—loom imminent in your life. Fore-knowing the resistance of much of mankind toward spiritual truth and the things of God, the living Creator has ordained a universal judgment during the "end times." God's Word has already pronounced the judgment; it has been impending for nearly 2,000 years; and, because of the "leaves" of world events bursting forth in such a way that the end-times prophecies can be fulfilled literally, it is now *imminent*. Consequently, you, the unbeliever, have a decision to make. Do you continue in your current false belief system (be it atheism, agnosticism, Deism, Judaism, Hinduism, Buddhism, Islam, Mormonism, Christian Science, astrology, humanism, relativism, self, good deeds, church membership, and so on) and face the fierce wrath of the imminent Tribulation? Or do you turn to the truth and put your faith in God's *only* provision for your inherent sin condition? Salvation is freely offered to men and women everywhere, regardless of nationality, race, or tongue, and it is received by *faith* (not good works): *"For God so loved the world that He gave His only begotten Son that whosoever believes in Him should not perish but have everlasting life" (John 3:16).*

God's Word is filled with examples of the love and mercy and forgiveness and tenderness and compassion of God toward all mankind—including His long-suffering love for even the vilest of sinners. As a result of this gracious love, many persons turn to Christ when they hear of the breadth and depth of the love of God for them personally. Others, however, come to God when they come face to face with the terrifying consequences ordained by God for all persons who refuse to turn their hearts to Him: eternal punishment and eternal separation from God in a place known as Hell. Both realities—God's perfect love and God's perfect justice—are legitimate motivating factors to cause a person to turn his heart back to God and to turn his life over to Jesus Christ. When God confronted the ancient Ninevites in approximately 750 B.C. with a pronouncement impending judgment ("in forty days you will perish"), the entire population of Ninevah—every single person—turned their hearts to God! God was so amazed at the magnitude and scope of this genuine, heart-felt repentance of these pagan people that He relented of the judgment.

But just as God once proclaimed impending judgment upon the Ninevites, God has also proclaimed impending judgment on the United States and the entire world. Most of the world and, lamentably, much of Christendom simply snickers at the thought of a future world-wide judgment. Yet such is the clear, irrefutable testimony of Scripture. Thus, whose side do you want to be on—the winning side or the losing side? Do you want a spiritually abundant life on this earth ("green pastures") and eternal heaven in the life after, or do you want a parched, empty life on this earth and eternal hell in the life after? Whatever your need, whatever your hurt, whatever your emptiness, whatever your crisis, the man who raised the dead and the man who was raised from the dead—Jesus Christ—stands ready to take you into His arms, to provide you with comfort and purpose and meaning and fulfillment. Only *He* can do it. If you have never invited Jesus Christ into your heart as Savior and Lord, then God's Word testifies that you have chosen the losing side. The impending horrors of the Tribulation and eternal damnation are your lot. On the other hand, if you choose to turn your heart to the truth of God's Word and the truth of the eternal gospel of Jesus Christ—that Christ died for your sins in order to give you abundant and eternal life starting right now—then you can instantly become a member of God's family, the winning team. Why not make that decision this very moment in the quietness of your heart? Simply acknowledge that you are a sinner in the eyes of God and that you desire not only to have your sins forgiven by God, but that you desire to enter into an eternal relationship with the living God by putting your faith in the Crucifixion and Resurrection of Jesus Christ for *you*.

B.   Catholic, Orthodox, and Protestant "Christians" who have never been born again

If you, the reader, are a person who calls yourself a "Christian" but have never consciously put your faith in the finished work of Jesus Christ for your sin problem, then you too face the horrors of the Tribulation period (and eternal judgment thereafter). Most Roman Catholic, Orthodox, or Protestant "Christians" of liberal denominations fall into this category.

Though the Catholic and Orthodox churches are to be commended for holding firm to the deity of Christ and the resurrection of Christ, they are in error over the core essence of the gospel—how a person is saved. To Catholics and Orthodoxes, a person is saved by membership in the Catholic or Orthodox church, and by the sacraments of these churches, and by good works rather than by simple faith—and faith alone—in God's provision of Jesus Christ for mankind's sins. Sadly, this "sacrament/good works" Christianity is not Biblical—and is leading millions of people into eternal damnation. The Catholic church claims to have 1.3 billion adherents worldwide; the Orthodox church claims to have about 260 million adherents. Thus, while Scripture makes it clear that some of these persons have put their faith in Christ alone and are saved (Rev. 3:4), most of them are lost: *"I know your deeds, that you have a name that you are alive, but you are dead. Wake up, and strengthen the things that remain, which were about to die, for I have not found your deeds completed in the sight of My God" (Rev. 3:1-2).* Of the 1.5 billion persons who call themselves Catholics or Orthodoxes, perhaps 1.4 billion of them are unsaved. They are "tares" (counterfeit Christians) rather than "wheat" (born-again children of God).

Being baptized as an infant into the Catholic or Orthodox church cannot save a Catholic or an Orthodox. The Scripture is categorical that *"faith comes from hearing, and hearing by the Word of God" (Rom. 10:17)*. It should be obvious to all that an infant cannot understand the substance of the gospel. Consequently, the belief of sacrament Christianity that infant baptism brings eternal salvation to that infant is conspicuous error and must be rejected. In addition, the Catholic doctrine which teaches that the wafer being eaten by a Catholic is the body of Christ and that the wine being taken a Catholic is the blood of Christ—and that somehow the "grace" of Christ is infused into the Catholic as he partakes of these sacraments—contradicts the plain teaching of the New Testament. In reality, sacrament Christianity is a theology of works rather than faith—because it teaches that the person must continually confess His sins and partake of the sacraments in order to be justified before God. Listen, however, to Paul's retort to such "works" systems as Sacrament theology: *"For by grace you have been saved through faith; and that, not of yourselves, it is the gift of God—not as a result of works, so that no one should boast. For we are His workmanship, created in Christ Jesus for good works, which God prepared beforehand, that we should walk in them" (Eph. 2:9-10)*. "Justification" (the judicial act of God of declaring the sinner righteous in His eyes upon the sinner's placing his faith in Jesus Christ) is a *one-time event*, not an on-going process (as sacrament Christianity teaches).

Thus, for the Catholic or Orthodox reader, your first challenge is to come to understand—and then put your faith in—the true gospel of grace. Salvation does not come through membership in the Catholic or Orthodox church or through the sacraments of these churches or through your good works. Salvation comes through repentance (a conscious turning away from your false belief system) and faith (a conscious turning to God's provision of Jesus Christ for your sin problem). Faith by definition is active. Faith, therefore, involves *accepting* God's free gift by inviting Jesus Christ to come into your life as your Savior. Have you, the Catholic or Orthodox reader, ever consciously put your faith in Christ alone for you salvation? If not, why not? Are you indifferent to the claims of Christ? Are you indifferent to the good news of salvation from sin and eternal life through faith in Jesus Christ? Are you trusting in your church membership or a wafer or your good works?

Jesus reserves some of His harshest words for the lukewarm Protestant—i.e., the Protestant who claims to be a "Christian" but who wants nothing to do with evangelical Christianity or being "born-again." Listen to Christ's fierce rebuke of the lukewarm or liberal Protestant: *"I know your deeds, that you are neither cold nor hot; I would rather that you were cold or hot. So because you are lukewarm, and neither hot nor cold, I will spit you out of My mouth. Because you say, 'I am rich, and have become wealthy, and have need of nothing,' and you do not know that you are wretched and miserable and poor and blind and naked, I advise you to buy from Me gold refined by fire, that you may become rich; and white garments, that you may clothe yourself and that the shame of your nakedness may not be revealed; and eye salve to anoint your eyes, that you may see" (Rev. 3:15-18).*

If you are a cultural, lukewarm, or liberal Protestant, what in reality is your belief system? Is it the fact that you think you are a "good" person? God's Word states emphatically that you are not: *"there is none righteous, not even one" (Rom. 3:10).* Is it because your supposed good deeds will outweigh your bad deeds? God's Word says they won't; in fact, God's Word says that your "good" deeds are but filthy rags before the perfectly holy, righteous, and sinless God (Isa. 64:6). Is it because you believe in "universalism"—that a "loving" God would not send anyone to Hell? God's Word states just the opposite: not only is God a God of perfect love, but He is also a God of perfect *justice.* Says Christ: *"for the gate is wide and the way is broad that leads to destruction, and many are those who enter by it; but the gate is small and the way is narrow that leads to life, and few are those who find it" (Matt. 7:13-14).* The problem, therefore, does not lie with God but with you, the liberal Protestant, who typically is not only ignorant of God's Word but is also ignorant of God's character. The Sacrament theology of the Catholics and Orthodoxes is in error because it teaches a false gospel—a salvation that is not by faith alone. On the other hand, the universalist, social theology of the liberal Protestantism is in error not only because it either rejects the need for salvation altogether (by teaching "universalism") or teaches salvation by good works, but also because it denies many or all of the other core doctrines of the faith: the deity of Christ, the resurrection of Christ, the sin nature of man, the inerrancy of the Scriptures, and the necessity of the new birth. As a result, the liberal Protestant never hears the true gospel. Instead the typical liberal Protestant flock on Sunday mornings hears nothing more than a feel-good social message that has little to do with the eternal truths of God's Word.

Are you a "Christian" who thinks you are going to make it to heaven because you're a morally upright person? The truth is that Jesus told Israel's most morally upright person that his righteousness was not good enough in God's eyes and that he too needed to be born again if he wanted to enter the kingdom of God (John 3:3-6). Tragically, the "morally upright" person is often the most difficult to reach with the gospel because such a person refuses to see that his own standard of righteousness falls so pitifully short of God's requirement of perfect righteousness. You and I can never live a perfectly righteous life. The only person who ever did was Jesus Christ, the Son of God. And because Christ lived a perfectly righteous life, God the Father imputes Christ's perfect righteousness for all eternity to any person who turns his heart back to God in true repentance and who puts his faith in the Crucifixion and Resurrection of Jesus Christ for his or her sin problem. Will you choose to exchange your supposed "goodness" for the imputed righteousness of Christ? When you make this choice—when you turn to Christ by faith and invite Him into your life—a supernatural transaction takes place: you are "born again." The Holy Spirit comes to indwell you for all eternity. You become a new creature in Christ. You have eternal life. Your sins are forgiven—past, present, and future. You are redeemed. You are reconciled with God. You are transferred out of the perishing kingdom of this world into the eternal kingdom of God. You become a child of God. You have direct access to God through prayer. You are delivered from spiritual darkness into light. You become the recipient of God's abundant grace. You become the object of Christ's perfect love—and much, much, more. Are not all of these incalculable and *true* riches compared to the temporal riches of this world? Says Jesus Himself: *"What does it profit a man if he gains the whole world but forfeits his soul?"* (Matt. 16:26).

C.   Born-Again Christians

For the born-again reader, salvation is not the issue confronting you in this book. Salvation for the born-again Christian centers on Evangelical theology (as opposed to sacrament theology or universalist theology or "good works" theology) and properly portrays the true grace-faith gospel of the Bible. Nevertheless, certain segments of evangelical Christianity teach error when it comes to a proper understanding of the end times. Let us examine some of the major errors.

Within evangelical Christianity, three positions are taught with regard to the end-times Millennial Kingdom of Jesus Christ. These positions are the "premillennial" position, the "postmillennial" position, and the "amillennial" position. Obviously, all three of these positions cannot be correct. Yet evangelical seminaries and evangelical theologians refuse to have a meeting of the minds over one of the basic issues of the end times—the true nature of the Millennial Kingdom.

Essentially, the premillennialist is a person who believes that Jesus Christ will return bodily to the earth before He establishes His reign of a thousand years upon the earth. The postmillennialist is a person who does not believe in a literal reign of Christ upon the earth after His Second Coming. Instead, he sees a kingdom of God being victoriously extended in the present world through the preaching of the gospel, and he believes that the world will be substantially Christianized prior to Christ's return. The amillennialist likewise is a person who does not believe in a literal reign of Christ upon the earth after His Second Coming, nor does he believe in a one-thousand-year period of world-wide peace and righteousness before the end of this present world order. Instead, he believes that Christ currently reigns over the earth from heaven, with the Church Age being a spiritual "millennium" of an undisclosed period of time. As does the postmillennialist, the amillennialist spiritualizes much of prophetic Scripture.

The postmillennial position is erroneous, however, for four basic reasons. First, the chronology of the book of Revelation—the definitive book on the end-times events—unequivocally teaches in Chapters 19 and 20 that Christ will return to earth *before* He establishes His one thousand year reign over the earth—the pre-millennial position. Second, Christ Himself teaches that His inter-advent kingdom will *not* be victoriously extended in the present world through the gospel nor will the world be eventually Christianized prior to His return. Instead, Christ states that (1) although His inter-advent kingdom (Christendom) will become the largest of the world's religions, it nevertheless will not take over the world entirely (Matt. 13:31-32) and (2) His inter-advent kingdom ("Christendom") will contain *counter-feit* Christians (sown by Satan) as well as true Christians (Matt. 13:24-30). Indeed, Christ in the Parable of the Sower (Matt. 13:18-23) states that many persons will *reject* the gospel between His advents. Third, Christ queries His disciples rhetorically in Luke 18:8: *"But when the Son of Man returns, will He find faith on the earth?"* The implication of the passage is that He will not find widespread faith when He returns. Today, even though perhaps as much as thirty percent of the world's population call themselves "Christian"—making Christianity the world's largest religion (just as Christ prophesied in His "Mustard Seed" parable), recent polls indicate that no more than ten to fifteen percent of the world's population is born-again and thus truly saved. Consequently, the postmillennial position not only contradicts the chronology given in the book of Revelation as well as the teachings of Christ in the Sower and Mustard Seed parables, it also contradicts the known empirical data. Fourth, Christ makes it clear that only a small percentage of people will be saved: *"the gate is small and the way is narrow which leads to life, and few will find it (Matt. 7:14)."*

The amillennial position is erroneous for several reasons as well. First, the book of Revelation clearly teaches—with six references—that Christ will reign over the earth for one thousand years (Rev. 20:4-6). Second, many of the Old Testament prophecies of the Millennial Kingdom simply cannot be spiritualized. For example, the Scripture passages presented in Appendix D (not an all-inclusive list) incontrovertibly describe the existence of a future *literal* Millennial Kingdom on earth. Third, the amillennialist, by cavalierly contending that the Church (because of Israel's corporate rejection of Christ) has now inherited God's promises to Israel, denigrates the irrevocable promises which God has made to Israel. The book of Romans refutes this amillenialist position by stating that God has not permanently rejected Israel but has only temporarily set her aside (Rom. 11:23-29). To be sure, when amillennial theologians and amillennial pastors choose to spiritualize the Bible's end-times prophecies rather than taking them at face value, they fall into eschatological quicksand—and, more importantly, rob their flocks of the grandeur and the truth of God's purposes for His covenant people Israel. God's Word teaches that Christ will reign over the earth for a thousand years (Rev. 20:4-6), that Israel will be the head of the nations during the thousand years (Isa. 49:22-23; 60:14-15; 61:6,7,9), and that Jerusalem will be the worship center of the world during the thousand years (Isa. 2:2-3; Mic.

4:1). Born-again Gentile Christians—including amillenialists—would do well to embrace these foundational truths in order to have an attitude of respect and joy toward Israel—both now and in the future when they, as resurrected Gentile Christians, return with Christ to serve Him during the Millennium Kingdom, a reign in which Israel will be exalted above the Gentile nations and will be the preeminent nation on earth (Isa. 49:22-23; 60:14-17; 61:6-9).

Here, then, is truth about the End Times: A terrifying and cataclysmic time of seven-year judgment will soon come upon the earth, during which time approximately three-fourths of the earth's post-Rapture population will be killed. Thirty days after the end of this seven-year Tribulation, Jesus Christ will return bodily to the earth to save Israel from annihilation at the hands of the earth's remaining armies who have maliciously gathered against her. Christ will quickly defeat these armies at the Battle of Armageddon. Shortly thereafter, Christ will gather to Jerusalem, and judge, all remaining persons on earth. Those who have put their faith in Him will be allowed to enter the Millennial Kingdom; those who have not will be slain. Forty-five days after His return to the earth, Jesus will then begin His Millennial reign over the earth, just as God's prophets foretold three thousand years ago.

Isn't it time for the Evangelical church to rid itself of the quicksand of post-millennialism and amillennialism once and for all? Isn't it time for the Evangelical church to awaken from its end-times slumber and begin telling the world of the horrors which await those who refuse to turn to Christ? Isn't it time for born-again Christians in the United States to get down on their knees in humble submission to Jesus Christ and to pray for national repentance? Isn't it time for born-again Christians throughout the world to center their lives around, and to focus their whole-hearted devotion on, the One whose return is so very near?

FOOTNOTES

1. Unger, Merrill F. *Unger's Bible Dictionary.* Chicago: Moody Press, 1978. pp. 114-115.

2. Boice, James Montgomery. *Genesis: An Expositional Commentary (Vol. 1).* Grand Rapids: Zondervan Publishing House, 1982. pp. 340-342.

3. Walvoord, John F. *The Revelation of Jesus Christ.* Chicago: Moody Press, 1966. pp. 250-251.

4. Marrs, Texe. *Mystery Mark of the New Age.* Westchester: Crossway Books, 1988. p. 23.

5. Huntington, Samuel P. *Foreign Affairs.* Summer 1993, Volume 73, Number 3. p. 22.

6. Huntington, Samuel P. *Foreign Affairs.* Summer 1993, Volume 73, Number 3. pp. 25-26.

COMMON END-TIMES ERRORS AND MISCONCEPTIONS

ERROR: the Battle of Armageddon takes place during the Tribulation period.

TRUTH: the Battle of Armageddon takes place after the Tribulation—when Christ returns bodily to the earth (thirty days later, Dan. 12:11-12) to save Jerusalem and Israel from annihilation (Rev. 19:11-21).

ERROR: "Babylon the Great" is a re-built city in Iraq.

TRUTH: The city of Babylon currently being built in present-day Iraq is 140 miles from the nearest seaport. It would thus be impossible for the laments of the shipmasters and passengers and sailors pictured in Revelation 18:17-19 to take place if the rebuilt city of Babylon is hit by a thermonuclear weapon (or a supernatural fire brought out of heaven from God) during the Tribulation. No passenger on a ship positioned 140 miles from a city could see the "smoke of her burning"—because such a ship is at least a hundred miles too far over the horizon. Instead, "Babylon the Great" is the revived Roman Empire—a Japhethite (i.e., from the line of Japheth) Western Empire (Dan. 2:36-43; 7:15:28; 9:24-27). Iraqis are Shemites (i.e., from the line of Shem).

ERROR: A Jew (a Shemite) could be the Antichrist.

TRUTH: The Antichrist cannot be a Jew; instead he will be a Japhethite (a Caucasian) and will be a descendent of the ancient Roman Empire (Dan. 9:26).

ERROR: An Arab (also a Shemite) could be the Antichrist.

TRUTH: The Antichrist cannot be an Arab; instead he will be a Japhethite (a Caucasian) and will be a descendent of the ancient Roman Empire (Dan. 9:26).

MISCONCEPTION: The Seal judgments and perhaps most of the Trumpet judgments take place during the first half of the Tribulation.

BETTER EXPLANATION: Only the *first* Seal judgment takes place during the first half of the Tribulation. The first Seal judgment depicts the Antichrist (the rider on the white horse) gaining control over a good portion of the earth (*"he went out conquering and to conquer"*) during the first forty-two months of the Tribulation. He does this by expanding his Empire peacefully beyond his ten-nation core to the entirety of present-day Christendom (i.e., those nations whose predominant religion is Christianity—principally the Western world). The second through fourth Seal judgments, on the other hand, result in the death of *one-fourth* of the earth's post-Rapture population (Rev. 6:3-8). The magnitude of such a death toll obviously suggests *great* tribulation and therefore best fits into the context of the second half of the Tribulation—the timeframe which Jesus describes in Matthew 24:22: *"and unless those days had been cut short, no life would have been saved."* As a result, the first Seal judgment is the only one of the Seals, Trumpets, or Bowls to take place during the first half of the Tribulation.

POSSIBLE MISCONCEPTION: the Antichrist's forty-two-month rule/authority takes place during the second half of the Tribulation.

BETTER EXPLANATIONS:

1. the Antichrist's authority over the earth (Rev. 13:1-5) perhaps best fits the first half of the Tribulation, when he goes out as an "angel of light" and expands his Empire peacefully (and beyond its ten-nation core) throughout present-day Christendom (Rev. 6:1-2). Because (1) the Antichrist cannot touch the inner court of the Jerusalem temple due to the power of God's two witnesses (Rev. 11:1-5); (2) the Antichrist is thwarted supernaturally in his efforts to destroy believing Jews who flee Jerusalem at the mid-point of the Tribulation (Rev. 12:13-16); and (3) the Antichrist's Empire is destroyed, utterly and forever, on the final day of the Tribulation (Rev. 16:17-20), it could be argued that the Antichrist does not have "authority" (or at least full authority) over the earth during the second half of the Tribulation. In fact, it could be suggested that the Antichrist has authority over the earth during the first half, but that the Lord's two Jerusalem witnesses are granted authority over the earth during the second half (Rev. 11:3-6): *"And I will grant authority to my two witnesses, and they will prophesy for twelve hundred and sixty days. . . . And if anyone desires to harm them, fire proceeds out of their and devours their enemies; and if anyone desires to harm them, in this manner he must be killed. These have power to shut up the sky, in order that rain may not fall during the days of their prophesying; and they have power over the waters to turn them into blood, and to smite the earth with every plague, as often as they desire."*

(or)

2. the forty-two months of the Antichrist's authority takes place *concurrently* (during the second half of the Tribulation) with the authority of the Lord's two Jerusalem witnesses. If this is the case, then the authority of the Antichrist—though great—is not unlimited (because of the supernatural powers of the two witnesses).

ERROR: the two Jerusalem "Witnesses" prophesy for God during the first half of the Tribulation.

TRUTH: the two Witnesses prophesy for God during the second half of the Tribulation (as well as supernaturally protect the inner court of the Jerusalem temple)—during the time when Israel and Jerusalem are overrun by the Antichrist's armies (Rev. 11:1-13).

ERROR: a Pope will be the Antichrist.

TRUTH: the Antichrist will be a world *political* figure, not a religious figure. Furthermore, the Antichrist will hate the "harlot" (Apostate Christendom) and will "devour" (kill) her (Rev. 17:16). If the Antichrist were a pope, then, according to Revelation 17:16, he would have to kill himself. This, of course, does not happen because the Antichrist is still alive at the Lord's bodily return after the Tribulation.

ERROR: a Pope will be the False Prophet.

TRUTH: the False Prophet will be an anti-Christian, New Age *occultist* (Rev. 13:11, 15-17). He will hate the pope and the pope's Apostate Christianity (Rev. 17:16), and will demand that the world worship the Antichrist rather than the Christ of the Apostate Church. Because the Antichrist will "devour" (kill) Apostate Christendom, the Antichrist would thus have to kill the False Prophet if he were a Pope. The False Prophet, however, is alive at the return of Christ (only to be consigned by Christ to the Lake of Fire after the Battle of Armageddon); thus, the False Prophet cannot be a Pope.

MISCONCEPTION: television will be the medium that broadcasts the return of Christ to the earth, so that "every eye can see" (Rev. 1:7).

BETTER EXPLANATION: much of the broadcasting capability of the world will have been destroyed during the Sino-Western (or Sino-Russo-Western) conflagration near the beginning of the seventh year of the Tribulation. Virtually all of the world's remaining broadcasting and viewing capability will be destroyed on the final day of the Tribulation when God strikes the earth with the most ferocious earthquake in human history (Rev. 16:17-20). Consequently, sufficient worldwide capacity will not likely exist in such a way that "every eye can see" the return of Christ by way of television. Instead, the return of Christ thirty days after the Tribulation (Dan. 12:11-12) will be preceded by signs in the sky (Matt. 24:29-30), will be a unique day in human history, and will be accompanied by His holy angels in flaming fire (II Thess. 1:7)—which every remaining person on earth will be able to look up and see.

ERROR: the Antichrist's Empire will be a ten-nation Arab Confederacy.

TRUTH: the Antichrist's Empire will begin as a ten-nation (predominantly) Western coalition—a revived Roman Empire—and will expand to encompass all of present-day Christendom by the mid-point of the Tribulation. After the mid-point of the Tribulation, the Antichrist will use military force to slaughter both the Islamic Middle East (including the Arab nations) and defenseless sub-Sahara Africa—causing the death of one-fourth of the earth's post-Rapture population (Dan. 11:40-43; Rev 6:3-8).

ERROR: the Antichrist's Empire will be a ten-nation Mediterranean Confederacy.

TRUTH: the nation's surrounding the Mediterranean Sea are not powerful enough militarily to fit the necessary end-times description, "who is like the Beast, and who is able to wage war with him?" Likewise, these Mediterranean nations are not wealthy enough to fit the necessary end-times description, "and your merchants were the great men of the earth."

MISCONCEPTION: the Antichrist's Empire will consist of ten Western European nations.

BETTER EXPLANATION: Western Europe, by itself, does not possess the military strength to fit the necessary end-times description, "who is like the Beast, and who is able to wage war with him?" The so-called "Group of Eight"—the United States, Russia, Great Britain, France, Germany, Italy, Japan, and Canada—better fits the necessary end-times "fingerprints" and descriptions at this point. Thus, the best conclusion with regard to the identity of the ten core nations of the Antichrist's Empire points to the "Group of Eight" expanding to a "Group of Ten."

ERROR: the Antichrist's Empire will be a German-led "Fourth Reich."

TRUTH: Germany, because it exterminated six million Jews during WW II, will never be trusted by Israel to broker a Middle East peace treaty. In addition, Germany does not have the military muscle to pull the strings of a ten-nation "world" empire. Germany, because of its advanced economy, will likely be a player in the Antichrist's ten-nation core, but it will not be the leading player.

MISCONCEPTION: the seventh "seal" judgment in the book of Revelation introduces the "trumpet" judgments, and the seventh trumpet judgment introduces the "bowl" judgments.

BETTER EXPLANATION: the seventh seal and the seventh trumpet are stand-alone judgments themselves. (see Appendix B)

ERROR: the seven bowl judgments take place during a thirty-day period immediately following the end of the seven-year Tribulation.

TRUTH: the seven bowl judgments will take place during (and near the end of) the seven-year Tribulation. The Tribulation lasts seven years, not seven years and thirty days. Daniel's "Seventieth Week" lasts seven years, not seven years and thirty days. The seventh bowl judgment takes place on the final day of the seven-year Tribulation.

THE OUTLINE OF REVELATION

THE REVELATION TO JOHN

Prologue [1:1-8]

I. THINGS PAST: "THE THINGS WHICH YOU HAVE SEEN" (CHAPTER 1)

    A. John's Patmos Vision and Command to Write [1:9-20]

II. THINGS PRESENT: "THE THINGS WHICH ARE" (CHAPTERS 2 AND 3)

    A. The Spiritual Condition of Seven First Century Churches [2:1 - 3:22]

III. THINGS FUTURE: "THE THINGS WHICH SHALL TAKE PLACE AFTER THESE THINGS"   (CHAPTERS 4 THROUGH 22)

    A. The Scene in Heaven before the First (of three) Series of Tribulation Judgments [4:1 - 5:14]

    B. The First Series of Tribulation Judgments on Earth: the Seven Seal Judgments [6:1-17]

    Parenthetical: The Calling Out of 144,000 Jews—and the Salvation of a Great Multitude during the Tribulation [7:1-18]

    B. The First Series of Tribulation Judgments on Earth: the Seven Seal Judgments (Continued) [8:1]

    C. The Scene in Heaven before the Second Series of Tribulation Judgments [8:2-6]

D. The Second Series of Tribulation Judgments on Earth:
the Seven Trumpet Judgments [8:7 - 9:21]

Parenthetical: The Mighty Angel and the Little Scroll [10:1-11]

Parenthetical: The Lord's Two Witnesses in Jerusalem [11:1-13]

D. The Second Series of Tribulation Judgments on Earth:
the Seven Trumpet Judgments (Continued) [11:14-19]

*Parenthetical: The Efforts of Satan to Thwart God's Purposes at the
First and Second Advents of Christ [12:1 - 13:1]*

*Parenthetical: The Rise and Reign of the Antichrist and the False
Prophet [13:2-19]*

*Parenthetical: A Foreshadowing of Christ's Victory Over All His
Enemies [14:1-22]*

E. The Scene in Heaven before the Third (and Final)
Series of Tribulation Judgments [15:1 - 16:1]

F. The Third Series of Tribulation Judgments on Earth:
the Seven Bowl Judgments [16:2-21]

*Parenthetical: The Destruction of Apostate Christendom ("The Great
Harlot") [17:1-18]*

*Parenthetical: The Destruction of the Antichrist's Godless World
Empire ("Babylon the Great") [18:1-24]*

G. The Scene in Heaven before the Second Coming of Christ [19:1-10]

H. The Second Coming of Christ to the Earth [19:11-16]

I.   The Battle of Armageddon—and Christ's Victory over All His Enemies [19:17-21]

J.   The Millennial Kingdom on Earth [20:1-3]

Parenthetical: The Resurrection of Tribulation Martyrs and Tribulation Saints to Reign with Christ for a Thousand Years [20:4-6]

K.   The Final Rebellion and Defeat of Satan [20:7-10]

L.   The Second Resurrection; The Destruction of the Present Heavens and Earth; and The Great White Throne Judgment [20:11-15]

M.   The Creation of the New Heavens and New Earth; and the Eternal Kingdom in Heaven [21:1-4]

Parenthetical: God's Invitation for Every Man and Woman to Receive the Free Gift of Salvation from Sin [21:5-8]

Parenthetical: A Prophetic Description of the New Jerusalem [21:9 - 22:5]

Epilogue [22:6-21]

THE TEXT OF THE OLIVET DISCOURSE

I. CHRIST'S PROPHECY ABOUT THE JERUSALEM TEMPLE (24:1-2)

And Jesus came out from the temple and was going away when His disciples came up to point out the temple buildings to Him. And He answered and said to them, "Do you not see all these things? Truly I say to you, not one stone here shall be left upon another which will not be torn down."

II. THE DISCIPLES' QUESTIONS ABOUT THIS PROPHECY (24:3)

And as He was sitting on the Mount of Olives, the disciples came to Him privately, saying, "Tell us, when will these things be, and what will be the sign of Your coming and of the end of the age?"

III. CHRIST'S ANSWERS TO THE DISICPLES QUESTIONS AND CHRIST'S EXPLANATION OF THE END-TIMES EVENTS (24:3 - 25:46)

A. The Church Age (24:4-8)

And Jesus answered and said to them, "See to it that no one misleads you. For many will come in My name, saying, 'I am the Christ,' and will mislead many. And you will be hearing of wars and rumors of wars; see that you are not frightened, for those things must take place, but that is not yet the end. For nation will rise against nation, and kingdom against kingdom, and in various places there will be famines and earthquakes. But all these things are merely the beginning of birth pangs.

B. The Tribulation Period (24:9-14)

"Then they will deliver you to tribulation, and will kill you, and you will be hated by all nations on account of My name. And at that time many will fall away and will deliver up one another and hate one another. And many false prophets will arise, and will mislead many. And because lawlessness is increased, most people's love will grow cold. But the one who endures to the end, he shall be saved. And this gospel of the kingdom shall be preached in the whole world for a witness to all the nations, and then the end shall come.

Parenthetical: Christ's Exhortation to Flee the Abomination of Desolation, and Christ's Pronouncement of the Severity of the Second Half of the Tribulation
(24:15-22)

"Therefore, when you see the abomination of desolation which was spoken of through Daniel the prophet, standing in the holy place (let the reader understand), then let those who are in Judea flee to the mountains; let him who is on the housetop not go down to get the things out that are in his house; and let him who is in the field not turn back to get his cloak.

"But woe to those who are with child and to those who nurse babes in those days! But pray that your flight may not be in the winter, or on a Sabbath; for then there will be a great tribulation, such as has not occurred since the beginning of the world until now, nor ever shall. And unless those days had been cut short, no life would have been saved; but for the sake of the elect those days shall be cut short.

Parenthetical: Christ's Exhortation to Avoid False Christs While He is Away
(24:23-28)

"Then if anyone says to you, 'Behold, here is the Christ,' or 'There He is,' do not believe him. For false Christs and false prophets will arise and will show great signs and wonders, so as to mislead, if possible, even the elect. Behold, I have told you in advance. If, therefore, they say to you, 'Behold, He is in the wilderness,' do not go forth, or, 'Behold, He is in the inner rooms,' do not believe them. For just as the lightning comes from the east, and flashes even to the west, so shall the coming of the Son of Man be. Wherever the corpse is, there the vultures will gather.

C.   The Second Coming of Jesus Christ to the Earth
(24:29-31)

"But immediately after the tribulation of those days the sun will be darkened, and the moon will not give its light, and the stars will fall from the sky, and the powers of the heavens will be shaken, and then the sign of the Son of Man will appear in the sky, and then all the tribes of the earth will mourn, and they will see the Son of Man coming on the clouds of the sky with power and great glory. And He will send forth His angels with a great trumpet and they will gather together His elect from the four winds, from one end of the sky to the other.

Parenthetical: The Parable of the Fig Tree—and the Sign of the End of the Age
(24:32-35)

"Now learn the parable from the fig tree: when its branch has already become tender, and puts forth its leaves, you know that summer is near; even so you too, when you see all these things, recognize that He is near, right at the door. Truly I say to you, this generation will not pass away until all these things take place. Heaven and earth will pass away, but My words shall not pass away.

Parenthetical: Christ's First Teaching on the Rapture and His Exhortation to be Alert for It at All Times
(24:36-44)

"But of that day and hour no one knows, not even the angels of heaven, nor the Son, but the Father alone. For the coming of the Son of Man will be just like the days of Noah. For as in those days which were before the flood they were eating and drinking, they were marrying and giving in marriage, until the day that Noah entered the ark, and they did not understand until the flood came and took them all away; so shall the coming of the Son of Man be.

"Then there shall be two men in the field; one will be taken, and one will be left. Two women will be grinding at the mill; one will be taken, and one will be left. Therefore, be on the alert, for you do not know which day your Lord is coming.

"But be sure of this, that if the head of the house had known at what time of the night the thief was coming, he would have been on the alert and would not have allowed his house to be broken into. For this reason you be ready too; for the Son of Man is coming at an hour when you do not think He will.

Parenthetical: Christ's Promise of Blessing and Reward for Faithful, Sensible Servanthood While He is Away
(24:45-51)

"Who then is the faithful and sensible slave whom his master put in charge of his household to give them their food at the proper time? Blessed is that slave whom his master finds so doing when he comes. Truly I say to you, that he will put him in charge of all his possessions.

"But if that evil slave says in his heart, 'My master is not coming for a long time,' and shall begin to beat his fellow slaves and eat and drink with drunkards; the master of that slave will come on a day when he does not expect him and at an hour which he does not know, and shall cut him in pieces and assign him a place with the hypocrites; weeping shall be there and the gnashing of teeth.

Parenthetical: The Parable of the Ten Virgins—the Picture of Christ's Coming for His Own at the Rapture (25:1-13)

"Then the kingdom of heaven will be comparable to ten virgins, who took their lamps, and went out to meet the bridegroom. And five of them were foolish, and five were prudent. For when the foolish took their lamps, they took no oil with them, but the prudent took oil in flasks along with their lamps.

"Now while the bridegroom was delaying, they all got drowsy and began to sleep. "But at midnight there was a shout, 'Behold, the bridegroom! Come out to meet him.' Then all those virgins rose, and trimmed their lamps. And the foolish said to the prudent, 'Give us some of your oil, for our lamps are going out.' But the prudent answered, saying, 'No, there will not be enough for us and you too; go instead to the dealers and buy some for yourselves.' And while they were going away to make the purchase, the bridegroom came, and those who were ready went in with him to the wedding feast; and the door was shut.

"And later the other virgins also came, saying, 'Lord, lord, open up for us.' But he answered and said, 'Truly I say to you, I do not know you.' Be on the alert then, for you do not know the day nor the hour.

Parenthetical: The Parable of the Talents (25:14-30)

"For it [the kingdom of heaven] is just like a man about to go on a journey, who called his own slaves, and entrusted his possessions to them. And to one he gave five talents, to another, two, and to another, one, each according to his own ability; and he went on his journey. Immediately the one who had received the five talents went and traded with them, and gained five more talents. In the same manner the one who had received the two talents gained two more. But he who received the one talent went away and dug in the ground, and hid his master's money.

"Now after a long time the master of those slaves came and settled accounts with them. And the one who had received the five talents came up and brought five more talents, saying, 'Master, you entrusted five talents to me; see, I have gained five more talents.' His master said to him, 'Well done, good and faithful slave; you were faithful with a few things, I will put you in charge of many things, enter into the joy of your master.' The one also who had received the two talents came up and said, 'Master, you entrusted to me two talents; see, I have gained two more talents.' His master said to him, 'Well done, good and faithful slave; you were faithful with a few things, I will put you in charge of many things; enter into the joy of your master.'

"And the one also who had received the one talent came up and said, 'Master, I knew you to be a hard man, reaping where you did not sow, and gathering where you scattered no seed. And I was afraid, and went away and hid your talent

in the ground; see, you have what is yours.' But his master answered and said to him, 'You wicked, lazy slave, you knew that I reap where I did not sow, and gather where I scattered no seed. 'Then you ought to have put my money in the bank, and on my arrival I would have received my money back with interest. Therefore, take away the talent from him, and give it to the one who has the ten talents.' For to everyone who has shall more be given, and he shall have an abundance; but from the one who does not have, even what he does have shall be taken away. And cast out the worthless slave into the outer darkness; in that place there shall be weeping and gnashing of teeth.

D.   The Judgment of the Remaining Nations by Christ (25:31-46)

"But when the Son of Man comes in His glory, and all the angels with Him, then He will sit on His glorious throne. And all the nations will be gathered before Him; and He will separate them from one another, as the shepherd separates the sheep from the goats; and He will put the sheep on His right, and the goats on the left.

"Then the King will say to those on His right, 'Come, you who are blessed of My Father, inherit the kingdom prepared for you from the foundation of the world. 'For I was hungry, and you gave Me something to eat; I was thirsty, and you gave Me drink; I was a stranger, and you invited Me in; naked, and you clothed Me; I was sick, and you visited Me; I was in prison, and you came to Me.' Then the righteous will answer Him, saying, 'Lord, when did we see You hungry, and feed You, or thirsty, and give You drink? And when did we see You a stranger, and invite You in, or naked, and clothe You? And when did we see You sick, or in prison, and come to You?' And the King will answer and say to them, 'Truly I say to you, to the extent that you did it to one of these brothers of Mine, even the least of them, you did it to Me.'

"Then He will also say to those on His left, 'Depart from Me, accursed ones, into the eternal fire which has been prepared for the devil and his angels; for I was hungry, and you gave Me nothing to eat; I was thirsty, and you gave Me nothing to drink; I was a stranger, and you did not invite Me in; naked, and you did not clothe Me; sick, and in prison, and you did not visit Me.' Then they themselves also will answer, saying, 'Lord, when did we see You hungry, or thirsty, or a stranger, or naked, or sick, or in prison, and did not take care of You?' Then He will answer them, saying, 'Truly I say to you, to the extent that you did not do it to one of the least of these, you did not do it to Me.' And these will go away into eternal punishment, but the righteous into eternal life."

MILLENNIAL KINGDOM VERSES

The following are some of the verses which attest to and describe the future literal reign of Jesus Christ over the earth:

Then a shoot will spring from the stem of Jesse, and a branch from his roots will bear fruit. And the Spirit of the Lord will rest on Him, the spirit of wisdom and understanding, the spirit of counsel and strength, the spirit of knowledge and the fear of the Lord. And He will delight in the fear of the Lord, and He will not judge by what His eyes see, nor make a decision by what His ears hear. But with righteousness He will judge the poor, and decide with fairness for the afflicted of the earth; and He will strike the earth with the rod of His mouth, and with the breath of His lips He will slay the wicked. Also righteousness will be the belt about His loins, and faithfulness the belt about His waist.

And the wolf will dwell with the lamb, and the leopard will lie down with the kid, and the calf and the young lion and the fatling together; and a little boy will lead them. Also the cow and the bear will graze; their young will lie down together; and the lion will eat straw like the ox. And the nursing child will play by the hole of the cobra, and the weaned child will put his hand on the viper's den. They will not hurt or destroy in all My holy mountain, for the earth will be full of the knowledge of the Lord as the waters cover the sea.

Then it will come about in that day that the nations will resort to the root of Jesse, who will stand as a signal for the peoples; and His resting place will be glorious (Isa. 11:1-10).

And the Lord will be king over all the earth; in that day the Lord will be the only one, and His name the only one. All the land will be changed into a plain from Geba to Rimmon south of Jerusalem; but Jerusalem will rise and remain on its site from Benjamin's Gate as far as the place of the First Gate to the Corner Gate, and from the Tower of Hananel to the king's wine presses. And people will live in it, and there will be no more curse, for Jerusalem will dwell in security (Zech. 14:9-11).

Then it will come about that any who are left of all the nations that went against Jerusalem will go up from year to year to worship the King, the Lord of hosts, and to celebrate the Feast of Booths. And it will be that whichever of the families of the earth does not go up to Jerusalem to worship the King, the Lord of hosts, there will be no rain on them (Zech. 14:16-17).

In that day there will be inscribed on the bells of the horses, "HOLY TO THE LORD." And the cooking pots in the Lord's house will be like the bowls before the altar. And every cooking pot in Jerusalem and in Judah will be holy to the Lord of hosts; and all who sacrifice will come and take of them and boil in them. And there will no longer be a Canaanite in the house of the Lord of hosts in that day (Zech. 14:20-21).

'Alas! for that day is great, there is none like it; and it is the time of Jacob's distress, but he will be saved from it. And it shall come about on that day,' declares the Lord of hosts, 'that I will break his yoke from off their neck, and will tear off their bonds; and strangers shall no longer make them their slaves. 'But they shall serve the Lord their God, and David their king, whom I will raise up for them.'

'And fear not, O Jacob My servant,' declares the Lord, 'and do not be dismayed, O Israel; for behold, I will save you from afar, and your offspring from the land of their captivity. And Jacob shall return, and shall be quiet and at ease, and no one shall make him afraid. For I am with you,' declares the Lord, 'to save you; for I will destroy completely all the nations where I have scattered you, only I will not destroy you completely. But I will chasten you justly, and will by no means leave you unpunished' (Jer. 30:7-11).

And they will no longer defile themselves with their idols, or with their detestable things, or with any of their transgressions; but I will deliver them from all their dwelling places in which they have sinned, and will cleanse them. And they will be My people, and I will be their God. And My servant David will be king over them, and they will all have one shepherd; and they will walk in My ordinances, and keep My statutes, and observe them. And they shall live on the land that I gave to Jacob My servant, in which your fathers lived; and they will live on it, they, and their sons, and their sons' sons, forever; and David My servant shall be their prince forever.

Therefore, I will deliver My flock, and they will no longer be a prey; and I will judge between one sheep and another. Then I will set over them one shepherd, My servant David, and he will feed them; he will feed them himself and be their shepherd. And I, the Lord, will be their God, and My servant David will be prince among them; I, the Lord, have spoken.

And I will make a covenant of peace with them and eliminate harmful beasts from the land, so that they may live securely in the wilderness and sleep in the woods. And I will make them and the places around My hill a blessing. And I will cause showers to come down in their season; they will be showers of blessing. Also the tree of the field will yield its fruit, and the earth will yield its increase, and they will be secure on their land. Then they will know that I am the Lord, when I have broken the bars of their yoke and have delivered them from the hand of those who enslaved them. And they will no longer be a prey to the nations, and the beasts of the earth will not devour them; but they will live securely, and no one will make them afraid (Eze. 34:23-28).

"Therefore, wait for Me," declares the Lord, "For the day when I rise up to the prey. Indeed, My decision is to gather nations, to assemble kingdoms, to pour out on them My indignation, all My burning anger; for all the earth will be devoured by the fire of My zeal. For then I will give to the peoples purified lips, that all of them may call on the name of the Lord, to serve Him shoulder to shoulder.

"From beyond the rivers of Ethiopia My worshipers, My dispersed ones, will bring My offerings. In that day you will feel no shame because of all your deeds by which you have rebelled against Me; for then I will remove from your midst your proud, exulting ones, and you will never again be haughty on My holy mountain. But I will leave among you a humble and lowly people, and they will take refuge in the name of the Lord. The remnant of Israel will do no wrong and tell no lies, nor will a deceitful tongue be found in their mouths; for they shall feed and lie down with no one to make them tremble."

Shout for joy, O daughter of Zion! Shout in triumph, O Israel! Rejoice and exult with all your heart, O daughter of Jerusalem! The Lord has taken away His judgments against you, He has cleared away your enemies. The King of Israel, the Lord, is in your midst; you will fear disaster no more. In that day it will be said to Jerusalem: "Do not be afraid, O Zion; do not let your hands fall limp. The Lord your God is in your midst, a victorious warrior. He will exult over you with joy, He will be quiet in His love, He will rejoice over you with shouts of joy" (Zeph. 3:8-17).

So many peoples and mighty nations will come to seek the Lord of hosts in Jerusalem and to entreat the favor of the Lord. Thus says the Lord of hosts, "In those days ten men from all the nations will grasp the garment of a Jew saying, 'Let us go with you, for we have heard that God is with you' " (Zech. 8:22-23).

"The wolf and the lamb shall graze together, and the lion shall eat straw like the ox; and dust shall be the serpent's food. They shall do no evil or harm in all My holy mountain," says the Lord (Isa. 65:25).

When the Lord will have compassion on Jacob, and again choose Israel, and settle them in their own land, then strangers will join them and attach themselves to the house of Jacob. And the peoples will take them along and bring them to their place, and the house of Israel will possess them as an inheritance in the land of the Lord as male servants and female servants; and they will take their captors captive, and will rule over their oppressors (Isa. 14:1-2).

Thus says the Lord God, "Behold, I will lift up My hand to the nations, and set up My standard to the peoples; and they will bring your sons in their bosom, And your daughters will be carried on their shoulders. And kings will be your guardians, and their princesses your nurses. They will bow down to you with their faces to the earth, and lick the dust of your feet; and you will know that I am the Lord; those who hopefully wait for Me will not be put to shame" (Isa. 49:22-23).

And the sons of those who afflicted you will come bowing to you, and all those who despised you will bow themselves at the soles of your feet; and they will call you the city of the Lord, The Zion of the Holy One of Israel. Whereas you have been forsaken and hated with no one passing through, I will make you an everlasting pride, a joy from generation to generation (Isa. 60:13-15).

But you will be called the priests of the Lord; you will be spoken of as ministers of our God. You will eat the wealth of nations, and in their riches you will boast. Instead of your shame you will have a double portion, and instead of humiliation they will shout for joy over their portion. Therefore, they will possess a double portion in their land, everlasting joy will be theirs. Then their offspring will be known among the nations, and their descendants in the midst of the peoples. All who see them will recognize them because they are the offspring whom the Lord has blessed (Isa. 61:6-7,9).

And it will come about in the last days that the mountain of the house of the Lord will be established as the chief of the mountains. It will be raised above the hills, and the peoples will stream to it. And many nations will come and say, "Come and let us go up to the mountain of the Lord and to the house of the God of Jacob, that He may teach us about His ways and that we may walk in His paths." For from Zion will go forth the law, even the word of the Lord from Jerusalem.

And He will judge between many peoples and render decisions for mighty, distant nations. Then they will hammer their swords into plowshares and their spears into pruning hooks; nation will not lift up sword against nation, and never again will they train for war (Micah 4:1-3).

Then the nations that are left round about you will know that I, the Lord, have rebuilt the ruined places and planted that which was desolate; I, the Lord, have spoken and will do it (Ezek. 36:36).

"At that time I will bring you in, even at the time when I gather you together; Indeed, I will give you renown and praise among all the peoples of the earth, when I restore your fortunes before your eyes," says the Lord (Zeph. 3:20).

For Zion's sake I will not keep silent, and for Jerusalem's sake I will not keep quiet, until her righteousness goes forth like brightness, and her salvation like a torch that is burning. And the nations will see your righteousness, and all kings your glory; and you will be called by a new name, which the mouth of the Lord will designate.

You will also be a crown of beauty in the hand of the Lord, and a royal diadem in the hand of your God. It will no longer be said to you, "Forsaken," nor to your land will it any longer be said, "Desolate"; but you will be called, "My delight is in her," and your land," Married "; for the Lord delights in you, and to Him your land will be married. For as a young man marries a virgin, so your sons will marry you; and as the bridegroom rejoices over the bride, so your God will rejoice over you.

On your walls, O Jerusalem, I have appointed watchmen; all day and all night they will never keep silent. You who remind the Lord, take no rest for yourselves; and give Him no rest until He establishes and makes Jerusalem a praise in the earth.

The Lord has sworn by His right hand and by His strong arm, "I will never again give your grain as food for your enemies; nor will foreigners drink your new wine, for which you have labored." But those who garner it will eat it, and praise the Lord; and those who gather it will drink it in the courts of My sanctuary (Isa. 62:1-9).

Then I saw an angel coming down from heaven, holding the key of the abyss and a great chain in his hand. And he laid hold of the dragon, the serpent of old, who is the devil and Satan, and bound him for a thousand years; and he threw him into the abyss, and shut it and sealed it over him, so that he would not deceive the nations any longer, until the thousand years were completed; after these things he must be released for a short time.

Then I saw thrones, and they sat on them, and judgment was given to them. And I saw the souls of those who had been beheaded because of their testimony of Jesus and because of the word of God, and those who had not worshiped the beast or his image, and had not received the mark on their forehead and on their hand; and they came to life and reigned with Christ for a thousand years. The rest of the dead did not come to life until the thousand years were completed. This is the first resurrection. Blessed and holy is the one who has a part in the first resurrection; over these the second death has no power, but they will be priests of God and of Christ and will reign with Him for a thousand years (Rev. 20:1-6).

On that day the Lord made a covenant with Abram, saying, "To your descendants I have given this land, from the river of Egypt [the Nile] a far as the great river, the river Euphrates (Gen. 15:18).

TRUMP – PUTIN – XI

[As of this writing, a tragic and destructive war rages in the Ukraine after an unprovoked invasion by Russia.]

Despite their obvious political differences, America's Donald Trump, Russia's Vladimir Putin, and China's Xi Jinping have one thing in common: each is an ardent nationalist. Donald Trump is a pro-business, "America first" nationalist; Vladimir Putin is an authoritarian, "Russia first" nationalist (who sometimes pays lip service to globalism), and Xi Jinping is a communist, "China first" nationalist (who also sometimes pays lip service to globalism). But none are true globalists.

In opposition to the nationalism of Trump, Putin, and Xi are such notable globalists (some deceased) as Nelson Rockefeller, Henry Kissinger, George H.W. Bush, Bill Clinton, Hillary Clinton, George W. Bush, Barack Obama, Joe Biden, Mikhael Gorbachev, Emmanuel Macron, Justin Trudeau, Angela Merkel, George Soros, Klaus Schwab, and Bill Gates. Mark it well, dear reader, the world political battle today is between nationalism and globalism—and the stakes are high.

As the Rapture and subsequent Tribulation period draw ever so close, the student of Bible prophecy can be certain that globalism will prevail: Forces in the West will be set in motion after the Rapture to establish a one-world government (led by the Antichrist) to pursue such utopian goals as universal human rights, more economic equity among nations, global sustainability, and saving the earth from environmental chaos.

Globalist forces in America have succeeded in removing Donald Trump from power, thus allowing America's political elites once again to further their globalist and one-world government intentions. Though America might see a return to nationalism in the short term, the long-term die is cast: America will be globalist. Furthermore, once the Rapture takes place (causing the departure of the born-again Christians, who for the most part vote nationalist), globalists will gain complete control of the United States.

Globalist forces, however, have not succeeded in reigning in Vladimir Putin. Putin sees the world as *tri-polar*—the leading players being the United States, Russia, and China. This is why Putin can "make nice" with the United States at times and, at other times, make handshake deals with Xi Jinping. In a January 27, 2021 virtual address to the World Economic Forum, Putin noted that a "normalization of relations with between Russia and the U.S. would meet the interests of both countries and, considering their special responsibility for maintaining global security and stability, of the entire international community." Yet, one year later Putin can shake hands Xi Jinping on what now appears be Xi's support of Russia's Ukraine invasion in exchange for Putin's support of what will likely be China's attempt to take over Taiwan. Globalists, in contrast, seek a *uni-polar* world, led by the West (principally, the United States,

Canada, Europe and Japan). Putin decries the uni-polarity of the West's framework for a New World Order and asserted on March 18, 2022 that the forces behind the New World Order "are deliberately creating economic hardships around the globe in order to push the 'Great Reset' on humanity."

Meanwhile, the Russian invasion of the Ukraine has turned into a nightmare for Putin, who in the eyes of most has overnight become a murderous villain. As such, it is doubtful that Putin can survive politically on the world stage. Indeed, the current hardships on Russia's citizenry caused by the world's sanctions will be blamed on Putin. As a result, it seems likely that Russia (perhaps with behind-the-scenes pressure from powerful non-Russian globalists) eventually will choose someone more in the mold of globalist Mikhael Gorbachev to succeed Putin. When this occurs (whether before or after the Rapture), both America and Russia will be led by globalists—and the vast majority of their respective post-Rapture citizenries will readily support the idea of combining forces (backed by their massive nuclear arsenals) to form a one-world government. The United States and Russia will be on the same side of the globalist net and will be the dominant countries in the Antichrist's initial ten-nation coalition. Today's tri-polar world of the United States, Russia, and China will become a bi-polar world of the Antichrist-led ten-nation coalition and China. In the eyes of many, the elusive goal of world peace will finally be within reach.

For sure, Xi Jinping will not allow himself to be brought into this Western-world attempt at a one-world government. Instead, Xi will continue to advance the interests of China throughout the world—and will continue to press forward with the eventual goal of Chinese global domination. These Chinese maneuvers will catalyze the alliance of Russia with the G-7—and, after the Antichrist's brilliant expansion of his Empire throughout much of the world (Chapter 25), will ultimately set the stage for the East-West (or East-North-West) conflagration prophesied in the sixth Trumpet judgment.

ABOUT THE AUTHOR

Steve Griffith was born again in the late 1970s when a series of personal set-backs caused him to turn to the Lord. After college, Steve enjoyed a twenty-year banking and management career. Before leaving the private sector, he served in a senior management position with a major U.S. transportation company.

Having read the Old Testament several times and the New Testament numerous times, Steve taught a citywide men's Bible study for six years and is a veteran of teaching an assortment of classes and electives at his home church and other churches. He also has served as an elder, elder chairman, and interim executive pastor at his church.

Steve's major theological influences are Charles Ryrie and John Walvoord. Christian Life influences, among others, include Phillip Keller, Ian Thomas, Elisabeth Elliot, A. Wetherell Johnson, Miles J. Stanford, A.W. Tozer, Andrew Murray, and Leslie Martin. Influences in helping to understand God's use of trials and testing in the life of a believer include Sandy Edmonson, Charles Stanley, Ron Dunn, R.T. Kendall, and Blaine Allen. Discernment influences include Jobe Martin, Warren B. Smith, Caryl Matrisciana, Dave Hunt, Roger Oakland, Keith Gibson, and T.A. McMahon.